The Supported Learning in Physics Project
has received major support from

Institute *of* **Physics**

ESSEX

Nuclear Electric

The project is also supported by
The Department for Education and
Employment

SUPPORTED
LEARNING
IN PHYSICS
PROJECT

PHYSICS FOR SPORT

This unit was written by
Kerry Parker and Malcolm Parry

Heinemann

D1386320

THE SUPPORTED LEARNING IN PHYSICS PROJECT

Management Group

Elizabeth Whitelegg, Project Director, The Open University

Professor Dick West, National Power Professor of Science Education, The Open University

Christopher Edwards, Project Coordinator

Professor Mike Westbrook, Vice-President for Education, Industry and Public Affairs, The Institute of Physics

George Davies, Manager, College Recruitment, Ford of Britain

Geoff Abraham, Project Trailing Manager

Dorrie Giles, Schools Liaison Manager, Institution of Electrical Engineers

Martin Tims, Manager, Education Programme, Esso UK

Catherine Wilson, Education Manager (Schools and Colleges), Institute of Physics

Production

This unit was written for the Project by Kerry Parker, Sheffield College, and Malcolm Parry, University of Durham

Other members of the production team for this unit were:

Elizabeth Whitelegg, Project Director and Academic Editor

Christopher Edwards, Project Coordinator

Andrew Coleman, Editor

John Coleman, Course Assessor

Alison George, Illustrator

Maureen Maybank, Unit Assessor

Julie Lynch, Project Secretary

Sian Lewis, Designer

Cartoons supplied by Dylan Jeavons

ISBN 0 435 68845 6

The Institute of Physics, 76 Portland Place, London, W1N 4AA.

First published 1997 by Heinemann Educational Publishers.

Printed in China

For further information on the Supported Learning in Physics Project contact the Information and Marketing Officer, The Centre for Science Education, The Open University, Walton Hall, Milton Keynes, MK7 6AA.

1.1

CONTENTS

The SLIPP units introduce you to a new method of studying – one that you probably won't have used before. They will provide you with a way of studying on your own, or sometimes in small groups with other students in your class. Your teacher will be available to guide you in your use of this unit – giving you advice and help when they are needed and monitoring your progress – but mainly you will learn about this topic through your own study of this unit and the practical work associated with it.

We expect that you will study the unit during your normal physics lessons and also at other times – during free periods and homework sessions. Your teacher will give you guidance on how much time you need to spend on it. Your study will involve you in a variety of activities – you won't find yourself just reading the text, you will have to do some practical work (which we have called 'Explorations') and answer questions in the text as you go along. (Advice on how long each exploration is likely to take is given.) It is very important that you do answer the questions as you go along, rather than leaving them until you reach the end of a section (or indeed the end of the unit!), as they are there to help you to check whether you have understood the preceding text. If you find that you can't answer a question, then you should go over the relevant bit of text again. Some questions are followed immediately by their answers but you should resist the temptation to read the answer before you have thought about the question. If you find this difficult it may be a good idea to cover up the answer with a piece of paper while you think about the question. Other slightly longer or more demanding questions have their answers at the back of the section. Some sections also have a few difficult questions at the end. You are likely to need help with these; this might be from a teacher or from working with other students.

It will be up to you to make notes on the physics you have learnt from this unit as you go along. You will need to use these notes to help you revise. You should also keep notes on how you arrived at your answers to the questions in the unit. It is important to show all your working out for each question and to set it out clearly. We try to do this in our answers to the questions in this unit.

Most sections start with a short 'Ready to Study' test. You should do this before reading any further to check that you have all the necessary knowledge to start the section. The answers for this test are also at the end of the section. If you have any difficulties with these questions, you should look back through your old GCSE notes to see if they can help you or discuss your difficulties with your teacher, who may decide to go over certain areas with you before you start the section or recommend a textbook that will help you.

The large number of practical explorations in the unit are designed to let you thoroughly immerse yourself in the topic and involve yourself in some real science. It is only after hands-on experiences that you really begin to think about and understand a situation. We suggest that you do some of these explorations with other students who are studying the unit and, when appropriate, present your results to the rest of the class. Because there are such a large number of these explorations it would be impossible for you to do all of them, so if everyone shares their results with others in the class you will all find out about some of the explorations that you are unable to do.

Your teacher will arrange times when the practical work can be undertaken. For health and safety reasons you must be properly supervised during laboratory sessions and your teacher will be responsible for running these sessions in accordance with your school's or college's normal health and safety procedures.

HEALTH AND SAFETY NOTE

The unit warns you about any potential hazards and suggests precautions whenever risk assessments are required of an employer under the Management of Health and Safety at Work Regulations 1992. We expect that employers will accept these precautions as forming the basis for risk assessments and as equivalent to those they normally advocate for school science. If teachers or technicians have any doubts, they should consult their employers.

However, in providing these warnings and suggestions, we make the assumption that practical work is conducted in a properly equipped and maintained laboratory and that field work takes account of any LEA or school or college guidelines on safe conduct. We also assume that care is taken with normal laboratory operations, such as heating and handling heavy objects, and that good laboratory practice is observed at all times.

Any mains-operated equipment should be properly maintained and the output from signal generators, amplifiers, etc., should not exceed 25 V rms.

1

Physics sets the agenda for absolutely all sports. The laws of physics are the ultimate rules of the game – competitors may cheat or play fairly, but no one can catch gravity out and no one can break Newton's laws of motion.

Sport science is a rapidly growing area of interest in which science is applied to sport so that athletes can improve their performance, and in the three sports we examine here (rock climbing, springboard diving and scuba diving) a thorough understanding of physics is important to make the activities safe and to help participants improve their skills. However, this is not a sport science book – this SLIPP unit has been written to teach physics by examining the physics of these three sports (we could have chosen many more), not to improve your sporting prowess.

So, whether your interest is in physics, sport or both, this unit will introduce you to some new ideas and show you the usefulness of some ideas that you have met before.

INTRODUCTION

Rock climbing is the fastest growing sport in Britain. It's an activity that used to be reserved for people who lived on fear and seemed intent on self-destruction, owing to the extreme risk and likelihood of injury and death. Now it has become a safe, but nevertheless still thrilling, sport. Modern equipment makes the drive to the climbing wall or rock face the most dangerous part of climbing. Falling off is now so safe that many climbers fall off on purpose so that they can go back and practice a certain move over and over again. Some mountaineers feel that the sport has been undermined in recent years as routes are made easier, but, judging by the number of people who regularly climb, it is clear that many disagree.

I

PHYSICS FOR
ROCK CLIMBING

If you can visit a local climbing wall, or can watch climbers on local rock faces, try to study their movements. You cannot fail to be impressed by the skill, strength and sheer athleticism of the climbers, who seem to defy gravity, clinging on to sheer rock faces with their fingernails, holding on to overhangs with their feet. It almost seems to cheat the laws of physics. But, of course, it doesn't: understanding the physics is the key to understanding how to push back the limits of climbing, and in this section we cover the rules that govern staying still and hanging on.

We're very concerned in this section with whether a climber will accelerate or not: a climber's main concern being to ensure that they do not do so downwards at 9.81 m s^{-2}!

READY TO STUDY TEST

During your study of this unit, you will be analysing the effects of forces acting on climbers by drawing triangles and determining unknown lengths and angles in them; for this, you will need to remind yourselves of some useful physics and maths. Before you begin this section you should be able to:

■ define sine, cosine and tangent of an angle and apply these trigonometrical functions to simple problems like finding the lengths of sides of triangles

■ state and use Pythagoras' theorem

■ recall Newton's statements about forces known as his laws of motion

■ distinguish between vector and scalar quantities and understand that vector quantities combine differently from scalar quantities

■ understand that the weight of a body may be taken as acting at a single point

■ calculate the moment of a force or pairs of forces about any point.

QUESTIONS

R1 Isaac Newton formulated three extremely important statements about forces (Newton's laws of motion): can you remember these? (a) Write out the first one. (b) Don't write out the second one, just write the most important formula in mechanics that results from the second law. If you can't remember these statements, look them up in your GCSE notes or a physics textbook, or consult your teacher. (Newton's laws of motion are given in Section 4 of the SLIPP unit *Physics On the Move*.)

R2 Here's an exercise that uses the trigonometry tools referred on page 10 and introduces two others that you may have also met before in your GCSE course.

In Figure 2.1(i)

$$\frac{\sin A}{a} = \frac{\sin B}{b} = \frac{\sin C}{c}$$

and

$$a^2 = b^2 + c^2 - 2bc\cos A$$

Find all the unknowns in the other triangles shown in Figure 2.1(ii)–(vii). (Give lengths and angles to two significant figures.)

R3 Add the missing word: 'Weight, pushes, pulls, tensions, loads, efforts are all ____'.

R4 What is the unit of force and what is its symbol?

R5 Complete the following law: 'If a body A exerts a force on body B, then body B ...'.

R6 If a mass of 5 kg is added to one of 15 kg the combined mass is 20 kg. If a 5 N force is combined with one of 15 N:

(a) Why can't you say that the combined force is 20 N without more information?

(b) What are the smallest and largest possible values of the combined forces?

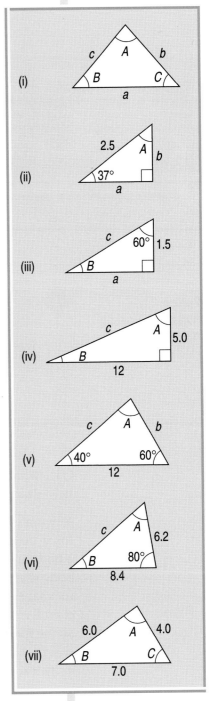

Figure 2.1
Find the unknowns

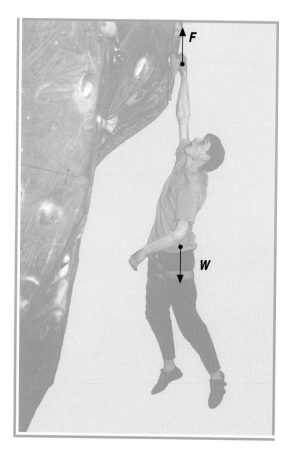

Figure 2.2
A climber holding
on with one hand

2.1 Vertical forces

We are all pulled towards the Earth by a force we call gravity. The size of this force, called weight, depends on our mass and how far away from the Earth's centre we are. On the Earth's surface gravity produces a force of 9.81 N for every kilogram of mass; this is known as the **gravitational field strength** of the Earth. Gravitational field strength is the force acting per unit mass on a body in a gravitational field. Its units are $N\,kg^{-1}$.

Thus

weight = mass × gravitational field strength

$$\boldsymbol{W} = m\boldsymbol{g}$$

and on Earth

weight = mass × 9.81 N kg^{-1}

 Calculate the weight of a 50 kg climber.

$$\text{Weight} = \text{mass} \times 9.81\,\text{N}\,\text{kg}^{-1}$$
$$= 50\,\text{kg} \times 9.81\,\text{N}\,\text{kg}^{-1}$$
$$= 491\,\text{N}$$
$$= 4.9 \times 10^{2}\,\text{N (to two significant figures)}$$

Q1 What would the climber weigh on the Moon, where the gravitational field strength is approximately one-sixth that on the Earth? ◆

Newton's laws of motion explain what forces can do. An unbalanced force, acting on a body, will cause it to accelerate. If the forces acting on a body are **balanced forces** the body does not accelerate, and if the body is already stationary it will stay still. For a climber hanging on to a rock face, staying still is infinitely preferable to falling off accidentally – even if modern equipment saves your life, falling off still means failure. So the fundamental aim for a climber is to counteract gravity, and to ensure that the climber's body is pulled upwards with a force that is equal to their weight.

You are hanging from a rope and you are stationary. If your mass is 60 kg, what is your weight, and what is the tension in the rope?

$$\text{Weight} = \text{mass} \times 9.81\,\text{N}\,\text{kg}^{-1}$$

$$= 60\,\text{kg} \times 9.81\,\text{N}\,\text{kg}^{-1}$$

$$= 5.9 \times 10^2\,\text{N} \text{ (to two significant figures) downwards}$$

The tension in the rope must be equal and opposite to this force, so that you stay still and don't accelerate anywhere, so the tension is 590 N upwards.

A point that is not accelerating, at which the forces balance, is said to be in **equilibrium**. One condition for the equilibrium of a point is that the forces that act on it should cancel out, so that there is no net force in any direction.

 Exploration 2.1   Forces in a line

Apparatus:
♦ two spring balances (e.g. 0–10 N) ♦ 1 m of climbing or similar rope

Set up the apparatus as shown in Figure 2.3(a). Adjust the two spring balances so that they both read zero. Now pull down on the lower spring balance. Compare the readings on the balances as you pull harder and harder.

Without adjusting the spring balances, attach the rope between them, as in Figure 2.3(b). Make a table of results to show the upper and lower balance readings for different amounts of tension as you pull on the lower balance.

Explain your results in terms of the condition for equilibrium of a point. Think about the end of each of the spring balances. Every time they were in equilibrium (i.e. stationary) what forces were acting on the points?

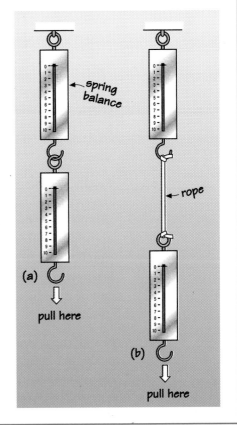

Figure 2.3   Arrangement of spring balances for Exploration 2.1: (a) without rope (b) with rope

How to set out solutions to physics problems

Many, but not all, physics problems are best answered in a structured way. Follow the steps set out below.

Step 1

First think carefully about what is being asked and think what physical principles and laws relate to what you are told and what you need to find out. After all, physics is very much to do with generalizations such as the conservation of energy or the principle of balanced forces – these generalizations must apply in many different situations. Choose the principle that relates what you know or are told to what you wish to know – usually the answer to the question. It helps to write this generalization out in words and to note any limitations on it. The following example shows the sort of limitations we mean:

> In an electric kettle, conservation of energy suggests that the energy given out by the element equals the energy absorbed by the water, *if no energy is lost to the surroundings including the kettle itself.* The italicized part shows the limitation.

Step 2

Try to write out the statement in algebraic form, explaining any unusual symbols (codes) you have used. Where possible stick to orthodox notation: for example, mass is usually represented by '*m*'. If you use *m* to represent, say, the length of a ladder, state 'where *m* is the length of the ladder', or draw a clear diagram showing how your code is used.

Step 3

The third stage should involve rearranging the algebra so that the thing you want to know is on the left of the equals sign and the things you know or are told are collected on the right.

Step 4

Finally, fill in numerical values, then work out your answer putting each stage of your calculation on a separate line. Each stage of the calculation should show the correct units and the answer should be given to an appropriate number of significant figures. (The appropriate number of significant figures will normally be the number of significant figures in the least precise data supplied in the question. Some books (but not this one) can be a bit hazy on this – stating 2 m when they mean 2.00 m, for example.)

Not all questions lend themselves to this outline: sometimes it is wiser to evaluate intermediate results before the end; sometimes it is better to do calculations with numbers rather than doing complex algebra with a lot of letters. This is especially true in situations where angles need to be found and then cosines etc. taken. So, don't treat this advice too rigidly.

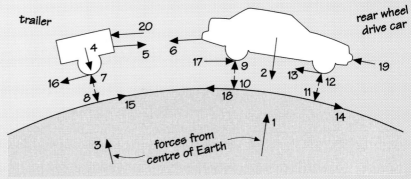

Using free body diagrams

When forces acting on a body need analysing, you should draw a **free body diagram**. Decide the limits of the system you want to consider. For example, take the case of a car pulling a trailer. This is shown in Figure 2.4. Here you can choose to limit the system to the car, or the car towing the trailer, or the car towing the trailer on a road attached to the Earth. Now draw the object or system floating above the Earth. Next draw the forces acting on it. If they are pull forces, show them as arrows with their tails originating where they act; if they are push forces, show them as arrows with their heads touching the point they act on. The reason for drawing the object or system floating above the Earth is that it is then clear what the forces act on and where they act.

Q2 A climbing rope has a mass of 70 g per metre.

(a) If a 30 m rope is hung over a sheer drop, calculate the tension in the rope (i) at the top, (ii) in the middle, (iii) at the bottom.

(b) If a 60 kg climber hangs on the bottom of the rope, calculate the new tension at the top of the rope. ◆

Q3 As you study this you are probably not hanging from a rope, but you are probably on planet Earth and in equilibrium. Draw a free body diagram of your position, and work out where the force comes from that stops you accelerating downwards because of your weight.

Show your sketch to your teacher and discuss the forces you have drawn. ◆

Key to figure

1 gravitational pull of the car on the Earth
2 gravitational pull of the Earth on the car
3 gravitational pull of the trailer on the Earth
4 gravitational pull of the Earth on the trailer
5 pull of the car on the trailer
6 pull of the trailer on the car
7 push of the ground on tyre of the trailer
8 push on the ground of tyre of the trailer
9 push of the ground on the rear tyre of the car
10 push on the ground of the rear tyre of the car
11 push on the ground of the front tyre of the car
12 push of the ground on the front tyre of the car
13 frictional force of the road on the front tyre
14 frictional force of the front tyre on the road
15 frictional force of the trailer tyre on the road
16 frictional force of the road on the trailer tyre
17 frictional force of the road on the rear tyre
18 frictional force of the rear tyre on the road
19 air resistance on the car body
20 air resistance on the trailer body

Forces on air are not shown; these are equal and opposite reactions to 19 and 20. The point of action of each force is accurate, but the line of action has been simplified.

Figure 2.4
A free body diagram showing forces acting in a system comprising a car, a trailer and the Earth

2.2 Pulling at angles

Climbers, unlike cavers, do not carry ropes to enable them to climb. Ropes are there for safety, to be used only if a climber fails to hold on using their own strength and skill. Using hands and feet, pushing and pulling on various hand- and foot-holds, a climber is rarely pushing upwards with one simple force to balance their weight. And yet they can still hold on, keeping in equilibrium.

Adding horizontal and vertical forces

Forces are a type of quantity in which direction, as well as size, is important. (If you have ever accidentally put a car into reverse instead of first gear you will appreciate the importance of direction!) These **vector** quantities add up quite differently from directionless **scalar** quantities because they also have a direction associated with them.

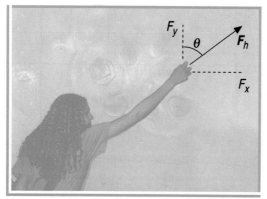

For example, a hand-hold may be just above a climber, but to their right (as in Figure 2.5). As the climber pulls on it, the hand-hold will pull them both upwards and to the right.

The size of the upwards part of this force depends on the size of the force from the hand-hold and also on the angle between the hand-hold and the vertical. The size of this upward part increases if the overall force increases or if the force is nearer to the vertical direction.

Figure 2.5
Climber pulling on a hand-hold that is above them and to the right

Since a single force can have several effects like this – a vertical part holding the climber up plus a horizontal part exerting a sideways pull – a technique for determining the size of the parts has been developed. This technique is called **resolving** a force into components.

Mathematically, we calculate the size of the vertical part of a force by drawing a triangle of forces, showing each force as a line in the direction of the force (see Figure 2.6). The length of the line is proportional to the size of the force. For example, if the force from the hand-hold was 100 N at an angle of 30° to the vertical, we could draw this as a line 10.0 cm long, with 1 cm representing 10 N.

We can find the length of y by measuring the scale drawing or, more accurately, using trigonometry:

In Figure 2.6(a)

$$\cos 30° = \frac{y}{10.0\,\text{cm}}$$

so

$$y = 10.0\,\text{cm} \times \cos 30°$$

$$= 8.66\,\text{cm}$$

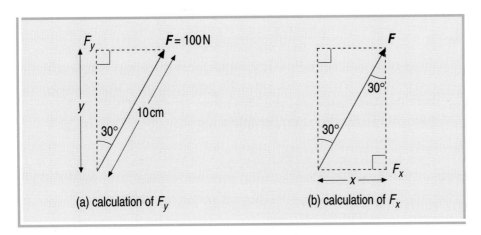

(a) calculation of F_y (b) calculation of F_x

Figure 2.6
Calculating vertical and horizontal components of a force

and this represents

$$8.66\,\text{cm} \times 10\,\text{N cm}^{-1} = 86.6\,\text{N}$$

You have probably noticed that we can miss out the scale part if we are using trigonometry.

Also in Figure 2.6(a)

$$\cos 30° = \frac{F_y}{100\,\text{N}}$$

so

$$F_y = 100\,\text{N} \times \cos 30°$$
$$= 86.6\,\text{N}$$

We can do the same sort of thing to find the horizontal component of the 100 N force (see Figure 2.6b):

$$\sin 30° = \frac{F_x}{100\,\text{N}}$$

so

$$F_x = 100\,\text{N} \times \sin 30°$$
$$= 50.0\,\text{N}$$

As a general rule, $F\cos\theta$ and $F\sin\theta$ (where θ represents the angle between the force $\boldsymbol{F}$ and the vertical) are two components of the force $\boldsymbol{F}$ at right angles to each other.

This is an application of the work on vectors that you will have done in your GCSE maths course.

Vectors are shown here in bold type. When you write them, you should draw a wavy line beneath them.

 Do 50.0 N and 86.6 N add up to 100 N?

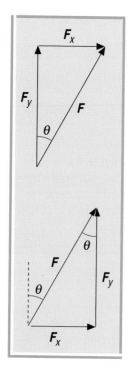

Figure 2.7
Adding the
horizontal and
vertical forces

They do not if we add them as if they were scalars. But these forces are vectors. They are the two components of the force F. Because they are at right angles the horizontal force does not contribute to the vertical force, and vice versa. So between them, these two forces have the same effect as the 100 N force, acting at 30°. So, as vectors, taking their direction into consideration they do add up to 100 N.

When resolving forces, it is often useful to separate the vector into two components that are perpendicular to each other, usually horizontally and vertically. This is known as resolving the vector into mutually perpendicular components.

To add the vectors we draw them as lines, as before, and place them end to end. Figure 2.7 shows clearly that adding the vectors F_y to F_x or adding F_x to F_y we always get F. The order in which we add them is not important.

We can check the size and direction of F mathematically.

Using Pythagoras' theorem:

$$(50\,N)^2 + (86.6\,N)^2 = F^2$$

$$F = \sqrt{10000\,N^2}$$

$$= 100\,N$$

Using trigonometry:

$$\tan\theta = \frac{50.0\,N}{86.6\,N}$$

so

$$\theta = 30°$$

Using the maths of vectors we are now able to work out how useful certain hand- and foot-holds might be to a climber.

Worked example

A hand-hold is above a climber at an angle of 60° to the vertical away from them. Calculate the force they must exert from the hand-hold in order to hold their vertical body weight of 700 N. Will this hand-hold do the job?

The force from the hand-hold must produce a vertical component of 700 N. So the vector diagram must be like the one in Figure 2.8.

By trigonometry:

$$\cos 60° = \frac{700\,N}{F}$$

so

$$F = \frac{700\,\text{N}}{\cos 60°}$$
$$= 1400\,\text{N}$$

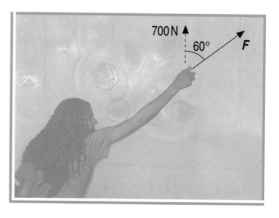

(When doing calculations with vectors it is always a good idea to check your answer with your diagram. Here the magnitude of the force, *F*, is much bigger than 700 N, as we would expect from Figure 2.8).

This is a force of twice the climber's body weight; it is unlikely that the climber will be strong enough to apply this size of force and therefore hold on to the climbing wall. Also, there is a horizontal component of the force; if the situation remains as we have described it, this force will accelerate the climber to the right, and they may well lose their grip. ◆

Figure 2.8
Reaching for a hand-hold

Adding more than two forces – to reach equilibrium

Because climbers have to use forces that are not perfectly vertical to hold up their weight they also have to cope with the sideways forces generated non-vertical forces.

If they are to stay balanced, in equilibrium, there must be no unbalanced force, in any direction. To find out about the forces needed to reach equilibrium we simply add them up by drawing them as vectors nose to tail – if the forces acting at a point add up to zero then the point is in equilibrium. This construction is called a **polygon of forces.**

Imagine that you are holding on to an overhang with both arms, as in Figure 2.9.

Adding the forces, putting them end to end, they make a closed triangle: i.e. the three forces between them have a total of zero.

When doing calculations with forces like this it is sometimes easier to work out the horizontal and vertical components of the forces. Then, if the point is in equilibrium the total of the horizontal forces must be zero and the total of the vertical forces must be zero.

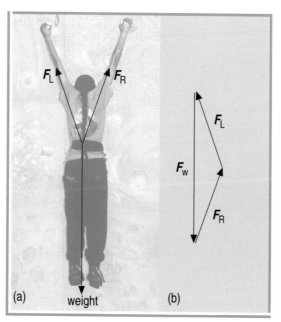

Figure 2.9
(a) Holding on to an overhang with both arms, (b) adding the forces in a triangle

◈ Exploration 2.2   Equilibrium of three forces

Part (i)

Apparatus:

◆ two climbing ropes each at least 2 m long

You need to work in groups of three for this part of the exploration.

Tie the climbing ropes carefully so that the second rope is knotted securely to the first rope halfway along the first rope. Pull the ropes so that they make the arrangements shown in Figure 2.10(a), (b) and (c).

This is not a test of strength! You don't need to pull hard to do this experiment. Make sure that you tie the ropes carefully so that they do not come apart, and take care not to slip on the floor when you are pulling the ropes.

10 MINUTES

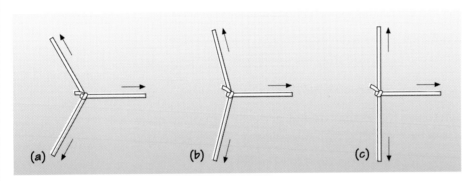

Figure 2.10 Arrangements of climbing ropes for Exploration 2.2

How hard is each student pulling to keep the knot in equilibrium? Tell each other what you are feeling. This is a very rough and ready experiment, but you should realize that in some of the arrangements the division of forces is not 'fair'.

Part (ii)

Apparatus:

◆ force board ◆ light, smooth string ◆ ten or more 100 g slotted masses with hangers
◆ 360° transparent protractor
◆ overhead projector

Set up the apparatus as shown in Figure 2.11, projecting an image of the centre of the protractor on to the knot K.

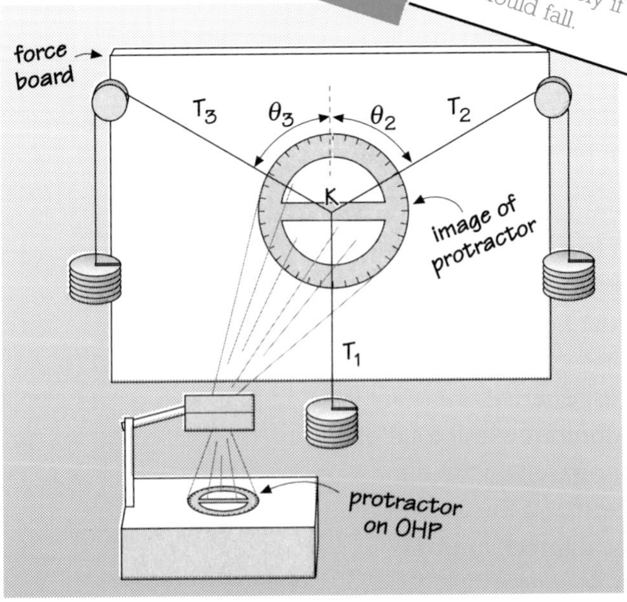

60 MINUTES

Devise a method (such as placing a cardboard carton on the floor) to catch the masses safely if they should fall.

force board

T_3 θ_3 θ_2 T_2

K

image of protractor

T_1

protractor on OHP

Figure 2.11   Force board for Exploration 2.2 part (ii)

Note down the size of the tensions (T_1, T_2, T_3), and the angles θ_2 and θ_3 between the strings. Repeat the experiment three more times for three new positions of the knot as you increase the masses. [*Note:* The tension will be (the mass on the string) $\times g$.]

Record your results in a table like Table 2.1.

Arrangement number	θ_2	θ_3	T_1 /N	T_2 /N		T_3 /N		Total forces
				$T_{2(y)}$	$T_{2(x)}$	$T_{3(y)}$	$T_{3(x)}$	
1								
2								
3								
4								

Table 2.1
Sample table for Exploration 2.2 part (ii)

Use trigonometry to calculate the horizontal (x) and vertical (y) component of each of the tensions. Finally, add the vertical forces and add the horizontal forces. They should both come to around zero. Discuss why you would not expect the forces to add up to 0.000 N. Are your results close enough to agree with the condition for equilibrium for the knot?

Part (iii)

Apparatus:

◆ force board with two pulleys ◆ three 100 g masses with hangers ◆ light, smooth string ◆ graph paper ◆ tracing paper

Make certain that the board is secure before you load it.

60 MINUTES

Set up the force board as shown in Figure 2.12.

Ensure that the knot K is held in equilibrium just by the tension from the three strings. It should not rub against the board, and all the masses should move freely. Move the knot slightly – it should return to approximately the same position. Put a piece of graph paper behind the knot and mark on it the direction of the three strings together with the tension in each string.

[*Note:* The tension will be (the mass on the string) $\times g$.]

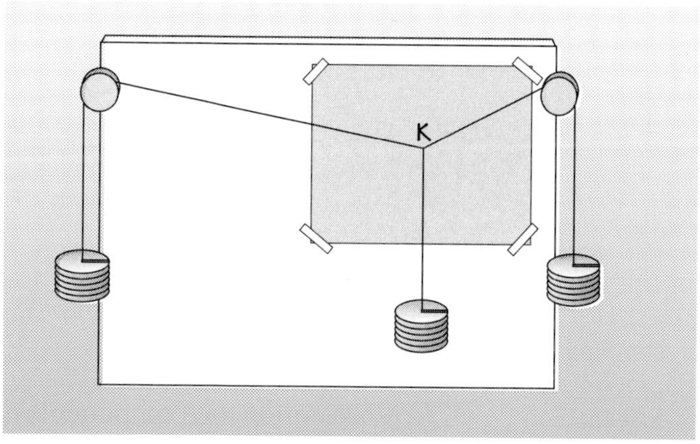

Figure 2.12 Force board for Exploration 2.2 part (iii)

Remove the graph paper from the board and put it on a desk so that you can draw on it carefully. Use a rule to draw a line along the line of each string representing the size of the tension in that string (e.g. use a scale of 1 cm representing 1 N), so that you get a diagram showing direction and length of the tension vectors T_1, T_2 and T_3.

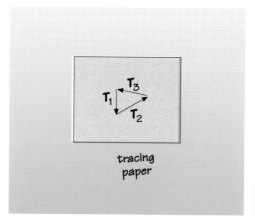

Figure 2.13 The force lines make a closed triangle

Put the tracing paper on the graph paper and copy the vectors you have drawn, placing them end to end and taking care to keep the side of the tracing paper lined up with the lines on the graph paper so that the direction of the lines is not altered, as shown in Figure 2.13.

You should find that the lines make, roughly, a closed triangle, proving that the forces add up to zero.

If it doesn't make a perfectly closed triangle why do you think this is?

Do you think your results are close enough to agree with the condition for equilibrium of a point?

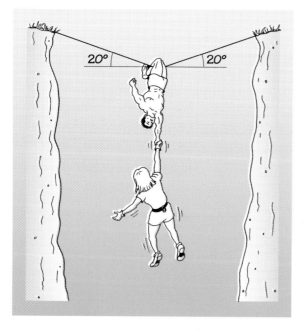

Figure 2.14
Sylvester Stallone holding a woman over a ravine

Q4   At the beginning of the film *Cliffhanger*, Sylvester Stallone (or rather the character played by him) (mass 130 kg) holds a woman (mass 60 kg) while hanging from a rope stretched across a ravine, as shown in Figure 2.14.

Draw the free body diagram (a) for Sylvester Stallone, (b) for the woman he is holding. Quantify (put in numerical values for) as many of the forces as you can.
(Use $g = 10$ N kg^{-1}.) ◆

Q5   Now 'lift' the forces from the free body diagram in Question 4(a) and sketch them nose to tail with appropriate angles between them. ◆

Q6   Should these arrows in Question 5 form a closed or an open triangle? Why? ◆

Q7   Considering the components on the original free body diagram in Question 4, work out the magnitude of the tension, *T*, in the rope. ◆

Q8 Unfortunately the woman falls. Draw the free body diagram for her just as she begins to descend. ◆

Q9 Find the new angles in your diagram for Question 5 now that Sylvester Stallone is lighter in body (if not in spirit!) and the tensions have reduced to 2200 N. ◆

Q10 A climber uses hand- and foot-holds as shown in Figure 2.15, leaving one hand free. Work out the unknown force, **F**, and the angle it makes to the horizontal. ◆

Q11 A climber who has not studied this SLIPP book has an accident and is airlifted by helicopter on a stretcher. The stretcher and climber weigh 1800 N. If the tension in the cable shown in Figure 2.16 is 2200 N at what acceleration will the casualty rise? What must the pilot do as the casualty is winched up? (Use $g = 10 \text{ N kg}^{-1}$.) ◆

Q12 The helicopter later flies forward at a steady velocity as shown in Figure 2.17. What is the drag force of the wind on the stretcher? ◆

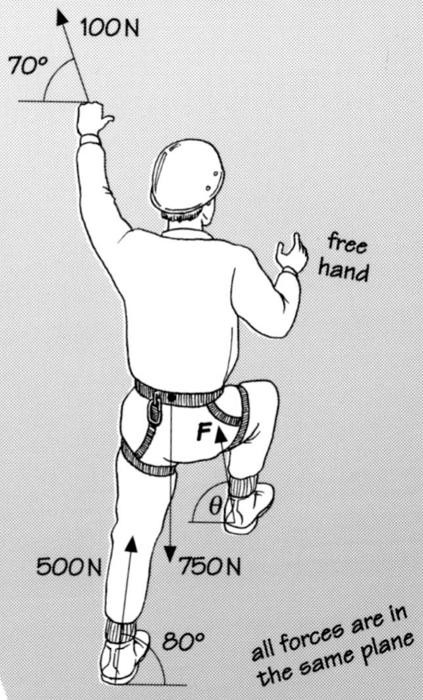

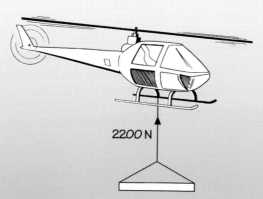

Figure 2.15
Climber using hand- and foot-holds

Figure 2.16
A helicopter hoisting a casualty

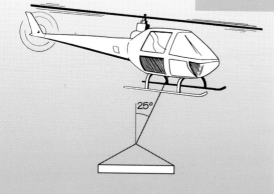

Figure 2.17
A helicopter flying forward with stretcher beneath

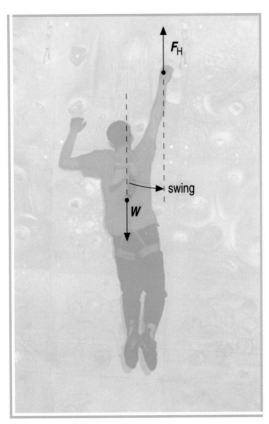

Figure 2.18
Swinging on a hand-hold. Although the magnitudes of **W** and F_H are the same, they are not in the same line, so the climber will swing round

2.3 Turning forces

So far we have only considered equilibrium of a point such as a knot. You have probably already realized that the climber we considered in Section 2.2, reaching for a hand-hold above them and to the right, could never hold themselves one-handed in that position, even if they were amazingly strong. Their body would swing round until it was underneath the hand-hold as in Figure 2.18.

This rotation is due to the fact that, unlike a knot, the climber is not a point. A climber has a body, which has size and shape. Forces can therefore act at different points on the climber, not only moving their body up and down, but also rotating it.

A turning force is called a **torque**; the turning effect of a force is called the force's **moment**. The moment of a force and the torque it produces are the same. Forces give rise to torques when the line of the force pushes at a point some distance from a pivot point. (You can find out more about torques and moments in Section 2 of the SLIPP unit *Physics On the Move*.)

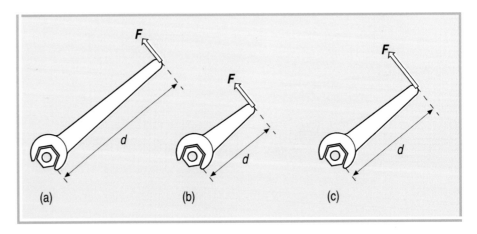

Figure 2.19 Torque exerted on a nut by a spanner

 Which spanner in Figure 2.19 produces the greatest torque?

The size of the turning force depends on two factors: the size of the force and the displacement d shown in Figure 2.19. Notice that d is measured along a line drawn from the pivot so that it is perpendicular to the line of the force. So spanner (a) produces the greatest torque.

Q13 Later, in hospital, the casualty from the climbing accident referred to in Question 11 has his leg placed in a sling, which is held up with a weight and pulleys, as shown in Figure 2.20. Calculate the moment of the tension about the hip joint in the cable holding up the patient's leg. (Use $g = 10$ N kg^{-1} and ignore friction in the pulleys and the mass of the cable.) ◆

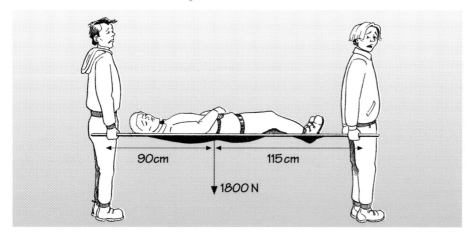

Figure 2.20
Patient's leg in hospital

For a climber to remain balanced, it is not enough that the forces up and down are balanced. For equilibrium of a body there must be no net force and no net turning force measured about any point.

It is often possible to have two equal but opposite forces acting on a body. They don't move the body along, but, because they don't act at the same point, they produce a turning effect. Such an arrangement of parallel forces is called a **couple**.

Q14 The climber's leg neither rises nor falls in the example in Question 13. (a) What does this tell you about the moment and line of action of the leg's weight (138 N) about the hip joint? (b) What is the distance from the hip joint (in Figure 2.20) to the **centre of gravity** of the leg? (For now, treat the hip joint as a simple loose 'pin' joint.) ◆

 Are there any other forces that exert a torque on the hip joint?

Yes – forces caused by the muscles of the upper leg and other, internal, factors. But we will assume that the casualty is very relaxed and flexible.

Q15 Back on the mountainside, before the helicopter arrived, the two companions carried the casualty (total mass 180 kg) down the mountain on an improvised stretcher, as shown in Figure 2.21. Work out the value of each of the forces the companions exert on the stretcher. ◆

Figure 2.21
Two companions carrying the casualty

2.4 Super boots and friction

Friction is the force that opposes motion when two surfaces touch. Without it, climbing would be impossible. When you push directly on a solid, even something like ice, or a banana skin on a wet floor, the solid resists deformation and pushes back. This force is always at right angles to the surface, pushing away from the surface, stopping it from being pushed in. Because it acts at right angles to the surface it is often called the **normal force**. If one solid pushes on another at an angle that is not perpendicular to the surface, the two surfaces may also resist movement parallel to the surfaces. Usually the two surfaces are not microscopically smooth, and the surfaces may interlock; they will also interact electrostatically (with a **Coulomb force**), allowing the surfaces to exhibit the force of friction. This normal force and friction almost always both act when two solids touch.

Worked example

A climber's foot pushes at an angle of 60° to the vertical, as shown in Figure 2.22, to gain an upward force of 800 N. Calculate the frictional force that must be produced between the boot and the rock.

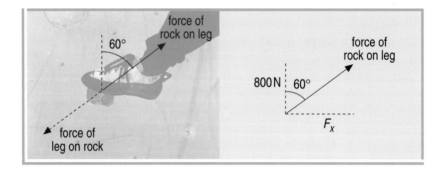

Figure 2.22
Friction between a boot and a rock

Applying trigonometry to the forces in Figure 2.22:

$$\tan 60° = \frac{F_x}{800\,\text{N}}$$

$$F_x = 800\,\text{N} \times \tan 60°$$

$$= 1.4 \times 10^3\,\text{N} \text{ (to two significant figures)} \blacklozenge$$

Q16 A climber is abseiling down an icy cliff and pauses in the position shown in Figure 2.23. Draw a triangle of forces for the centre of gravity and work out each force acting. (Assume that there is no friction at the ice wall so there will be no upward or downward force at this point.) ◆

The three forces must act at the same point, why?

Because there must be no total moment about this point. If the forces acted as in Figure 2.24, a turning effect would result.

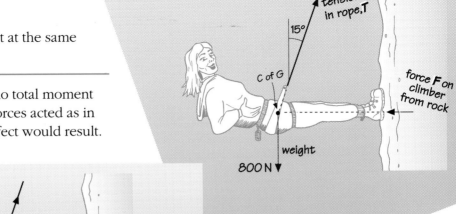

Figure 2.23
Climber with rope

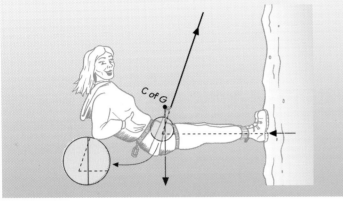

Figure 2.24 Disequilibrium from three forces

Q17 Earlier in the descent, the climber's boots had been in contact with rock so that a fourth, frictional, force of 150 N acted upwards, as shown in Figure 2.25. Draw a force polygon and evaluate the unknown forces. ◆

Clearly, in climbing it is essential to be able to depend on large frictional forces from the rocks. Many rocks are unsuitable for climbing because they crumble before they can sustain such large forces, and climbing in wet conditions limits free climbing activities. The huge growth in the popularity of purpose-built climbing walls is due to the dependability of the climbing surface.

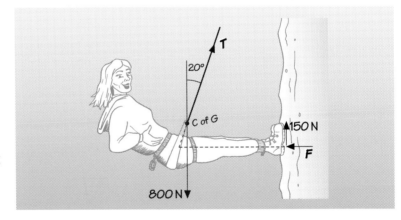

Figure 2.25
Climber – showing frictional force

The size of the frictional force between a rock and a climber depends on the force the climber places on the rock and on the nature of the two surfaces. The frictional force that a rock can give to a climber can be increased by increasing the size of the normal reaction force – i.e. by (i) pushing the surfaces together harder, (ii) wearing rubber shoes (climbing shoes have rubber soles that are made from the soft, sticky rubber used in aircraft tyres), and (iii) keeping hands sweat-free using chalk.

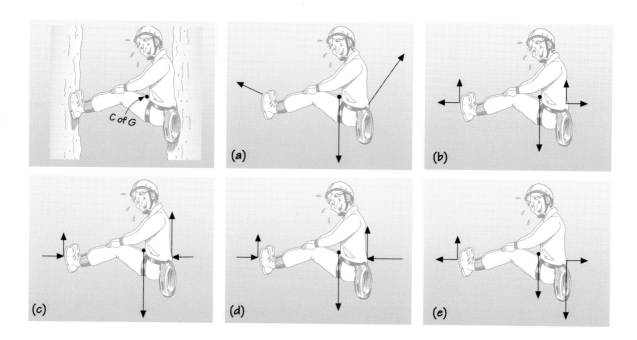

Figure 2.26
Free body diagram options

Q18 While climbing a chimney as shown in Figure 2.26, a climber pushes on the rough walls of the chimney and remains at rest. Which of the free body diagrams for the climber best represents the forces acting on the climber. Explain your reasons. ◆

Achievements

After working through this section you should be able to:

- set out a solution to physics problems at this level
- analyse force situations leading to static situations using trigonometry, Pythagoras' theorem and graphical methods
- resolve a force into vector components
- draw free body diagrams
- apply conditions for the equilibrium of forces acting at a point
- apply the principle of moments
- draw a force polygon.

Glossary

Balanced forces   The forces that act when a body is in equilibrium. When forces are balanced they form a closed vector polygon, and their components (vertical and horizontal) add independently to zero. Forces being balanced is a necessary, but not sufficient, condition of equilibrium. Furthermore, the equilibrium may be unstable, stable or neutral.

Centre of gravity   The point through which an object's entire weight can be considered to act. It coincides with the centre of mass unless the object is in a non-uniform gravitational field.

Coulomb force   The force of attraction or repulsion resulting from interaction of two or more charged particles.

Couple   Unit: newton metre (N m). The sum of the moments of two equal but opposite forces acting along parallel lines of action. The numerical value of the couple equals the product of each force and their separation. The unit is always N m, never J.

Equilibrium   Equilibrium exists for a body if it is not accelerating. That occurs when all the forces acting on the body add up (as vectors) to zero *and* when all the moments of the forces acting on the body about any point add up to zero. When the forces add up to zero the vector polygon of all the forces is closed *or*, perhaps more usefully, components of forces vertically balance and the components of forces horizontally balance. Sometimes it makes sense to consider components of forces in other directions. To say that the moments add up to zero means that clockwise moments of forces about any point balance the anticlockwise moments about the same point. If they don't, the body spins with an accelerating rotation. *If* these conditions are satisfied, then Newton's first law tells us that the body will either be stationary or be moving at a uniform velocity. Another issue is how stable is the equilibrium – will the body *remain* stationary? To answer this we need to consider how the potential energy of the body changes for a small disturbance: if it falls, the body is unstable; if it rises, the body is stable; if it remains constant, the body is said to be in neutral equilibrium.

Free body diagram   A diagram of one part (usually a body) in a system drawn in isolation from surfaces or other bodies with which it is in contact or interaction, so that only the forces acting on the body can be drawn without ambiguity.

Friction   The force acting on both of two bodies opposing relative motion of the surfaces in contact. Static friction exists until relative motion takes place. Dynamic friction is the minimum force required to maintain constant relative motion.

Gravitational field strength The force acting per kilogram (i.e. per unit mass) on a test body placed in the gravitational field. Provided no other forces act on a test mass, the net or resultant force on the mass will then be equal to the gravitational force, and, from Newton's second law, will produce an acceleration equal to the gravitational field strength.

Moment Unit: newton metre (N m). The turning effect of a force defined as the product of a force and the perpendicular displacement of the line of action of the force from the axis about which the moment is being calculated. The unit is always N m, never J.

Normal force A force acting perpendicular to a surface.

Polygon of forces A diagram in which vectors are drawn nose to tail in scale and preserving the proper angles between them (it is rare at this level to need more than a triangle).

Resolving Splitting a vector (often a force) into the vector sum of two or more components (usually two at right angles, usually vertically and horizontally). In effect, this means that the problem can subsequently be dealt with using scalar (non-vector) methods.

Scalar A directionless quantity that obeys ordinary rules of algebra (e.g. speed as opposed to velocity; distance as opposed to displacement).

Torque Unit: newton metre (N m). The turning effect of a force, defined as the product of the force exerted by a turning effect and the perpendicular displacement of the force from the axis of rotation. Usually applied to rotary machines. (Technically this is a vector but such rigour is beyond A-level.) The unit is always N m, never J.

Vector A quantity embodying direction as well as magnitude (e.g. velocity as opposed to speed; displacement as opposed to distance).

Answers to Ready to Study test

R1

(a) Every object remains at rest or in uniform motion in a straight line unless acted upon by an unbalanced force.

(b) $\boldsymbol{F} = m\boldsymbol{a}$

R2

The equations $\dfrac{\sin A}{a} = \dfrac{\sin B}{b} = \dfrac{\sin C}{c}$

and $a^2 = b^2 + c^2 - 2bc\cos A$ apply to all triangles, *but* they are most useful for those with no right angle in them, i.e. examples (v), (vi) and (vii).

Triangle (ii)

To find a:

$$\cos 37° = \frac{a}{2.5}$$

so

$$a = 2.5\cos 37°$$
$$= 2.0 \text{ (to two significant figures)}$$

To find b:

$$\sin 37° = \frac{b}{2.5}$$

so

$$b = 2.5\sin 37°$$
$$= 1.5 \text{ (to two significant figures)}$$

$$A = 180° - 90° - 37°$$
$$= 53°$$

Triangle (iii)

To find a:

$$\tan 60° = \frac{a}{1.5}$$

so

$$a = 1.5 \tan 60°$$
$$= 2.6 \text{ (to two significant figures)}$$

To find c:

$$\cos 60° = \frac{1.5}{c}$$

so

$$c = \frac{1.5}{\cos 60°}$$
$$= 3.0$$

$$B = 180° - 90° - 60°$$
$$= 30°$$

Triangle (iv)

$$c = \sqrt{\left(5.0^2 + 12^2\right)}$$
$$= 13$$

To find B:

$$\tan B = \frac{5.0}{12}$$
$$= 0.417$$

so

$$B = 23° \text{ (to two significant figures)}$$

To find A:

$$\tan A = \frac{12}{5.0}$$
$$= 2.4$$

so

$$A = 67° \text{ (to two significant figures)}$$

Triangle (v)

$$A = 180° - 40° - 60°$$
$$= 80°$$

To find b:

$$\frac{b}{\sin 40°} = \frac{12}{\sin 80°}$$

so

$$b = \frac{12 \sin 40°}{\sin 80°}$$
$$= 7.8 \text{ (to two significant figures)}$$

To find c:

$$\frac{c}{\sin 60°} = \frac{12}{\sin 80°}$$

so

$$c = \frac{12 \sin 60°}{\sin 80°}$$
$$= 11 \text{ (to two significant figures)}$$

Triangle (vi)

$$c = \sqrt{\left(6.2^2 + 8.4^2 - 2 \times 6.2 \times 8.4 \cos 80°\right)}$$
$$= 9.5 \text{ (to two significant figures)}$$

To find B:

$$\frac{9.5}{\sin 80°} = \frac{6.2}{\sin B}$$

so

$$\sin B = \frac{6.2 \sin 80°}{9.5}$$

so

$$B = 40° \text{ (to two significant figures)}$$

To find A:

$$\frac{8.4}{\sin A} = \frac{9.5}{\sin 80°}$$

so

$$\sin A = \frac{8.4 \sin 80°}{9.5}$$

so

$$A = 60.55°$$
$$= 61° \text{ (to two significant figures)}$$

or use

$$A = 180° - 80° - 40°$$
$$= 60°$$

(Errors caused by rounding numbers to two significant figures cause the two values of A to differ by 1°.)

Triangle (vii)

To find C:

$$\cos C = \frac{4.0^2 + 7.0^2 - 6.0^2}{2 \times 4.0 \times 7.0}$$

so

$C = 59°$ (to two significant figures)

To find A:

$$\cos A = \frac{4.0^2 + 6.0^2 - 7.0^2}{2 \times 4.0 \times 6.0}$$

so

$A = 86°$ (to two significant figures)

To find B:

$$\cos B = \frac{6.0^2 + 7.0^2 - 4.0^2}{2 \times 6.0 \times 7.0}$$

so

$B = 35°$ (to two significant figures)

Of course, once you have found two angles you can find the third by subtracting the known angles from 180°.

R3

Forces.

R4

The newton, N.

R5

… exerts an equal and opposite force on body A.

R6

(a) Force is a vector quantity and therefore requires a direction as well as a size.

(b) 10 N, 20 N.

Answers to questions in the text

Q1

Weight, $\boldsymbol{W} = m\boldsymbol{g}_{\text{moon}}$

so

$$W = \frac{50\,\text{kg} \times 9.81\,\text{N kg}^{-1}}{6}$$
$$= 81.75\,\text{N}$$
$$= 8 \times 10^1\,\text{N (to one significant figure)}$$

Q2

(a) (i) Tension, $\boldsymbol{T} = m\boldsymbol{g}$

and

$$m = 30\,\text{m} \times 70\,\text{g m}^{-1}$$
$$= 2100\,\text{g}$$
$$= 2.1\,\text{kg}$$

so

$$T_{top} = 2.1\,\text{kg} \times 9.81\,\text{N\,kg}^{-1}$$

$$= 20.60\,\text{N}$$

$$= 21\,\text{N (to two significant figures)}$$

See Figure 2.27.

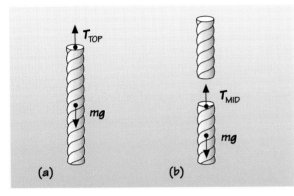

Figure 2.27 Answer for Question 2.
(a) Tension at the top, (b) tension in the middle

(ii) In the middle, the weight of rope below is half of previous value, as is the tension.

$$T_{mid} = \frac{20.60\,\text{N}}{2}$$

$$= 10.30\,\text{N}$$

$$= 10\,\text{N (to two significant figures)}$$

(iii) At the bottom of the rope, no rope is below this point so there is nothing for gravity to attract and therefore no tension in rope at this point.

(b) The new tension at the top of the rope is given by

$$T_{top} = \text{weight of rope and climber}$$

$$= \left(2.1\,\text{kg} + 60\,\text{kg}\right) \times 9.81\,\text{N\,kg}^{-1}$$

$$= 609.2\,\text{N}$$

$$= 6.1 \times 10^2 \,\text{N (to two significant figures)}$$

Q3

See Figure 2.28.

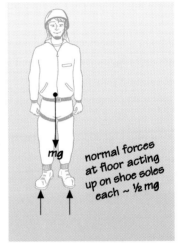

Figure 2.28
Answer for
Question 3

Q4

See Figure 2.29.

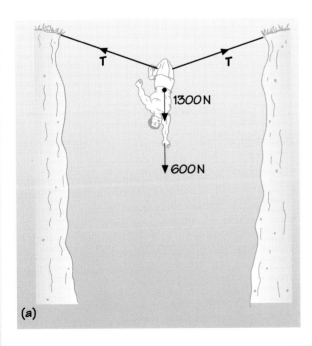

(a)

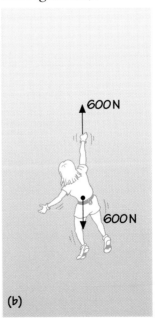

(b)

Figure 2.29
Answer for
Question 4

Q5

See Figure 2.30.

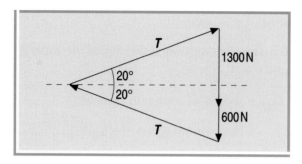

Figure 2.30 Answer for Question 5

Q6

Closed. An open triangle would imply that an unbalanced force or resultant acts and Stallone would accelerate.

Q7

The vertical components of T balance the downwards weights.

$$\frac{T_y}{T} = \sin 20°$$

and

$$T_y = T \sin 20°$$

$$2T \sin 20° = 1300 \, \text{N} + 600 \, \text{N}$$
$$= 1900 \, \text{N}$$

so

$$T = \frac{1900 \, \text{N}}{2 \sin 20°}$$
$$= 2778 \, \text{N}$$
$$= 2.8 \times 10^3 \, \text{N} \text{ (to two significant figures)}$$

Or, from the sine rule

$$\frac{1900 \, \text{N}}{\sin 40°} = \frac{T}{\sin\left(\frac{180° - 40°}{2}\right)}$$

so

$$T = \frac{\sin 70°}{\sin 40°} \times 1900 \, \text{N}$$
$$= 2800 \, \text{N}$$
$$= 2.8 \times 10^3 \, \text{N} \text{ (to two significant figures)}$$

Q8

See Figure 2.31.

Figure 2.31
Answer for Question 8

Q9

The calculation is as before, but with a new (unknown) angle, and no 600 N force.

$$2 \times 2200 \, \text{N} \sin\theta = 1300 \, \text{N}$$

so

$$\sin\theta = \frac{1300 \, \text{N}}{4400 \, \text{N}}$$
$$= 0.295$$

therefore

$$\theta = 17.18°$$
$$= 17° \text{ (to two significant figures)}$$

See Figure 2.32.

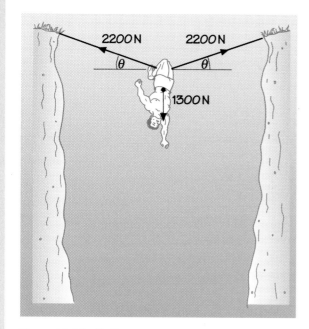

Figure 2.32 Stallone alone

Q10

Vertical forces are balanced so

$$F \sin\theta + 500\,\text{N} \sin 80° + 100\,\text{N} \sin 70° = 750\,\text{N}$$

so

$$F \sin\theta = 163.6\,\text{N (upwards)}$$

Horizontal forces are balanced so

$$F \cos\theta + 100\,\text{N} \cos 70° = 500\,\text{N} \cos 80°$$

so

$$F \cos\theta = 52.62\,\text{N (to the left)}$$

Now

$$\sin\theta = \frac{\text{opposite}}{\text{hypotenuse}}$$

and

$$\cos\theta = \frac{\text{adjacent}}{\text{hypotenuse}}$$

so

$$\frac{\sin\theta}{\cos\theta} = \frac{\text{opposite}}{\text{hypotenuse}} \times \frac{\text{hypotenuse}}{\text{adjacent}}$$

$$= \frac{\text{opposite}}{\text{adjacent}}$$

$$= \tan\theta$$

If

$$\tan\theta = \frac{\sin\theta}{\cos\theta}$$

then

$$\tan\theta = \frac{F \sin\theta}{F \cos\theta}$$

$$= \frac{163.6\,\text{N}}{52.62\,\text{N}}$$

$$= 3.11$$

therefore

$$\theta = 72.2°$$

Substituting θ into

$$F \sin\theta = 163.6\,\text{N}$$

gives

$$F = 172\,\text{N (to three significant figures)}$$

The unknown force is therefore 172 N, making an angle of 17.8° to the vertical.

Q11

See Figure 2.33 overleaf. The resultant upward force, **F**, is given by

$$F = 2200\,\text{N} - 1800\,\text{N}$$

$$= 400\,\text{N}$$

The weight of the stretcher and casualty is 1800 N. Since

$$\boldsymbol{W} = m\boldsymbol{g}$$

the mass of the stretcher and casualty is given by

$$m = \frac{1800\,\text{N}}{10\,\text{N}\,\text{kg}^{-1}}$$

$$= 180\,\text{kg}$$

As

force = mass × acceleration

acceleration of the stretcher is given by

$$a = \frac{F}{m}$$

$$a_{\text{upwards}} = \frac{400\,\text{N}}{180\,\text{kg}}$$

$$= 2.222\,\text{m}\,\text{s}^{-2}$$

$$= 2.2\,\text{m}\,\text{s}^{-2} \text{ (to two significant figures)}$$

The pilot should increase the lift slightly or the helicopter could be 'winched' down!

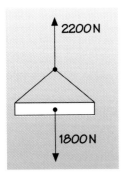

Figure 2.33
Free body diagram for the stretcher

Q12

From Figure 2.17, the cable makes an angle of 25° with the vertical. By definition

$$\tan 25° = \frac{D}{1800\,\text{N}}$$

where D is the magnitude of the drag force of the wind on the stretcher. So

$$D = 839.4\,\text{N}$$

$$= 8.4 \times 10^2\,\text{N} \text{ (to two significant figures)}$$

See Figure 2.34.

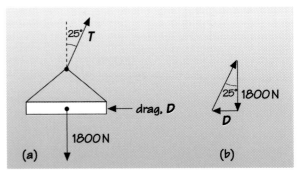

Figure 2.34 (a) Free body diagram, (b) triangle of forces

Q13

The tension, T, is given by

$$T = mg$$

so

$$T = 6.0\,\text{kg} \times 10\,\text{N}\,\text{kg}^{-1}$$

$$= 60\,\text{N}$$

The moment due to T is given by

$$\text{moment} = 60\,\text{N} \times 0.80\,\text{m}$$

$$= 48\,\text{N}\,\text{m}$$

Q14

(a) The moment of the leg's weight about the hip joint must be equal and opposite in turning effect to the moment of the tension in the cable due to the weight.

(b) The moment of the leg's weight is equal in magnitude to the moment of the tension in the cable, so

$$138\,\text{N} \times l = 48\,\text{N}\,\text{m}$$

where l is distance from the hip joint to the centre of gravity of the leg. Therefore

$$l = \frac{48\,\text{N}\,\text{m}}{138\,\text{N}}$$

$$= 0.347\,8\,\text{m}$$

$$= 35\,\text{cm} \text{ (to two significant figures)}$$

Q15

See Figure 2.35. We know that $F_1 + F_2 = 1800$ N, but this is not enough to find F_1 and F_2 individually. We will take moments about x because for equilibrium

sum of clockwise moments = sum of anticlockwise moments

$$1800\,\text{N} \times 0.90\,\text{m} = F_2 \times (0.90 + 1.15)\,\text{m}$$

so

$$F_2 = \frac{1800\,\text{N} \times 0.90\,\text{m}}{2.05\,\text{m}}$$

$$= 790.2\,\text{N}$$

$$= 7.9 \times 10^1\,\text{N (to two significant figures)}$$

(F_1 has *no* moment about x.)

Then

$$F_1 + F_2 = 1800\,\text{N}$$

so

$$F_1 = 1800\,\text{N} - F_2$$

$$= 1800\,\text{N} - 790\,\text{N}$$

$$= 1010\,\text{N}$$

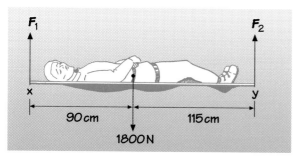

Figure 2.35 Forces acting on the stretcher

Q16

To find T:

For the triangle of forces in Figure 2.36

$$\cos 15° = \frac{800\,\text{N}}{T}$$

so

$$T = \frac{800\,\text{N}}{\cos 15°}$$

$$= 828.2\,\text{N}$$

$$= 8.3 \times 10^2\,\text{N (to two significant figures)}$$

To find F, from Figure 2.36

$$\tan 15° = \frac{F}{800\,\text{N}}$$

so

$$F = 800\,\text{N}\tan 15°$$

$$= 214.4\,\text{N}$$

$$= 2.1 \times 10^2\,\text{N (to two significant figures)}$$

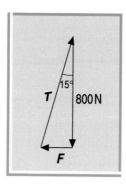

Figure 2.36
Triangle of forces for climber

Q17

See Figure 2.37.

Resolving vertically

$$T\cos 20° + 150\,\text{N} = 800\,\text{N}$$

so

$$T\cos 20° = 650\,\text{N}$$

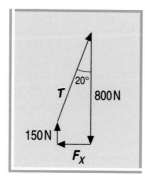

Figure 2.37
Polygon of forces

Therefore

$$T = \frac{650\,\text{N}}{\cos 20°}$$

$$= 691.7\,\text{N}$$

$$= 6.9 \times 10^2\,\text{N (to two significant figures)}$$

Resolving horizontally

$$T\sin 20° = F_x$$

so

$$F_x = 691.7\,\text{N}\sin 20°$$

$$= 236.6\,\text{N}$$

$$= 2.4 \times 10^2\,\text{N (to two significant figures)}$$

Q18

Remember the criteria for equilibrium:

- horizontal forces must add up to zero (or be balanced)

- vertical forces must add up to zero (or be balanced)

- moments of forces about any point must add up to zero (or be balanced).

Alternatively, for three forces, they must add up vectorially to zero and pass through the same point.

(a) The forces do seem to add up to zero and pass through the same point, but they place the climber under tension – clearly wrong. The climber pushes on the walls so the walls push back with equal but opposite forces on the climber – remember that free body diagrams show the forces on the body under analysis, in this case not the walls.

(b) Vertical forces are balanced as are horizontal forces, but moments are not. Given that the climber's weight is mainly at the right hand end, the vertical force due to the wall must be higher at this end.

(c) Correct answer; all criteria are met.

(d) Horizontal forces are not balanced; the climber would accelerate to the left.

(e) Vertical forces are not balanced; the climber would accelerate downwards. The climber would also tend to rotate clockwise.

Rock climbing is tough – it is hard work. Physics defines work as the action of moving along the line of the force. Lifting your body weight against gravity is work, because you are moving your body mass against the force of gravity. Falling down, on the other hand, is easy, but dangerous: the energy stored from doing work is released – and is potentially lethal to a falling climber. Understanding and applying the physics of forces, energy and materials is vital to the design, use and effectiveness of climber protection. This section covers the physics of these all-important mechanical energy transfers.

READY TO STUDY TEST

Before you begin this section you should be able to:

- write down Newton's second law and explain each of the terms used
- use Newton's second law to define the newton
- define linear momentum and give its units of measurement
- write down and use the equations of uniform acceleration
- state and use Hooke's law.

QUESTIONS

R1 In the last section, we were mainly concerned with situations of static equilibrium when the forces are balanced. What about when forces aren't balanced? Newton's second law tells us what happens then. (a) Explain Newton's second law in words and write out the algebraic expression for this law. (b) Define the newton.

R2 It is useful to be able to relate the common terms that turn up in dynamics (i.e. displacement, velocity, acceleration and time) to each other. There are three classic relationships that apply to uniform accelerated motion. Write down these three equations of motion.

R3 Remember the injured climber in Question 11 in Section 2 being picked up from the ground by helicopter? Suppose this time that the tension in the cable is 2600 N and the climber, kit and stretcher have mass 170 kg. (Use $g = 9.81$ N kg^{-1}.)

(a) What is the weight of the climber, kit and stretcher?

(b) What is the total (resultant) force acting on them?

(c) At what rate does the climber accelerate?

(d) After 4.0 s how fast is the climber rising, assuming they start from rest?

(e) How high are they now above the ground?

(f) Horrors! The cable snaps. (Sad, but true, many accidents occur just after the casualty has been saved, during the airlift to hospital!) How fast do they strike the ground?

R4 When a force of 0.5 N is applied to the end of a spring, the length is increased from 10 cm to 12 cm. If the spring obeys Hooke's law and the load is increased by the addition of 0.25 N, what is the new length of the spring?

3.1 Physics and work

Work is the transfer of energy that occurs when a force moves a point (see Figure 3.1) or, more strictly

work = force × displacement

where the displacement is in the direction of the force.

work = force × displacement

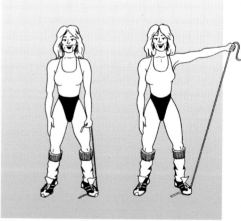

Figure 3.1
Examples of work

Worked example

Suppose an 80 kg athlete climbs a vertical cliff 30 m high. (a) How much work have they done against gravity? (b) If the athlete climbed 30 m, but some of this was not vertically upwards, would the **work done** be the same? (Use $g = 9.81$ N kg^{-1}.)

(a) The weight, $\mathbf{W}$, of the athlete = mass × $\mathbf{g}$

so

$$W = 80 \, \text{kg} \times 9.81 \, \text{N} \, \text{kg}^{-1}$$

$$= 784.8 \, \text{N}$$

Work done = force × displacement

$$= 784.8 \, \text{N} \times 30 \, \text{m}$$

$$= 23\,544 \, \text{N} \, \text{m}$$

$$= 2.4 \times 10^4 \, \text{N} \, \text{m} \text{ (to two significant figures)}$$

(b) No, much less work is done by going more horizontally. Work is done only when the force moves with a component of its movement in the direction of the force, parallel to the force field. For example, if the athlete moved along a cliff at an angle of 30° to the horizontal (see Figure 3.2) their vertical displacement would be:

$$h = 30 \, \text{m} \times \sin 30°$$

so, since work = force × displacement

$$\text{work} = 784.8 \, \text{N} \times 30 \sin 30° \, \text{m}$$

$$= 11\,772 \, \text{N} \, \text{m}$$

$$= 1.2 \times 10^4 \, \text{N} \, \text{m} \text{ (to two significant figures)} \quad \blacklozenge$$

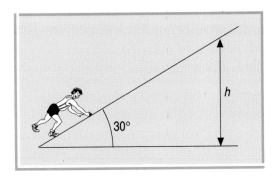

Figure 3.2 Athlete moving at 30° along the cliff

Work and energy

Work measures transfer of energy. When a force of 1 newton moves a distance of 1 metre in its own direction, then 1 joule of energy is transferred. This statement defines the joule, the unit of energy.

1 joule = 1 newton metre.

 What is the joule, in terms of the fundamental SI units, the kilogram, the second and the metre?

From the definition of the newton $1 \, \text{N} = 1 \, \text{kg} \, \text{m} \, \text{s}^{-2}$

therefore, since $1 \, \text{J} = 1 \, \text{N} \, \text{m}$,

$$1 \, \text{J} = 1 \, \text{kg} \, \text{m} \, \text{s}^{-2} \, \text{m}$$

$$= 1 \, \text{kg} \, \text{m}^2 \, \text{s}^{-2}$$

What energy is transferred in the case of the climber climbing vertically in the above example?

Chemical energy in their muscles converts to 24 kJ of gravitational potential energy. (Because we can't do this work with 100% efficiency and we use much more chemical energy than this.)

3.2 The work of climbing – gaining gravitational potential energy

The examples of work studied so far have all involved converting energy into **gravitational potential energy**. When any object is lifted, work must be done against gravity. An object that has been lifted has the potential to do work. For example, some old clocks are wound up by lifting weights – as the weights fall they do the work of running the clock. Energy from the Sun lifts water from the sea to the hills and this falling water can do work driving water wheels and hydro-electric power stations.

A climber who has almost conquered a 50 m wall is unlikely to do any useful work with the gravitational potential energy they have gained. Unfortunately for the tired climber, they cannot use this energy to climb further. The energy will be released only if they move back down the wall, and that only happens in a climb if they fall off.

The amount of the gravitational energy gained during a climb depends on the work that is done, so it depends on the force (the weight of the climber and their equipment) and their vertical displacement (the vertical height of the climb).

Thus

gain in gravitational potential energy = weight × upwards displacement

we know that

weight, $\boldsymbol{W}$ = mass × $\boldsymbol{g}$

so, if m is the mass of the climber with their equipment and h is the vertical height climbed upwards, their gain in potential energy is

$\Delta E_\text{p} = mgh$

Gain in potential energy is

$\Delta E_\text{p} = mgh$

Calculate (a) the gain in potential energy of a 65 kg climber when they ascend a 40 m gritstone wall, (b) the energy the climber gives to their 15 kg of kit.

(Use $g = 9.81$ N kg^{-1}.)

(a) The gain in potential energy is

$$\Delta E_p = mgh$$

$$= 65\,kg \times 9.81\,N\,kg^{-1} \times 40\,m$$

$$= 25\,506\,J$$

$$= 2.6 \times 10^4\,J \text{ (to two significant figures)}$$

(b) The gain in the kit's potential energy is

$$\Delta E_p = mgh$$

$$= 15\,kg \times 9.81\,N\,kg^{-1} \times 40\,m$$

$$= 5886\,J$$

$$= 5.9 \times 10^3\,J \text{ (to two significant figures)}$$

Q1 Two climbers travel from point A to B by the routes shown in Figure 3.3. One climbs vertically upwards; the other, having lost their nerve, slides along the rock shelf, along which the mean frictional force is 1600 N in the direction shown. How much work does each of them do? Both have mass 90 kg. (Use $g = 10\ N\ kg^{-1}$.) ◆

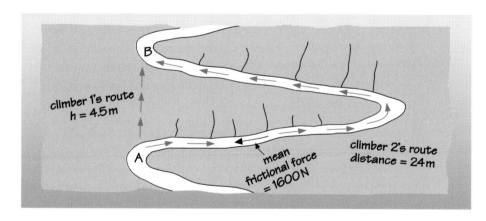

Figure 3.3
The climbers' routes

Q2 A small 100 ml serving of orange juice contains 182 kJ. If all this energy was converted into the potential energy of the climber climbing the gritstone wall (without carrying the kit), how many times could the climber make the ascent after one small cup of orange juice? ◆

 Why do climbers have to drink more than orange juice for energy?

The human body is inefficient. Not all of the energy from the food and drink we consume goes into doing the work we want to do. Among other things, energy is used breathing, keeping us warm and thinking. The muscles of the body also produce considerable amounts of thermal energy when they contract to do work.

(a) What energy will be released when the gritstone wall climber descends 40 m? (b) What forms may that released energy take?

(a) The loss of gravitational potential energy is the same as the gain: 2.6×10^4 J (without kit). The climber has 'gained' -2.6×10^4 J, because of their negative displacement upwards (i.e. they went downwards).

Gain in potential energy $\Delta E_p = mgh$

$$= 65\,\text{kg} \times 9.81\,\text{N}\,\text{kg}^{-1} \times (-40\,\text{m})$$

$$= -2.6 \times 10^4\,\text{J (to two significant figures)}$$

(b) If they fall into thin air the energy would all turn into movement energy, called **kinetic energy**. If they descend safely the energy would all be converted into thermal energy – for example, as their shoes rubbed the path and as their muscles controlled their legs.

3.3 The work of falling – gaining kinetic energy

All moving bodies possess a kind of energy. It takes work to make a body move. Work must be done *on* a body to make it move; work must be done *by* a body (on something else) to make it to stop. The energy a moving body possesses because of its movement is called its kinetic energy. The size of this energy depends on how fast the body is going and also the mass of the body.

To develop an equation for the size of the kinetic energy of a body we must calculate the work that is done in getting it moving. If we have a body of mass m, and we accelerate it up to velocity v, we will do work equal to the kinetic energy gained by the body (if there are no frictional forces opposing the movement and converting kinetic energy into thermal energy).

Figure 3.4
A body gaining kinetic energy

Let's suppose the body in Figure 3.4 accelerates with a uniform acceleration a, moving through a displacement s as it accelerates from rest.

We know that work = Fs, from the definition of work, and that $F = ma$, from Newton's second law.

Combining these we get

$$\text{work} = mas \qquad\qquad\qquad\qquad (3.1)$$

We may also apply the equations of uniform acceleration so $v^2 = 0 + 2as$ (the initial velocity being zero),

Rearranging this equation we get

$$as = \frac{v^2}{2}$$

We can then substitute for as in Equation (3.1) giving

$$\text{work} = m\frac{v^2}{2}$$

As we said earlier, this work must equal the gain in kinetic energy, so the kinetic energy of a body of mass m, travelling at velocity v, is given by

$$E_k = \frac{mv^2}{2}$$

 Calculate the kinetic energy of a stone of mass 0.50 kg falling from a cliff at 10 m s^{-1}.

$$E_k = \frac{mv^2}{2}$$

$$= \frac{0.50\,\text{kg} \times \left(10\,\text{m s}^{-1}\right)^2}{2}$$

$$= 25\,\text{J}$$

Notice that the units of energy are always joules, and that to get the right answer in these calculations SI units are essential.

Q3 Calculate the kinetic energy of a 100 kg climber falling at 15 km hour^{-1}. ◆

3.4 The universal law – energy conservation in falling

If a climber falls, the energy that they have gained as gravitational potential energy during the climb will be converted to other forms of energy as they fall. The further they fall downwards, the more energy will be transferred to other forms. To begin with, as the climber is accelerated by gravity, virtually all of the energy will transfer into kinetic energy. Sooner or later, however, the climber will encounter other forces – maybe from rocks or from their safety ropes. They will be stopped by something, and the energy will eventually transfer into thermal energy.

 In the example in Section 3.2 we calculated that a 65 kg climber ascending a 40 m gritstone wall gained 2.6×10^4 J of gravitational potential energy. If they fell vertically downwards again, without any protection, calculate the speed at which they would hit the ground.

Assuming that all their gravitational potential energy transfers into kinetic energy, and that they are stationary when they fall:

loss in potential energy = gain in kinetic energy

$$E_k = \frac{mv^2}{2}$$

$$v^2 = \frac{2E_k}{m}$$

$$= \frac{2 \times 2.6 \times 10^4 \text{ J}}{65 \text{ kg}}$$

$$v = 28 \text{ m s}^{-1} \text{ (to two significant figures)}$$

So they would hit the ground at 28 m s^{-1}.

Any climber is bound to be concerned not to release energy in such a way. The problem is that this energy cannot be destroyed, it can't be switched off – the **law of conservation of energy** tells us that. It is a universal law that no one can break – *energy cannot be created or destroyed, it can only be transferred from one form to another.* It would be nice if this energy could be put to some useful purpose, but, like much of the energy in the Universe, it is too difficult and energy consuming to do this. All a climber wants to do, anyway, is to survive a fall with a minimum of pain. It is vital that the energy of their fall does not stay as kinetic energy.

Q4 A 60 kg climber ascends 12 m vertically. (Use $g = 10$ N kg^{-1}.)

(a) How much work is done by the climber?

(b) How much gravitational potential energy does the climber now possess?

The climber then free falls 9.0 m.

(c) How much potential energy does the climber lose?

(d) How much kinetic energy does the climber gain?

(e) What is the climber's total energy at this point?

Luckily, at this point, their rope straightens and extends 0.60 m as the climber comes to rest.

(f) What work is done on the rope?

(g) What mean force is experienced by the climber from the rope?

(h) What mean acceleration is experienced by the climber? ◆

Using frictional forces of various types it is relatively easy to transfer kinetic energy to thermal energy. The energy of a 50 m fall, if it all transferred to thermal energy in a climber, would heat their entire body by less that 0.1° C. This is much kinder than hitting the ground at 28 m s^{-1}!

 I have a friend with badly scarred hands from the burns he received while breaking a fall. What do you think caused the burns?

The scars are from rope burns. Although the energy of a fall would not burn a climber if it were spread throughout their body, in a small volume of skin intense heating can occur, because skin is a rather poor conductor. So safety procedures must guard against this; if you are holding a rope for another climber you should always wear gloves.

Chris Bonington belaying in the Lemon Mountains, Greenland, 1991 (Source: Chris Bonington Picture Library)

Exploration 3.1   Measuring the velocity of falling objects

Apparatus:

◆ pieces of card or sheet metal   ◆ light gate   ◆ electronic timer or a computer
◆ Action Man, Barbie doll or alternative doll   ◆ metre rule

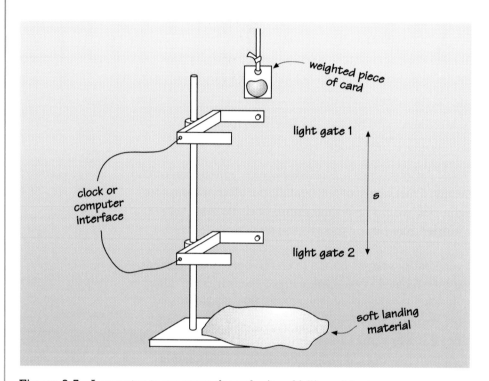

Figure 3.5   Apparatus to measure the velocity of falling objects

Set up the apparatus as shown in Figure 3.5 to time a piece of card weighted with Blu-Tack (or sheet metal) falling from rest as it drops through a light gate (if using sheet metal, it should be dropped so as to fall into a bucket of sand). Take care that the light gates are connected to the required voltage (this should be indicated on your apparatus – it isn't necessarily standard).If you have a computer, program it to calculate the final velocity of the card.

Measure times and calculate the final velocity of the card (v_f) as it falls through increasing distances, s. (Ask your teacher to explain how to do this if you have not used a computer to calculate velocities before.)

Tabulate your results and plot a graph to show how v_f and s are related. Use the equations you have studied in this section to choose the axes for a graph that will give you a straight-line graph. Plot this graph to test your results against the theory.

Do you expect to see any differences in velocity between the doll and the card? Write down a hypothesis and work out how to test it.

Climbers have used ropes for centuries to make climbing safer. You don't have to study physics to realize that if you are held in place by a rope you won't fall very far when you lose your footing, and you may not get hurt. Sadly, owing to the nature of climbing, it is impossible for climbers always to be protected by a rope which is kept taut from a secure fixture, and many climbers have lost their lives because of this. The most vulnerable climber is always the leader, who is roped to the rest of the team. In years past, if the leader fell off they fell a long way, and sometimes took other members of the party with them. The rule was 'the leader never falls'. Unlike the laws of physics, however, this rule could be broken! In the next section we will discuss the properties of climbing ropes and how they can be designed to keep climbers as safe as possible.

3.5 Strain energy – the route to safety

For a falling climber, the only chance of survival is to convert the kinetic energy they have gained into **thermal energy**. This must occur slowly and in a controlled manner. We have already mentioned the problem of rope burns. Climbers have also been injured, sometimes fatally, by receiving internal injuries from the ropes that were designed to protect them.

When an object is squashed, stretched or deformed in any way, work is being done on it. It is taking in some sort of energy. **Strain** is a measurement of how deformed something becomes when a force acts on it. The work that is done to deform an object is called **strain energy.**

Elastic strain energy

When a spring is stretched, most of the strain energy that is stored in it can be released later. Stretched springs are very useful in wind-up toys, catapults, car suspension systems and pogo sticks for that very reason. The strain energy stored in objects that are deforming elastically is called **elastic potential energy**. A perfectly elastic material deforms under a load and, when the load is removed, it springs back into shape, releasing all the strain energy it had stored. A low stiffness material deforms a lot when a force is applied and work done on it; a high stiffness material deforms little when a force is applied and work done on it.

Strain energy $E = \dfrac{1}{2}Fx$

or

$\dfrac{1}{2}kx^2$

where k is the stiffness.

 If a climber fell on to a perfectly elastic material, what would happen?

When the climber hit the material it would deform as it brought the climber's body to rest. Almost all of the kinetic energy of the climber would be transferred into the strain energy of the material (a little deforms the body of the climber). The material would then spring back into its original shape, forcing the climber back into the air, with almost the original amount of kinetic energy. It would be like a perfectly elastic trampoline.

 Would falling on to this sort of material make a safer landing for the climber?

Probably not. If it was an elastic material with low stiffness, forces acting on the climber could be small, but they would still be catapulted back into the air and might end up in worse trouble. If the material was of high stiffness (e.g. steel, which is also elastic) it would deliver very high forces to their body, which would undoubtedly damage it!

Plastic strain energy

The opposite extreme from a spring is a material like putty or Plasticene. When you squash it doesn't spring back at all. You still do work in deforming it but the energy is transferred to the thermal energy of the putty, which gets warmer. The energy that is used to deform the object is called **plastic strain energy**.

 Would falling on to a plastic material guarantee a safe landing for a climber?

Not necessarily. We have touched on the sizes of forces that climbers could experience – if high enough, these could be fatal. But we can be sure that the climbers would not bounce. Indeed, we carefully control our muscles so that an impact deforms our body safely when we can.

Exploration 3.2 Measuring the elasticity of materials

EXPLORATION DESIGN
20 MINUTES

CARRYING OUT
60 MINUTES

Apparatus:

◆ blocks of polystyrene, clay, foam rubber, steel (these should all be about the same size) ◆ ball-bearings of about 1 cm diameter ◆ rule

Devise an experiment to measure the change in velocity of a ball-bearing as it bounces against different materials. (*Hint:* how would the height of the ball-bearing be related to its velocity?) This will give a measure of the **elasticity** of the materials.

Q5 This question is larger than most of the previous questions and so you should allow plenty of time to do it, take it step by step and use your calculator. A bungee rope company wishes to design a rope for a drop from a bridge 100 m above a river. A 2.00 m tall, 80.0 kg jumper plunges from the bridge until the rope, length 50 m, just begins to tauten. The jumper falls until the rope is fully stretched, then bounces upwards, oscillating many times until they reach an equilibrium position. Assume **Hooke's law** holds true and use $g = 10.0 \text{ N kg}^{-1}$ for your calculations. It is intended that the jumper should come to a halt with their ankles just 5.0 m above the water, then travel back up. Assume that the jumper's centre of gravity is mid-way between their feet and head.

(a) What kinds of energy do they have at points A to F in Figure 3.6? Take the zero level of gravitational potential energy as the river surface and the centre of gravity of the jumper as 1.0 m below their ankles. Quantify these three kinds of energy in a table for each of the positions shown, along with values of height, velocity, acceleration and extension of the rope.

(b) Draw free body diagrams for the jumper at each of the positions shown in Figure 3.6, quantifying the forces in each case.

(c) To be sure of remaining dry, our 2 m jumper must be below a certain maximum mass. What is that mass? ◆

In order to design the safest climbing equipment possible we need to understand how materials respond to forces. Materials science is a whole area of science principally devoted to understanding why materials behave the way they do when subjected to forces, and it should come as no great surprise to you that materials science has played an important part in the development of climbing equipment.

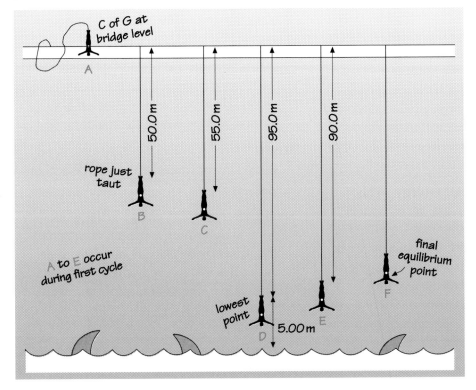

Figure 3.6
A bungee jumper

Achievements

After working through this section you should be able to:

- recall units and expressions for the main types of mechanical energy
- define work and recall its units
- recall and apply the principle of conservation of energy
- use the principle of conservation of energy to solve simple problems
- apply Newton's first and second laws
- use Hooke's law to determine work done in an elastic stretch and thus the elastic potential energy or strain energy.

Glossary

Elastic potential energy   The energy stored in a sample of material that has been stretched within its elastic limit.

Elasticity   Ability of a material to return to its original dimensions after the removal of a stress.

Gravitational field   Each object that has mass has its own gravitational field. This field extends through the whole of space. If another mass enters this field it will experience a force. We think of a gravitational field as a set of imaginary arrowed lines that show the direction of the force on any mass within the field. The closeness of these lines indicates the size of the force per unit mass.

Gravitational potential energy   The energy gained by a mass, m, when it is separated from another mass or raised in a **gravitational field**. It is equal to work done in raising the mass over a height, h, near the Earth's surface, where the gravitational field may be considered reasonably uniform. The energy change is expressed as $E = mgh$.

Hooke's law   The extension of a sample is proportional to the force applied. A graph of force against extension would therefore be a straight line. The gradient of such a graph depends on the dimensions and composition of the sample and is called its stiffness in $N\,m^{-1}$. This law applies (by definition) only up to the **limit of proportionality**.

Kinetic energy   Unit: joule (J). The energy a body has by virtue of its motion. This energy is equal to the work done in accelerating it. $E = \frac{1}{2}mv^2$, where v is the magnitude of the velocity of the body and m is its mass. Kinetic energy is a scalar quantity.

Law of conservation of energy   Energy may be transferred from one form or site to another but may not be created or destroyed. To transfer energy is to do *work* if it is mechanical, or to *heat* if it is thermal.

Limit of proportionality   The limit of force or extension beyond which Hooke's law no longer applies; the end of the straight part of a force–extension graph.

Plastic strain energy   Energy absorbed by a sample stretched beyond its elastic limit. Such work done beyond the elastic limit in deforming a sample reveals itself as thermal energy within the material.

Strain   A measurement of how deformed something becomes when a force acts on it.

Strain energy   This energy is the work done in deforming a sample of material and arises by displacement of atoms or molecules within each other's electrostatic fields. Up to the limit of proportionality,

$E = \frac{1}{2}kx^2$ or $E = \frac{1}{2}Fx$, where F is the magnitude of the force, x the extension and k the stiffness of the sample. When the sample relaxes, this energy may be transferred out of the sample. If stretched beyond the elastic limit, work is done internally on the sample and the energy cannot be recovered.

Thermal energy   When thermal energy is absorbed by a gas, its random molecular motion is speeded up. This is observed as a rise in temperature. In a solid or liquid, both molecular kinetic energy and potential energy increase, manifesting themselves as a rise in temperature or change of phase.

Work   Unit: newton metre (N m) or joule (J). This quantity gives a measure of energy transferred by the action of a force applied over a distance. Movement is always involved, even if it is only a change of shape. Work is a scalar quantity.

Work done   Unit: newton metre (N m) or joule (J). The product of magnitude of force and the displacement of the point of action of the force in the direction of the force. $W = Fs$, where W is work done, F is the magnitude of the force and s is displacement in the direction of the force. Work of 1 J is done if 1 N moves through 1 m in the direction of the force. For example, if an average apple is lifted one metre above the ground, approximately one joule of work is done and one joule of gravitational potential energy is gained by the apple.

Answers to Ready to Study test

R1

(a) Newton's second law states that the rate of change of momentum of a body is proportional to the resultant force acting on it and takes place in the direction of the force. Momentum, the product of mass and velocity, is a vector quantity, measured in $kg\ m\ s^{-1}$. The algebraic expression is $\boldsymbol{F} = m\boldsymbol{a}$ or in calculus notation $\boldsymbol{F} = \dfrac{d(m\boldsymbol{v})}{dt}$.

(b) $1\ N = 1\ kg\ m\ s^{-2}$.

R2

The three main equations of motion for uniform accelerated motion are:

$$\boldsymbol{v} = \boldsymbol{u} + \boldsymbol{a}t$$

$$\boldsymbol{s} = \boldsymbol{u}t + \frac{1}{2}\boldsymbol{a}t^2$$

$$v^2 = u^2 + 2as$$

where $\boldsymbol{u}$ is the initial velocity in $m\ s^{-1}$, $\boldsymbol{v}$ is the final velocity in $m\ s^{-1}$, $\boldsymbol{a}$ is the acceleration in $m\ s^{-2}$, t is the time taken in seconds and $\boldsymbol{s}$ is the displacement in metres.

There is also a fourth, less frequently used, equation:

$$\boldsymbol{s} = \boldsymbol{v}t - \frac{1}{2}\boldsymbol{a}t^2$$

R3

(a) Weight is given by

$$\boldsymbol{W} = m\boldsymbol{g}$$

so

$$W = 170\,kg \times 9.81\,N\,kg^{-1}$$
$$= 1700\,N \text{ (to two significant figures)}$$

(b) Resolving vertically

$$\text{force up} - \text{force down} = 2600\,N - 1700\,N$$
$$= 900\,N$$

The resultant force is therefore 900 N upwards.

(c) From Newton's second law $F = ma$, so

$$a = \frac{F}{m}$$

$$a_{upwards} = \frac{+900\,\text{N}}{1700\,\text{kg}}$$

$$= 0.529\,\text{m}\,\text{s}^{-2}$$

$$= +0.53\,\text{m}\,\text{s}^{-2}$$

(to two significant figures)

So the climber accelerates at 0.53 m s^{-2} upwards.

(d) Using the first equation of motion

$$v = u + at$$

so

$$v_{upwards} = 0 + 0.529\,\text{m}\,\text{s}^{-2} \times 4.0\,\text{s}$$

$$= +2.116\,\text{m}\,\text{s}^{-1}$$

$$= +2.1\,\text{m}\,\text{s}^{-1}$$

(to two significant figures)

So the climber is rising at a rate of 2.1 m s^{-1}.

(e) Using the second equation of motion

$$s = ut + \frac{1}{2}at^2$$

so

$$s_{upwards} = 0.0\,\text{m}\,\text{s}^{-1} \times 4.0\,\text{s}$$

$$+ \frac{1}{2} \times 0.529\,\text{m}\,\text{s}^{-2} \times (4.0\,\text{s})^2$$

$$= +4.232\,\text{m}$$

$$= +4.2\,\text{m}$$

(to two significant figures)

So the climber is 4.2 m above the ground.

(f) The equations of motion are vector equations and we can take this into account as long as we use a rigid sign convention, e.g. up is positive and down is negative.

$$u = +2.116\,\text{m}\,\text{s}^{-1}$$
$$a = -10\,\text{m}\,\text{s}^{-2}$$
$$s = -4.232\,\text{m}\,\text{s}^{-1}$$

Using the third equation of motion

$$v^2 = u^2 + 2as$$

so

$$\left(v_{upwards}\right)^2 = \left(2.116\,\text{m}\,\text{s}^{-1}\right)^2$$

$$+ 2 \times \left(-9.81\,\text{m}\,\text{s}^{-2}\right) \times \left(-4.232\,\text{m}\right)$$

$$v_{upwards} = \sqrt{87.51\,\text{m}^2\,\text{s}^{-2}}$$

$$= \pm 9.4\,\text{m}\,\text{s}^{-1}$$

(to two significant figures)

So they strike the ground at 9.4 m s^{-1} ($v_{upwards} = -9.4$ m s^{-1}).

Technically, we must take the negative square root, since the stretcher is falling downwards.

R4

$$F = kx$$

so

$$0.5\,\text{N} = k \times 0.02\,\text{m}$$

therefore

$$k = \frac{0.5\,\text{N}}{0.02\,\text{m}}$$

$$= 25\,\text{N}\,\text{m}^{-1}$$

If the extension is x, then

$$0.25\,\text{N} = 25\,\text{N}\,\text{m}^{-1} \times x$$

so

$$x = \frac{0.25\,\text{N}}{25\,\text{N}\,\text{m}^{-1}}$$

$$= 0.01\,\text{m}$$

The spring extends by 0.01 m = 1 cm. The new length of the spring is 3 cm.

Answers to questions in the text

Q1

The first climber simply works against gravity, gaining potential energy, so

$$mgh = 90\,\text{kg} \times 10\,\text{N}\,\text{kg}^{-1} \times 4.5\,\text{m}$$
$$= 4050\,\text{J}$$
$$= 4.1 \times 10^3\,\text{J (to two significant figures)}$$

The second climber does the same work against gravity and also work against friction. Work against friction is given by $W = Fs$, where F is the magnitude of the force and s is the magnitude of the distance travelled. So

$$W = 1600\,\text{N} \times 24\,\text{m}$$
$$= 38\,400\,\text{J}$$

Therefore

$$\text{total work done} = 38\,400\,\text{J} + 4050\,\text{J}$$
$$= 42\,450\,\text{J}$$
$$= 4.2 \times 10^4\,\text{J}$$
$$\text{(to two significant figures)}$$

Q2

$$\text{Number of ascents} = \frac{\text{total energy}}{\text{energy for one ascent}}$$
$$= \frac{182 \times 10^3\,\text{J}}{2.6 \times 10^4\,\text{J}}$$
$$= 7.0$$
$$\text{(to two significant figures)}$$

So the first climber (A) could make seven complete ascents.

Q3

Before you start the calculation you must convert the non-SI unit (km hour^{-1}) into the SI unit (m s^{-1}).

1 km = 1000 m

1 hour = 3600 s, so

$$15\,\text{km}\,\text{hour}^{-1} = \frac{15 \times 1000\,\text{m}}{3600\,\text{s}}$$
$$= 4.167\,\text{m}\,\text{s}^{-1}$$
$$= 4.2\,\text{m}\,\text{s}^{-1}$$
$$\text{(to two significant figures)}$$

Now we can do the calculation:

$$E_\text{k} = \frac{1}{2}mv^2$$
$$= \frac{100\,\text{kg} \times \left(4.17\,\text{m}\,\text{s}^{-1}\right)^2}{2}$$
$$= 8.7 \times 10^2\,\text{J (to two significant figures)}$$

Q4

(a) The climber gains potential energy equal to work done

$$mgh = 60\,\text{kg} \times 10\,\text{N}\,\text{kg}^{-1} \times 12\,\text{m}$$
$$= 7200\,\text{J}$$
$$= 7.2 \times 10^3\,\text{J (to two significant figures)}$$

(b) 7200 J.

(c)

$$\text{Potential energy} = mgh$$
$$= 60\,\text{kg} \times 10\,\text{N}\,\text{kg}^{-1} \times 9.0\,\text{m}$$
$$= 5400\,\text{J}$$
$$= 5.4 \times 10^3\,\text{J}$$
$$\text{(to two significant figures)}$$

So the climber has lost potential energy of 5400 J.

(d) By the principle of conservation of energy, no other work is done so

kinetic energy gained = potential energy lost

$$= 5400\,\text{J}$$

(e) Taking zero level of potential energy to be the starting-point, the climber has total energy

$$E = mgh + \frac{1}{2}mv^2$$

where $\frac{1}{2}mv^2 = 5400\,\text{J}$, $h = 3.0\,\text{m}$.

so total energy

$$E = 60\,\text{kg} \times 10\,\text{N}\,\text{kg}^{-1} \times 3.0\,\text{m} + 5400\,\text{J}$$

$$= 7200\,\text{J}$$

$$= 7.2 \times 10^3\,\text{J}$$

(to two significant figures)

(*Note:* Total energy at any point in the climber's descent is equal to initial potential energy gained.)

(f) The rope absorbs 5400 J of energy plus potential energy lost as body falls 0.60 m.

Work done = transfer of energy

$$= 5400\,\text{J} + mgh$$

$$= 5400\,\text{J} + 60\,\text{kg} \times 10\,\text{N}\,\text{kg}^{-1} \times 0.60\,\text{m}$$

$$= 5760\,\text{J}$$

$$= 5.8 \times 10^3\,\text{J}$$

(to two significant figures)

(g) The work done on the rope = *Fs*, where F is the magnitude of the mean force and $s = 0.60$ m. Therefore

$$5760\,\text{J} = F \times 0.60\,\text{m}$$

rearranging gives

$$F = \frac{5760\,\text{J}}{0.60\,\text{m}}$$

$$= 9600\,\text{N}$$

$$= 9.6 \times 10^3\,\text{J} \text{ (to two significant figures)}$$

So the climber experiences a mean force of 9600 N from the rope.

(h) Mean acceleration *a* is found from Newton's second law.

Net force up $= 9600\,\text{N} - 600\,\text{N}$

$$= ma_{\text{upwards}}$$

so

$$a_{\text{upwards}} = \frac{9000\,\text{N}}{60\,\text{kg}}$$

$$= 150\,\text{m}\,\text{s}^{-2} \text{ (upwards)}$$

Q5

(a) See Table 3.1

Table 3.1

	A	B	C	D	E	F
h/m	**100**	**49.0**	**44.0**	**4.0**	**9.0**	$38.5^{(i)}$
gravitational potential energy/kJ	**80.0**	**39.2**	**35.2**	**3.2**	**7.2**	$30.8^{(iii)}$
kinetic energy/kJ	**0**	**40.8**	$43.9^{(vi)}$	**0**	$12.1^{(vii)}$	**0**
elastic potential energy/kJ	**0**	**0**	$0.948^{(iv)}$	**76.8**	$60.7^{(v)}$	$4.22^{(ii)}$
$v_{downwards}$/m s^{-1}	**0**	**31.9**	$33.1^{(viii)}$	**0**	$17.4^{(ix)}$	**0**
$a_{upwards}$/m s^{-2}	**10.0**	**10.0**	$-5.26^{(x)}$	$32.7^{(xi)}$	$27.9^{(xii)}$	**0**
extension/m	0	0	5	45	40	x^*

The bold results can be obtained by noting that gravitational potential energy (zero at water level) = mgh, kinetic energy = $\frac{1}{2}mv^2$ and that because of the law of conservation of energy, the sum of kinetic, gravitational and elastic energies should be constant at any instant during the first few oscillations. (Later in the motion, decay occurs because mechanical energy becomes thermal energy.) Also, of course, when stationary $v = 0$, but h must be adjusted for the position of centre of gravity. Note, however, that $v = 0$ does not imply that $a = 0$ always! To obtain the other values, first work out the stiffness, k (the spring constant), of the rope for the rope to operate as required. Then calculate the height above the water at which they will finally come to rest. At D the extension, x, of the rope must be 100 m – 50.0 m – 5.00 m = 45 m.

According to the law of conservation of energy, during the fall potential energy is lost as the jumper does work on the rope. Since the kinetic energy is zero both at the beginning and at the lowest point in the motion it can be ignored here.

So

$$mgh = \frac{1}{2}kx^2$$

rearranging gives

$$k = \frac{2mgh}{x^2}$$

therefore

$$k = \frac{2 \times 80.0\,\text{kg} \times 10.0\,\text{N kg}^{-1} \times 96.0\,\text{m}}{(45.0\,\text{m})^2}$$

$$= 75.85\,\text{N m}^{-1}$$

$$= 75.9\,\text{N m}^{-1} \text{ (to three significant figures)}$$

In the final equilibrium position, F, tension in rope = weight of jumper, so

$$kx = mg$$

$$x = \frac{mg}{k}$$

$$= \frac{80.0\,\text{kg} \times 10.0\,\text{N kg}^{-1}}{75.85\,\text{N m}^{-1}}$$

$$= 10.547\,\text{m}$$

$$= 10.5\,\text{m} \text{ (to three significant figures)}$$

(x is marked with an asterisk in Table 3.1.)

The values identified by a roman numerals in the table can be calculated as follows:

(i) At point F, the jumper's ankles will be 10.5 m + 50 m below the bridge and centre of gravity will be 1.0 m below this, i.e. 61.5 m below the bridge, so $h = 38.5$ m.

(ii) At point F, elastic potential energy is given by

$$\frac{1}{2}kx^2 = 75.85\,\text{N}\,\text{m}^{-1} \times \frac{(10.547\,\text{m})^2}{2}$$

$$= 4219\,\text{J}$$

$$= 4.22\,\text{kJ (to three significant figures)}$$

(iii) At point F, gravitational potential energy is given by

$$mgh = 80.0\,\text{kg} \times 10.0\,\text{N}\,\text{kg}^{-1} \times 38.5\,\text{m}$$

$$= 30.8\,\text{kJ (to three significant figures)}$$

(*Note:* The sum of energies does not equal initial mechanical energy because thermal energy has resulted from decay of oscillations.)

(iv) At point C, elastic potential energy is given by

$$\frac{1}{2}kx^2 = \frac{75.85\,\text{N}\,\text{m}^{-1} \times (5.00\,\text{m})^2}{2}$$

$$= 0.9481\,\text{kJ}$$

$$= 0.948\,\text{kJ (to three significant figures)}$$

(v) At point E, elastic potential energy is given by

$$\frac{1}{2}kx^2 = 75.85\,\text{N}\,\text{m}^{-1} \times \frac{(40.0\,\text{m})^2}{2}$$

$$= 60.68\,\text{kJ}$$

$$= 60.7\,\text{kJ (to three significant figures)}$$

(vi) At point C, kinetic energy (during first oscillation) approximately equals (initial gravitational potential energy) – (gravitational potential energy at C) – (elastic potential energy at C). So

kinetic energy = 80.0 kJ – 35.2 kJ – 0.948 kJ

$$= 43.9\,\text{kJ}$$

(to three significant figures)

(vii) At point E, kinetic energy (during first oscillation) approximately equals (initial gravitational potential energy) – (gravitational potential energy at E) – (elastic potential energy at E). So

kinetic energy = 80.0 kJ – 7.2 kJ – 60.7 kJ

$$= 12.1\,\text{kJ}$$

(to three significant figures)

(viii) At point C, kinetic energy $= \frac{1}{2}mv^2$

so

$$v = \sqrt{\frac{2 \times E_K}{m}}$$

$$= \sqrt{\frac{2 \times 43.9 \times 10^3\,\text{J}}{80.0\,\text{kg}}}$$

$$= 33.1\,\text{m}\,\text{s}^{-1} \text{ (to three significant figures)}$$

(ix) At point E,

$$v = \sqrt{\frac{2 \times 12.1 \times 10^3\,\text{J}}{80.0\,\text{kg}}}$$

$$= 17.4\,\text{m}\,\text{s}^{-1} \text{ (to three significant figures)}$$

(x), (xi) and (xii) Upwards forces at points C, D and E are obtained from

$$F = kx$$

for a spring.

At point F,

$$\boldsymbol{F} = m\boldsymbol{g}$$

for equilibrium.

Acceleration, $\boldsymbol{a}$, can now be obtained for (x), (xii) and (xiii) from (force up) − (force down) = ma_{upwards}

(x) At point C,

$$a_{\text{upwards(C)}} = \frac{(379 - 800)\,\text{N}}{80.0\,\text{kg}}$$

$$= -5.26\,\text{ms}^{-2}$$

(to three significant figures)

(xi) At point D,

$$a_{\text{upwards(D)}} = \frac{(3413 - 800)\,\text{N}}{80.0\,\text{kg}}$$

$$= 32.7\,\text{ms}^{-2}$$

(to three significant figures)

(xii) At point E,

$$a_{\text{upwards(E)}} = \frac{(3034 - 800)\,\text{N}}{80.0\,\text{kg}}$$

$$= 27.9\,\text{ms}^{-2}$$

(to three significant figures)

(b) See Figure 3.8.

(c) In this case we again use the equation $mgh = \frac{1}{2}mv^2$, but this time we want to find the value of m. We know that

$$x = 50\,\text{m} - (\text{height of person})$$

$$= 48\,\text{m}$$

where x is the extension of the rope before the jumper enters the water. So

$$m = \frac{kx^2}{2gh}$$

$$= 75\,\text{N}\,\text{m}^{-1} \times \frac{(48\,\text{m})^2}{2 \times 10\,\text{N}\,\text{kg}^{-1} \times 100\,\text{m}}$$

$$= 86.4\,\text{kg (to two significant figures)}$$

This means that anyone whose mass is less than 86.4 kg should keep dry on a windless day with no waves!

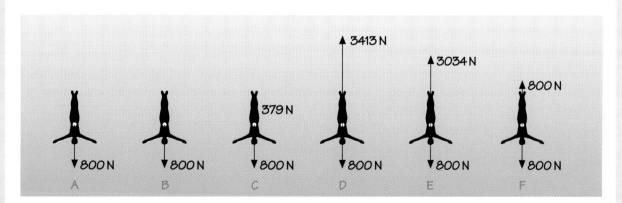

Figure 3.8 Answer for Question 5(b)

4

THE CLIMBER'S LIFELINE – THE PHYSICS OF ROPE DESIGN

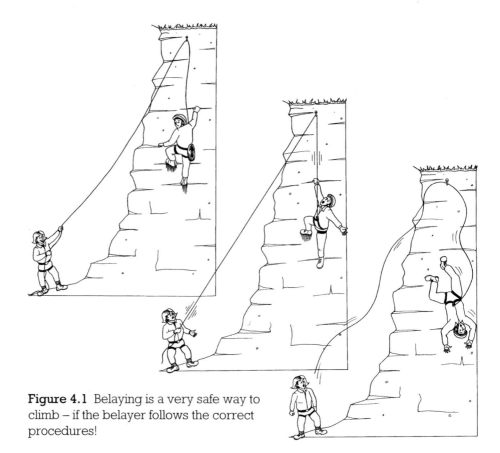

Figure 4.1 Belaying is a very safe way to climb – if the belayer follows the correct procedures!

Most people think that a good climbing rope simply needs to be strong enough to take the weight of a climber. After further consideration, they may realize that the rope will be subjected to much greater forces if the climber has a bad fall. But a strong rope could still kill a climber by decelerating their body too quickly, subjecting it to forces that cause internal injuries, or causing the bolts to which the rope is attached to be ripped from the rock. To design good equipment, and to use it properly, we need to understand the way in which the braking force of a rope can bring a falling climber safely to rest. In this section we will look at how to compare materials for their usefulness in different applications, and how to explain the differences in behaviour of these materials from our understanding of atomic bonding.

Most climbers connect their rope to a belay point above them and on to a partner who acts as a belayer (see Figure 4.1). The belayer should hold the rope, keeping it as short as possible so that if the climber falls, they don't fall very far. A secure belay point offers the best protection to a climber, as long as the belayer concentrates and remembers to keep hold!

READY TO STUDY TEST

Before you begin this section you should be able to:

- describe the structure of an atom as a positive nucleus surrounded by a 'cloud' of orbiting electrons
- recall that an ion is a neutral atom that has become charged by losing or gaining electrons
- recall that like charges repel, whilst opposites attract, and that the size of the force gets bigger as the size of each charge increases and gets smaller as the charges get further apart
- describe how intermolecular bonds arise
- carry out calculations of extensions, loads and energies using Hooke's law
- calculate elastic strain energy
- define stiffness
- remember and use the formula for the area of a disc
- state the definition of the pascal
- understand and use Newton's third law.

QUESTIONS

R1 Sketch a simple model of an atom showing the location of the constituent particles, and their relative masses and charges.

R2 An atom of carbon contains six protons in its nucleus. How many electrons orbit the nucleus in a neutral atom?

R3 The ion, Al^{3+} contains 10 electrons in one ion. How many protons are in the nucleus of this ion?

R4 In Figure 4.2, A has a single positive charge. To which ion will it be most attracted? From which will it be most repelled?

R5 List the main ways by which atoms and molecules are bonded in a solid and explain briefly how they arise.

R6 A climber falls and the rope extends and saves the climber while exerting a 1900 N force on them. What force does the climber exert on the rope? What force does the rope exert on the bolt on the rock face?

R7 A part of the climber's harness is made of cylindrical metal with a diameter of 10.0 mm. What is the cross-sectional area of the harness in (a) mm^2, (b) m^2?

R8 Give the equation for pressure and name the SI unit that it is measured in.

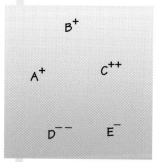

Figure 4.2
Charged ions

4.1 Testing ropes – the requirements

No other piece of equipment is more important to climbers than the skinny nylon line that separates us from eternity. Yet, of all the toys on which our lives depend, climbing ropes are probably the least understood. Many climbers have only a vague concept of the testing process of ropes and therefore don't understand what those numbers on the hangtags actually mean.

(Clyde Soles, *Rock and Ice*, vol. 117, July/August 1995)

Rope manufacturers use sophisticated analyses for developing their products, but all ropes are subjected to nationally and internationally recognized tests. Modern ropes are tested and certified by the Union Internationale des Associations d'Alpinisme (UIAA). The tests were designed to set performance standards by Professor Dodero in France in the late 1950s.

There are two types of rope used for climbing: static and dynamic. Static ropes are not meant to take falls, being designed simply to take the weight of a roughly stationary climber. They are used extensively by cavers to allow them to climb up and down vertical and near-vertical drops. The static rope acts for a short time, stopping the climber quickly, generating higher impact forces. Dynamic ropes are designed to cope with fast-moving falling climbers: it is these ropes that we will consider in this section.

In the drop test for single ropes, an 80 kg mass is dropped 4.8 m (see Figure 4.3). The section of the rope that catches the mass is only 2.5 m long, so the test represents a very severe fall for a climber. The rope is also held under conditions that will cause it to experience the maximum force it could expect in use. It is clamped so that it cannot move at one end, wrapped three times around an anchor bar and passed over an edge formed by a rod with a radius of 10 mm to catch the falling mass. If the rope is being used when a climber falls, the end of the rope will be allowed to move slightly by the person who is holding it. This is called a dynamic belay and it helps to cushion the fall, as do the cushioning properties of the rope.

Before testing, the ropes are stored at fixed conditions of temperature and humidity for four days.

To pass the test, three samples of rope from the same production batch must hold after at least five consecutive falls without breaking or deforming.

Impact forces

It is obviously vital that the rope does not break when a climber hangs from it, but the other factor that is extremely important is the **impact force**. This is a measure of the force applied to the end of the rope by the

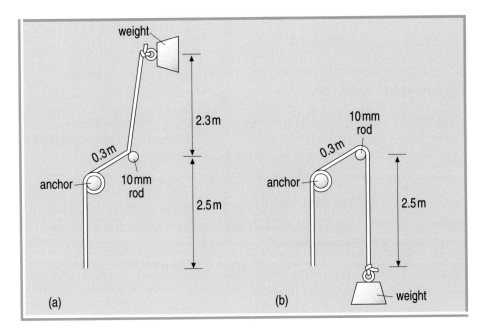

Figure 4.3
The drop test

falling mass, and is therefore the maximum force experienced by the falling climber, which far exceeds their weight. A high impact force will stop a climber quickly, but it will hurt. If the impact force is too high it could kill the climber. When climbers are choosing ropes they can find out about the quality of the rope from the information about the impact force delivered as the rope catches a fall, and in general the rule is 'the lower the better'. A lower impact rope means a gentler, softer catch and less chance that the bolts will be pulled out by the rope, and less problems for the belayer – the person holding the rope from below.

To illustrate impact forces, we will consider ropes from three companies: Bluewater, New England and Beal. These were recently tested at four different, theoretically identical, drop towers by the magazine *Rock and Ice* (July/August 1995)

The four testing centres were each supplied with pieces of rope that had been divided into four equal lengths. Measurements of maximum impact force (F_{max}) and number of falls the rope held for (n_{max}) were recorded as shown in Table 4.1.

Table 4.1 Drop test results for 10.5 mm diameter climbing ropes

Drop tower	Bluewater F_{max}/kN	n_{max}	New England F_{max}/kN	n_{max}	Beal F_{max}/kN	n_{max}
1	6.94	8	8.17	6	7.11	5
2	8.90	N/A	9.79	8	9.12	8
3	7.99	9	9.61	7	8.27	7
4	N/A	6	9.85	7	8.43	6

Q1 Which rope would you choose to get the lowest impact force during a fall? Explain your choice. ◆

Q2 Suggest reasons for the differences in the results between the different drop towers. ◆

It might at first seem surprising that a given weight, falling a given distance, can generate different impact forces depending on the type of rope. To understand this, we need to remember that

$$\text{change in momentum } (\Delta \boldsymbol{mv}) = \text{force } (\boldsymbol{F}) \times \text{time } (t)$$

The momentum of the falling weight is the same in every case, so the change is the same for every rope. If the time for the catch is extended, however, the force is smaller.

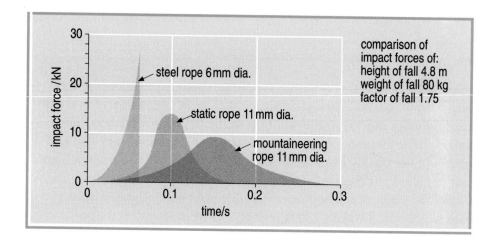

Figure 4.4
Comparison of impact forces

The area under each graph in Figure 4.4 equals force × time, i.e. change in momentum.

 How can you tell from the area under the steel graph that the steel rope broke?

The area is smaller so all the momentum is not lost, i.e. the fall continued. (You can also tell that the steel rope broke because the shape of the graph changes abruptly at about 0.06 s.)

4.2 Designing ropes – comparing materials

When ropes were first used for mountaineering in the mid-1800s they were made from natural fibres such as hemp. They were relatively weak, they stretched very little, rotted, and became heavy and difficult to work when wet; to avoid carrying a huge weight of rope, climbers used ropes of approximately 7 mm diameter (much thinner than modern ropes.)

If we are deciding on the best material for the job, we often want to compare the **strength** of materials of different shapes and sizes, so instead of simply measuring the force exerted on a material, we measure the stress.

The **tensile stress** exerted on a material, σ (the lower-case Greek letter sigma), is the force per unit area, so

$$\sigma = \frac{F}{A} \qquad (4.1)$$

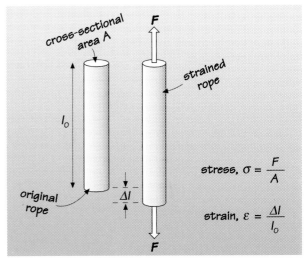

Figure 4.5
Finding stress and strain

where F is the tensile (pulling) force on the material, and A is its cross-sectional area, as shown in Figure 4.5.

 It is obvious that a climbing rope has to be strong, but why is the stretchiness and the diameter important?

A more stretchy rope will increase the stopping time of a falling climber. A longer time will produce a smaller impact force and so less chance of injury. If the rope did not stretch at all a falling climber would suffer a massive deceleration when the rope became taut and would consequently suffer massive forces. The diameter of a rope will influence its strength and also determine the stress sustained when the rope exerts a given force on a falling climber.

For example, the stress on a 10 mm diameter rope, holding the 700 N weight of a climber is worked out as follows:

The cross-sectional area of the rope is given by

$$A = \frac{\pi (d)^2}{4} \qquad (4.2)$$

so

$$A = \frac{\pi \left(10 \times 10^{-3}\,\mathrm{m}\right)^2}{4}$$

$$= 7.9 \times 10^{-5}\,\mathrm{m}^2 \text{ (to two significant figures)}$$

The stress exerted on the rope is given by

$$\sigma = \frac{F}{A}$$

$$= \frac{700\,\mathrm{N}}{7.9 \times 10^{-5}\,\mathrm{m}^2}$$

$$= 8.9 \times 10^{6}\,\mathrm{N\,m}^{-2} \text{ (to two significant figures)}$$

1 **pascal** is defined as 1 N m^{-2}, so the stress on the rope may also be written as 8.9 MPa.

 A climber's harness experiences a force of 1900 N distributed over a cross-sectional area of 6.5×10^{-5} m^2. What is the stress experienced by the harness in pascals?

$$\sigma = \frac{F}{A}$$

$$= \frac{1900\,\text{N}}{6.5 \times 10^{-5}\,\text{m}^2}$$

$$= 2.9 \times 10^7 \,\text{N}\,\text{m}^{-2}$$

$$= 2.9 \times 10^7 \,\text{Pa (to two significant figures)}$$

The stretchiness of a material depends on the length of the sample, as well as the material itself, so, to compare the stretch (or give) in a material we compare its fractional extension or **strain** at a given stress, or when it breaks.

Strain, ε (the lower-case Greek letter epsilon), is given by

$$\varepsilon = \frac{\Delta l}{l_0}$$

where Δl is the change in the length of the sample and l_0 is the original length of the sample.

 What are the units of strain?

There are no units, length divided by length will be dimensionless. However, rather than write the answer as a fraction, or a small number, strain is often quoted as a percentage

$$\text{percentage strain} = \frac{\Delta l}{l_0} \times 100\% \qquad\qquad (4.3)$$

For example, a 10 mm diameter rope gives a strain of 2.5% after an 80 kg drop test. If the rope was initially 7.0 m long, we can calculate the extension of the rope as follows.

$$\text{Percentage strain} = \frac{\Delta l}{l_0} \times 100\%$$

$$\Delta l = \frac{\text{percentage strain} \times l_0}{100\%}$$

$$= \frac{2.5\% \times 7.0\,\text{m}}{100\%}$$

$$= 0.18\,\text{m (to two significant figures)}$$

 Someone tells you that they have invented a new material for a rope that is strong enough to take the weight of a bus, and stretches less than 2 mm. Can you tell whether the material is likely to be useful?

The rope as described will not be of much use to a climber. It stretches so little that a falling climber would be stopped in a very short time and would experience damagingly high forces.

In fact, to answer this fully we would have to make assumptions about the rope, as we have not really been given enough information. Any rope can be made to take the weight of a bus if it is made thick enough. If it were then made short enough it could be made to stretch less than 2 mm.

Climbing Mont Blanc, late nineteenth century (Source: Chris Bonington Picture Library)

Exploration 4.1
Comparing stress–strain curves for materials

Apparatus: ◆ fishing wire (2–3 m long)
◆ thin copper wire (2-3 m long) ◆ long rubber band
(anything over 20 cm) ◆ micrometer ◆ metre rule
◆ G-clamp ◆ 100 g masses and hanger ◆ Sellotape
◆ pulley ◆ two C-cores (usually used for electromagnets)

Set up the apparatus as shown in Figure 4.6. With only the hanger
holding the test piece straight, measure its length, l_0 (from the clamp to the
Sellotape maker), and the diameter in several places. Record the measurements in a
table like Table 4.2. Use the mean diameter to calculate the cross-sectional area A.

Add the 100 g masses one at a time. Each time you add a mass, measure the *extension*
of the sample from the *original position*, when it was only holding the weight of the
hanger. Record the results in a table like Table 4.3, using a new table for each material.
Calculate the force applied to the sample using the equation $\boldsymbol{F} = m\boldsymbol{g}$, and calculate
stress and strain using the Equations (4.1)–(4.3).

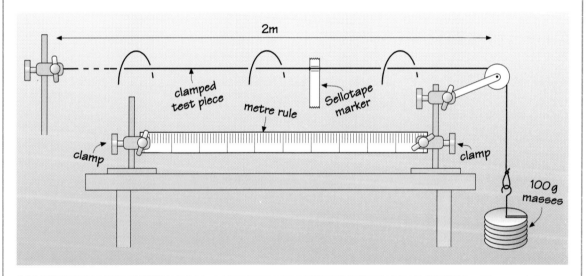

Figure 4.6
Apparatus for
measuring stress
and strain

Material	Fishing wire		Thin copper wire		Rubber band		
Diameter/mm							
Mean diameter/mm							
Cross-sectional area/x 10^{-6} m^2							
Original length/m							

Table 4.2

Mass added/kg	Extension/ mm	Force applied/N	Stress/MPa	Strain/%
0	0	0	0	0
0.1				
0.2				
0.3				
etc.				

Table 4.3

Repeat the experiment for the other materials.

Plot your data as several stress–strain graphs on the same piece of graph paper to enable you to compare the behaviour of the materials – use the same axes if the data fits sensibly. (Stress is placed on the y-axis, strain on the x-axis. This is because the machines used routinely in materials testing laboratories control the extension and measure the load.)

Join the points for each material in a smooth curve. Label the curves clearly.

Some typical stress–strain graphs are shown in Figure 4.7; you will notice that different materials cannot always be fitted on the same axes.

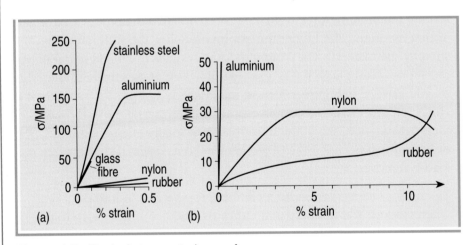

Figure 4.7 Typical stress–strain graphs

We know that metal, rubber and nylon have a very different 'feel'. This is principally because, when we subject them to stress, they deform by different amounts.

 Look at Figure 4.7(b). Which material deforms most easily with the smallest force? How can you tell from the graph?

Rubber extends most easily. At a given stress, e.g. 10 MPa, it has the largest strain.

 Why is a stress–strain graph more useful than a single value of strain at a given stress?

We can see from the stress–strain graph that although rubber is very stretchy at low stresses, it becomes much less extensible at higher stresses. Steel, on the other hand, suddenly gives and starts to stretch much more once the stress has exceeded a certain amount.

It is cumbersome and difficult to keep comparing materials by their stress–strain graphs, so engineers often compare materials by using the ratio of stress–strain: the gradient of a stress–strain graph. This is known as the **Young modulus**, E, so

$$E = \frac{\sigma}{\varepsilon}$$

All other things being equal, a material with a large Young modulus will require much more force to make it stretch than a material with a small Young modulus. The higher the Young modulus, the stiffer and less stretchy the material. The Young modulus equals the initial gradient of the stress–strain graph if it is a straight line that passes through the origin. As you can see in Figure 4.7, most materials do not produce straight lines! However, most materials do give straight lines during the early stages of their deformation, while the deformation is totally elastic. (**Elastic deformation** occurs if the object returns to its original shape when the load is removed.)

The most crucial criterion for a climbing rope is that it does not break when loaded. The quantity that indicates whether a rope is up to the job is the **ultimate tensile stress (uts)**. Knowing this value enables a rope of sufficient cross-section to be specified. Ultimate tensile stress is not necessarily the stress at failure; sometimes the stress on a failing rope can be reduced and it will still snap. Ultimate tensile stress is the maximum stress applied during testing.

 The ultimate tensile stress of a new plastic material is found to be 400 MPa. What minimum diameter should a rope composed of this material be so that it won't fail when a force, F, of magnitude 2.2 kN is applied to it?

$$\sigma = \frac{F}{A}$$

so

$$A = \frac{F}{\sigma}$$

where cross-sectional area, $A = \frac{\pi d^2}{4}$ and d is the diameter.

Substituting for A in the second of these equations gives

$$\frac{\pi d^2}{4} = \frac{F}{\sigma}$$

so

$$d = \sqrt{\frac{4F}{\pi \times \sigma}}$$

$$= \sqrt{\frac{4 \times 2.2 \times 10^3 \, \text{N}}{3.14 \times 400 \times 10^6 \, \text{Pa}}}$$

$$= 2.64 \times 10^{-3} \, \text{m}$$

$$= 2.6 \, \text{mm (to two significant figures)}$$

All loads cause materials to deform, but designers are usually concerned with designing objects so that in use they don't become permanently deformed. Chairs, cars, buildings, saucepans – we expect most of the things we use to keep their normal shape when we use them. If we want to predict how much they will deform while they are being used, we can use the Young modulus. However, if we want to know what happens to the material when it becomes deformed, when it passes its **elastic limit**, then we had best look at its stress–strain graph for more detail. Many elements of this type of graph are important and have names to indicate their significance.

Figure 4.8 shows that the elastic limit (2) (the point beyond which permanent elongation occurs), the **yield point** (3) (the point at which sudden deformation may take place) and the limit of proportionality (1) (the point below which Hooke's law holds) are not in the same place. In some materials, the line isn't straight at all; in others no yield point, as such, exists. Since these three points are often so close, however, little harm is done if they are assumed to be coincident, but the terms should not be used interchangeably. Broadly speaking, then, behaviour is **elastic** for the portion

Figure 4.8
A stress–strain graph

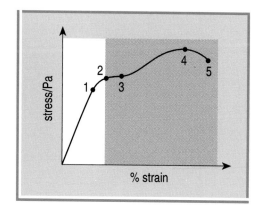

71

of the graph to the left, when a material returns to its original dimensions after the removal of a stress, and **plastic** to the right, when a material may flow and change shape permanently under the action of a stress.

Several other elements of this figure are important to us. The ultimate tensile stress is the breaking stress. It tells us how strong the material is in tension and whether the material will fail or not. It sets a minimum cross-sectional area for a rope experiencing a given force. The maximum stress before failure is also shown on the figure (4), but note that after this point the stress may be reduced, yet the sample still fail (5). The slope of the straight part of the graph in Figure 4.8, since it goes through the origin, is stress/strain, which equals the Young modulus in N m^{-2} or Pa.

The relative extent of the plastic and elastic regions

If the plastic region is small compared with the elastic region, the material will be **brittle**, like glass or high-carbon steel.

If the plastic region is more extensive, the sample may stretch considerably and permanently; if it does we might call it **ductile**. How a material behaves depends very much on what kind of intermolecular bonding it has, the resulting structure, and, if crystalline, the number and location of defects. It is the interplay between the intrinsic properties of materials and the chemical, thermal and mechanical treatments that technology applies to them that leads to characteristics such as:

- **hardness** – the ability of a material to resist abrasion or indentation; it usually rises with tensile strength

- **malleability** – when a material may be deformed in all directions by hammering or squeezing without cracking

- **toughness** – the ability of a material to withstand shock loading or fracture; it is the opposite of brittleness.

 The graphs in Figure 4.9 show the stress–strain curves for two brittle materials. (a) Which is the stiffer of the two materials? Explain your choice. (b) Which of the two materials is the stronger? Explain your choice.

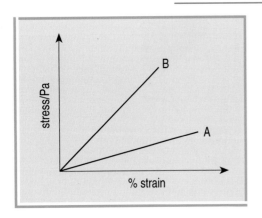

(a) Material B is stiffer because it has a higher Young modulus as shown by the steeper gradient of the graph. (b) Material B is also stronger, for the same reason.

Figure 4.9 Stress–strain curves for two brittle materials

Table 4.4 The Young modulus (E) and ultimate tensile stress (uts) of various materials

Material	E/ GPa	uts/MPa	Density/kg m$^{-3} \times 10^3$
Aluminium alloy (2024)	71	150	2.7
Copper-based alloy	110	42	–
Stainless steel	200	1500	7.8
Nylon 66	2.0	80	1.14
High-density polyethylene	1.0	~3.5	0.91
Polystyrene	3.5	~55	1.05
Glass	70	up to 40*	2.5
Natural rubber	0.02	~30	

*This value varies a great deal.

Q3 Suppose that you were testing 10 m ropes made of each of the five materials in Figure 4.7 by gradually adding more and more weights. Work out the lengths of each rope if they were subjected to a stress of (a) 20 MPa, (b) 40 MPa, (c) 100 MPa. ◆

Karabiners

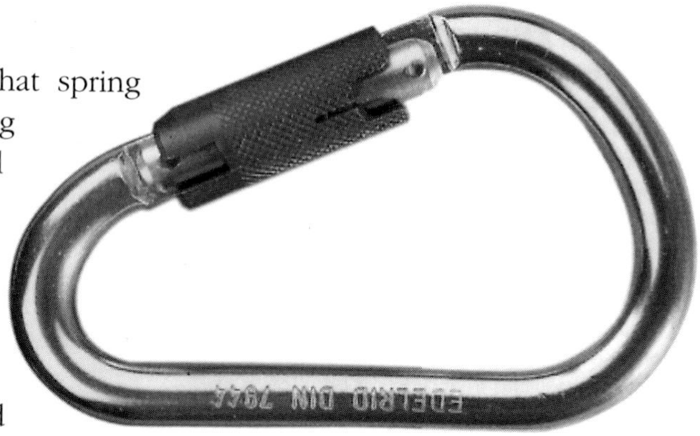

'Krabs' are metal snaplinks, with opening gates that spring shut. They are used to connect pieces of climbing equipment. They are sometimes made from steel or from a less hardwearing aluminium alloy, which is lighter.

Worked example

Suppose a manufacturer is considering developing a karabiner that would be lighter and cheaper than aluminium alloy. Calculate why aluminium alloy has been such a successful material so that comparisons can be made with other materials.

A 1 cm diameter karabiner needs to be able to withstand a force of about 2.0×10^4 N without breaking or distorting so badly that it becomes unclipped. (We will assume that the krab simply stretches without bending during this example.)

We can work out the stress this force produces as follows.

Figure 4.10
A karabiner
Source: Edelrid

If the diameter of the krab is 1 cm, its cross-sectional area, A, is given by

$$A = \frac{\pi d^2}{4}$$

$$= \frac{\pi \left(1 \times 10^{-2} \text{ m}\right)^2}{4}$$

$$= 7.9 \times 10^{-5} \text{ m}^2$$

So, when a force of 1.0×10^4 N (i.e. $\frac{2.0}{2} \times 10^4$ N) pulls on the krab, the stress on each side of the krab is

$$\sigma = \frac{F}{A}$$

$$= \frac{1.0 \times 10^4 \text{ N}}{7.9 \times 10^{-5} \text{ m}^2}$$

$$= 127 \text{ MPa}$$

This is less than the uts of the aluminium alloy so the karabiner will not break.

From Table 4.4, aluminium alloy has a Young modulus of 71 000 MPa.

Young modulus, $E = \dfrac{\sigma}{\varepsilon}$

So, at this stress, the strain of the krab is given by

$$\varepsilon = \frac{\sigma}{E}$$

$$= \frac{127 \times 10^6 \text{ Pa}}{71000 \times 10^6 \text{ Pa}}$$

$$= 1.8 \times 10^{-3} \text{ or about } 0.2\% \text{ (to two significant figures)}$$

So, if the karabiner was 8.0 cm long, and since strain is given by

$$\varepsilon = \frac{\Delta l}{l_0}$$

change in length will be

$$\Delta l = \varepsilon l_0$$

$$= 1.8 \times 10^{-3} \times 8.0 \text{ cm}$$

$$= 0.015 \text{ cm}$$

This increase of 0.15 mm is unlikely to cause the karabiner to unclip, so aluminium is a good material to use for a karabiner. ◆

Q4 If the krab has to cope with a stress of 127 MPa, use the data from Table 4.4 to decide whether it would be safe to use the same shape of karabiner made from any of the other materials listed. ◆

 Why is stainless steel not often used to make karabiners?

Stainless steel is much denser than aluminium, so a karabiner made from stainless steel in the same shape as one made from aluminium would be much heavier. Because stainless steel is stronger (with higher uts and Young modulus) the design could be slimmed down safely, but a krab of the same strength would still be heavier.

 Why is the Young modulus of materials used for ropes relatively unimportant?

The ropes are meant to deform permanently when a climber falls, so the ropes will be used beyond their elastic limit and the stress–strain graph will not be a straight line.

 If a climber takes a heavy fall on a rope, what should they do with the rope?

They should discard it – or use it for unimportant jobs. It will have lost its ability to 'give' and is therefore unsafe.

Q5 It is *possible* to make strong karabiners from plastics. They obviously can't be made of 1 cm diameter plastic, because that would not withstand a 1.0×10^4 N force. However, using thicker plastic will make polyethylene krabs stronger and stiffer.

(a) If the krab material is 8.0 cm long and it must extend only 0.15 mm, calculate its strain.

(b) Calculate the stress that will cause this strain (use the Young modulus of polyethylene from Table 4.4). Compare this stress with the uts of polyethylene.

(c) Calculate the cross-sectional area and hence the diameter of the polyethylene needed.

(d) Comment on your final answer. ◆

Exploration 4.2 Work done in stretching a spring

30 MINUTES

Apparatus:

◆ spring ◆ spring balance ◆ metre rule

You should do this experiment with a partner. Set up the apparatus as shown in Figure 4.11.

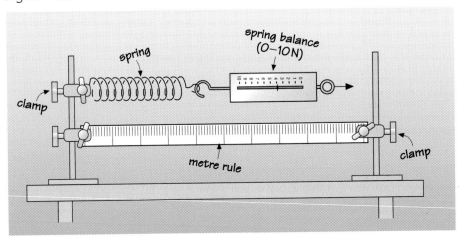

Figure 4.11 Apparatus for Exploration 4.2

Pull the spring so that it extends 5 cm, looking carefully at the spring balance as you do this. Estimate how much work is done in producing this extension.

(*Hint:* Move the spring balance 1 cm at a time. Remember that work done = force × distance moved.)

Take a series of readings for force and extension of the spring balance, moving the spring balance 1 cm at a time. Plot a graph of force versus extension.

For every position of the spring balance the force is different, but each time you move it the work done = force × distance moved.

Use the graph to estimate work done.

It is easy to calculate the work done in moving a constant force, such as a weight. Force × distance is the area under the graph.

It might not be so obvious that the work done is the area under the graph in *all* force versus extension graphs – because the force varies we usually can't take an average value easily. However, imagine dividing the area below the curve into very thin vertical strips. The forces can be considered to remain constant over the tiny displacements covered by these thin strips. So, for each of the tiny displacements, work done = force × displacement, i.e. the area of the tiny strip. Adding all these together will give the total area under the whole curve, and this will represent the total work done for the whole extension. This method of calculating the area under a non-uniform curve is discussed on pages 50–1 of the SLIPP unit *Physics On the Move*.

From your own experience, think about the work done in breaking a piece of metal compared with that done in breaking a piece of glass. Now look at the graphs in Figure 4.7. How does the amount of work done in breaking each compare?

Glass is brittle – it is easily broken. Once a piece of glass is bent too far it breaks totally. Metals, on the other hand, are usually tough. Even if they are dented, it takes much more work to separate the two pieces. The graphs in Figure 4.7 show that glass has a very small area under the curve (little work done in breaking it) whereas the metal has a very large area (lots of work done in breaking it).

When a climber falls whilst attached to a rope, where does the energy come from to do work stretching the rope?

The kinetic energy of the falling climber must all be converted into other forms by the force of the rope. At the instant the climber first becomes stationary, all their kinetic energy has been transferred to the rope.

A glass rope, even if it were very strong, would be disastrous. The glass extends so little that massive forces would be generated in the rope (and also in the climber) to do the work required to stop the climber.

As glass is stretched beyond its elastic limit, plastic stretching occurs. Glass has a fairly high Young modulus and, also importantly, it has a high yield stress. So, even when it is under a lot of stress it will not 'give' much, leading to extremely high stresses at the tips of any tiny scratches on the surface. Once a scratch starts to give, it becomes a crack. The stress at the crack tip is then enormous. As the crack grows the stress gets even bigger, so the glass fails catastrophically, all at once, in brittle failure. The lack of any cushioning effect coupled with sudden, no-warning, catastrophic failure (if it does fail) makes glass a terrible material for climbing ropes.

Q6 Which of the materials in Figure 4.7 you would recommend as a possible material for a climbing rope. Explain the reasons for your choice. ◆

Q7 A rope with a cross-sectional area of 1.2×10^{-4} m^2 and a Young modulus of 5.0×10^{9} Pa is stretched elastically, extending by 0.15 m with a force, F, of magnitude 22.5 kN.

(a) What stress exists in the rope?

(b) What strain exists?

(c) How long is the rope? ◆

Q8 (a) What does the area under a force–extension graph represent?

(b) What does gradient of a force–extension graph represent?

(c) What does the area under a stress–strain graph represent?

(d) What does the gradient of a stress–strain graph represent? ◆

Q9 Estimate the energy per unit volume absorbed before failure for the glass-fibre and nylon in Figure 4.7. ◆

Q10 The table below shows typical values of stress and corresponding strain for different materials.

	Stress/N m^{-2}	Strain/%
Rubber	4.5×10^6	200
Steel	5.2×10^8	0.25
Tendon	7.5×10^7	5.0

(a) Calculate the value for the Young modulus for each of these materials under these particular applied stresses.

(b) Calculate the energy stored per unit volume for each material.

(c) Your answer for rubber will only be an approximate one. Why? ◆

4.3   What holds rope together?

Materials scientists classify materials into four main groups: metals, **ceramics**, glasses and **polymers**. Metals and ceramics are both **crystalline**: they are made of crystals, usually many tiny crystals. Within each crystal is a well-organized arrangement of atoms or molecules, chemically bonded in a regularly repeated three-dimensional pattern (see Figure 4.12).

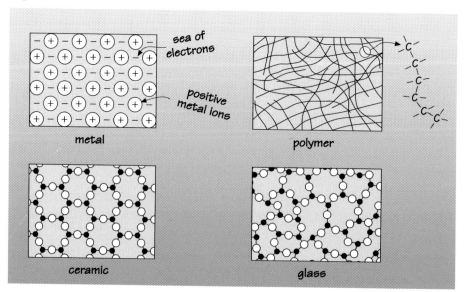

Figure 4.12
Atoms/molecules in metals, ceramics, glasses and polymers

Metals have very different properties from ceramics. As we know, metals are tough – they can be bent and stretched into shape, making them excellent tools. Ceramics, on the other hand, are hard and brittle – they are useful because of their hardness and high melting points, but they are difficult to use as engineering materials. The reason for this is the type of bonding between molecules. (However, because of their lower density, high melting points and hardness, ceramics are often hailed as the engineering materials of the future, and are the subject of much research.)

Metals are all made from atoms that easily lose one or two electrons. Positive metal ions bind together because they are attracted to a 'sea' of these electrons which move around freely, not limited to staying near any one particular atom. Ions are not attracted to the 'sea' in any particular direction. Indeed, if external forces are great enough they make the mass slide over one another – allowing the metal to change shape without falling apart. The electron 'sea' also gives metals unique properties, such as very high thermal and electrical **conductivity**.

Ceramics are non-metallic, polycrystalline materials in which the atomic elements are bonded by chemical bonds where there are no loose electrons. The bonds hold the molecules or ions rigidly in fixed positions, and they cannot change position without falling apart. The bonds are very strong and rigid – giving ceramics great hardness, high Young modulii and high melting points.

Glasses are materials that are non-crystalline. Their molecules are not arranged in a regularly repeated pattern. Lacking any long-range structure they are **amorphous** materials (see Figure 4.12). Liquids are also amorphous. Glasses can be made from most materials if they are cooled fast enough, so that the molecules do not have time to move to their lowest energy position. It is even possible, though very difficult, to make metallic glasses. Ordinary glasses are made of non-metallic compounds that are extremely viscous liquids close to their freezing point, so that the molecules cannot move over one another very easily. It is therefore quite difficult to form crystals as a molten glass is cooled – it tends to form a glass.

Polymers are made of long chains of molecules. Within each chain the molecules are tightly held together by chemical bonds. Because the molecules are so long it is difficult for them to line up in straight rows and form large crystals – the ends get tangled. Imagine trying to organize a plate of spaghetti into straight rows (see Figure 4.12). Polymers usually have crystalline and non-crystalline regions, although the proportion of each varies depending on the chemistry and on the treatment of a sample.

The forces that cause molecules to bond together are all due to the same fundamental force – the attraction of opposite charges, which is known as electrostatic attraction or the **Coulomb force.** All molecules contain positive and negative charges. The positive charges attract the negative charges in adjacent molecules, and vice versa.

 Why don't molecules merge together as their constituent parts attract?

There is also a repulsive force – the positive charges in the molecule will repel the positive charges in the adjacent molecule. The negative charges repel the adjacent negative charges.

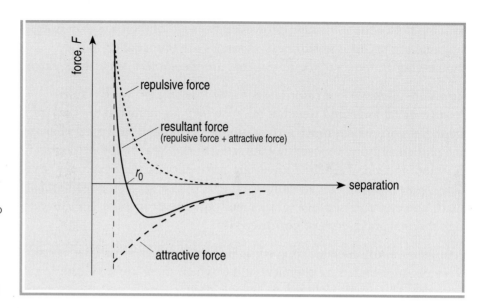

Figure 4.13
Forces between two adjacent molecules at close separation – attractive, repulsive and resultant (net) force

If we apply the laws of electrostatic forces to the attractive and repulsive forces of two typical molecules we get a graph such as Figure 4.13

In Section 4.2 we saw that when materials start to deform their stress–strain curve is always a straight line. If you look at Figure 4.13 you can see why. Molecules usually occupy a balanced **equilibrium position**, at a separation where the attractive and repulsive forces exactly balance – this is shown as r_0 on Figure 4.13. If an external force pulls the molecules to a slightly larger separation the attractive forces become larger than the repulsive forces, and there is a net attractive force. The net force forms a straight line through the equilibrium position, so the attractive force must be proportional to the displacement from the equilibrium position – hence the straight line on the stress–strain curve.

Figure 4.14
Energy separation graph of two molecules

Both the attractive and the repulsive forces (especially the repulsive force) vary a great deal with very small changes in separation; therefore the new equilibrium is achieved with only a very small change in separation.

Hence, the Young modulus is large: a large stress is required to produce a small strain.

We can also apply our knowledge of physics to calculate the energy needed to separate two molecules. By calculating the area under the force/separation graph we can see how much energy is released when the molecules move from 'infinite' separation to their equilibrium positions. The separated molecules start with zero energy, so the energy of the bonded molecules is negative, as shown in Figure 4.14.

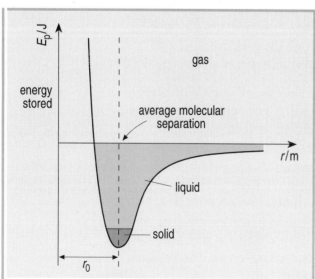

80

This graph explains yet more about the behaviour of solids. As they get hotter they expand and melt. This is because as they get more thermal energy they have more than the minimum energy, and the molecules vibrate between the limits of the **energy well**. This increases the average separation of the molecules – as shown in Figure 4.14.

Eventually the energy increases sufficiently so that some of the molecules can move over one another and the material is able to flow – it becomes liquid.

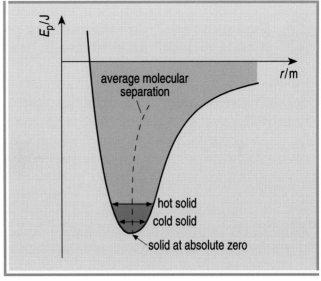

Q11 Look at Figure 4.15 for the combined effect of the attraction and repulsion between molecules in a solid. Consider what happens if the two molecules are compressed slightly from a separation of r_0. Write down your answers to the following questions.

Figure 4.15
The effect of increasing the energy of a pair of molecules

(a) Under a compression, the molecules move closer together. What happens to the resultant force between them?

(b) In the case of compression, an external force moves the particles closer together. Is energy transferred *to* the particles, or is it transferred *from* the particles?

(c) Now consider what happens if the material is stretched and the molecules are moved slightly further apart. Describe the energy transfer for an expansion.

(d) In both examples above, *compression* in part (ii) and *stretching* in part (iii), what happens when the force is released?

(e) Complete the gaps in the following passage.

If an external force is applied to a material to stretch it, or to compress it, then _____ is done _____ the material. Energy is stored because of the _____ of the molecules relative to each other. When the force is removed the molecules return to their _____ positions. The strain energy may do _____ and/or be transferred to _____ energy. ◆

Exploration 4.3 Are the melting point and the Young modulus of metals related? An exercise in developing a hypothesis

40 MINUTES

Develop a hypothesis about the way the Young modulus and melting point may be related in a material. Explain the reasons behind your ideas.
(*Hint:* Think about what controls the Young modulus on an atomic scale. What controls the melting point on an atomic scale? Would you therefore expect to see any relationship between E and melting point? What would it be – direct? linear? inverse?)

If you have no idea at this stage, guess.

Plan a series of experiments to test your hypothesis. (You will not actually be doing the experiments, so you may imagine that you have access to metal wires of various shapes and sizes (you won't have access to huge pieces of gold or platinum), strong tensile testing machines (up to 10 000 N load), furnaces that heat up to 2000° C with suitable temperature measuring equipment. You would also have normal physics laboratory apparatus.)

Make sure you give details about the number of experiments, the size of the samples, the materials you might choose (suggest some metals).

How would you process the information to check your hypothesis – what graphs would you plot? What would you do with the graphs – what lines would you draw? Would you do anything mathematical with them?

When you have finished your design, ask your teacher for the data in the Teachers' Guide to check your hypothesis without getting your hands sweaty and dirty!

4.4 Choice of materials for ropes

When mountaineering first became popular in the nineteenth century, the ropes the climbers used were made from natural fibres, such as hemp. Artificial polymers hadn't been invented. Roping techniques were so unreliable that roping offered little security, so the ropes were made relatively thin (7 mm diameter) in order to keep the weight down. Until climbing equipment was revolutionized by modern materials and design, the motto for climbers was always 'the leader never falls'.

After the Second World War a new polyamide synthetic fibre called 'Nylon' came on the market and was soon used not only for ladies' stockings but also for ropes. It proved to be an ideal material for climbing ropes. It has a low density and is very strong. It has a relatively low Young modulus, and once past its elastic limit it undergoes considerable deformation before breaking. It also repels water and does not rot.

Nylon fibres woven together like traditional ropes became the standard climbing rope for several decades.

But these nylon ropes are not without faults. If a climber is left dangling at the end of a rope it gradually untwists, spinning the climber round, and the rope fibres are easily snagged on rocks. Also, although Nylon repels water, Nylon rope can still absorb water amongst the fibres, and the outer shape of the rope produces a large amount of friction over the rock.

In 1951, the manufacturer Edelrid introduced the *kernmantle* rope, which has now become the standard climbing rope (see Figure 4.16). The inner *kern* contains the core of strong nylon fibres (usually twisted or braided together). The outer *mantle* is a woven casing, designed to protect the fibres, reduce friction and repel water. This type of construction makes it possible to tailor the cushioning of a rope and to customize ropes for different purposes. The inner fibres are designed to slip within the sheath when the rope sustains a heavy fall. The friction within the rope is another means of dissipating the kinetic energy of the falling climber.

4.5 Fall factors and belays – the physics of roping techniques

The severity of a fall is described by the fall factor. The fall factor is defined as the ratio of the vertical distance fallen in free-fall to the length of rope holding the fall. The worst fall factor that can possibly be sustained is 2 (see Figure 4.17(i) overleaf). Climbers use their ropes so that they never risk such a severe fall. Several such methods are shown in Figure 4.17(ii) to (iv).

Q12 (a) Place the four roping techniques in order of safety – most dangerous first. Give your reasons. (b) Roughly estimate the fall factors sustained by the climbers in Figure 4.17(iii) and (iv). ◆

Q13 If two climbers with ropes of different lengths (but otherwise identical) fall the same distance in free fall, why does the longer rope lessen the severity of the fall? ◆

Until the 1930s, mountaineers roped themselves together, often simply tying ropes around their waist and so tying one climber to the next. To improve protection, climbers also tied themselves to boulders and other fixed objects that would hold a climber still (statically). In the 1930s, the Sierra Club (a non-profit-making organization dedicated to the preservation of wilderness and improving the quality of life) introduced the dynamic belay. This allowed controlled slippage of the rope through the belayer's gloved hands, and is essentially the technique that is still used today. In the roping techniques shown in Figure 4.17(ii) and (iii), the most dangerous situation occurs when the leader falls, but the use of longer, better quality and thicker ropes and improved technique (such as the controlled, dynamic belay) have greatly improved safety.

Figure 4.16
The construction of a modern kernmantle rope
Source: Edelrid

Figure 4.17 Roping styles

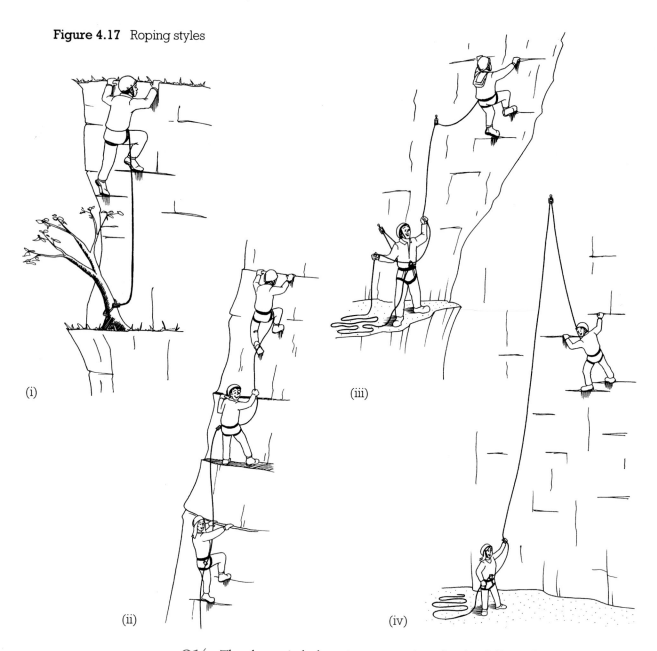

(i)

(ii)

(iii)

(iv)

Q14 The dynamic belay gives more time for the falling climber to be slowed down, reducing the impact forces on their body. Why isn't the belayer who is holding the rope at the bottom pulled up into the air by the falling climber, particularly if the falling climber is heavier than the belayer? (Occasionally a very heavy climber taking a bad fall will lift a belayer, but this is very unusual.) ◆

 Suggested further exploration

Design an experiment to compare the potential of materials for a range of climbing ropes. Use Plasticene models for climbers, and drop them in different ways using the 'ropes' made from different materials.

Achievements

After working through this section you should be able to:

- explain the relevance of bonding and structure to the strengths of different materials

- explain the relevance of the different parameters associated with material behaviour under stress to their suitability for climbing ropes

- define stress, strain and the Young modulus and perform calculations using the Young modulus

- describe the behaviour of different materials appropriately as brittle, tough, elastic, ductile, malleable, plastic or stiff

- interpret stress–strain graph plots for typical ductile, brittle, elastic and polymeric material

- calculate energy stored per unit volume of a material

- distinguish between elastic and plastic deformation of a material

- describe, qualitatively, the force–molecular separation graph between two molecules

- identify important features on a force–separation graph for two particles, such as *equilibrium separation*.

Glossary

Amorphous   Non-crystalline material.

Brittleness   The inability of a material to absorb energy without breaking. It is the opposite of *toughness*. (Hard materials are often brittle.)

Ceramics   Non-organic, non-metallic materials, e.g. porcelain.

Conductivity   A measure of the ability of a material to conduct electricity or heat.

Coulomb force   Force of attraction or repulsion resulting from interaction of two or more charged particles; for point charges, force is proportional to each of the charges and inversely proportional to their separation.

Crystalline   Composed of crystals (structures in which atoms or molecules are arranged in a regular manner).

Ductility   Ability of a material to be cold-worked (e.g. drawing or extruding) without cracking.

Equilibrium position   A point where the forces and moments of forces (taken about any point) acting on a body add up to zero. Equilibrium may be stable, neutral or unstable, depending on whether the energy of the system rises, remains uniform or falls when the system is perturbed.

Elastic deformation   Deformation that occurs in the elastic region of a stress–strain graph before the elastic limit is reached. The sample will revert to its original shape and size following the removal of stress.

Elastic limit   Value of stress and/or strain below which a material returns to its original size after a stress is removed. The elastic limit is usually close to both the yield point and the limit of proportionality, the point beyond which the stress–strain graph is no longer straight.

Elasticity   Ability of a material to return to its original dimensions after the removal of a stress.

Energy well   If work must be done on an object to move it in any direction, it is said to reside in an energy well. Unless energy (measured in joules) equal to the depth of the well is supplied the object is trapped. An example would be an electron orbiting a proton or a satellite orbiting a planet:

work must be done to remove either from the influence of the central body. They each reside in 'potential wells'.

Hardness   The ability of a material to resist abrasion or indentation. Increased tensile strength usually results in increased hardness.

Impact force   The force sustained by a body during a collision or other intense, short-lived interaction.

Malleability   The ability to be deformed in all directions by hammering or squeezing without cracking.

Pascal   Symbol: Pa. The unit of stress defined as $N\,m^{-2}$.

Plasticity   The ability of a material in a solid state to flow and change shape permanently under the action of a stress.

Polymer   A material built up of 100 to 100 000 or more monomers – smaller units (e.g. Polythene is made up of ethene).

Strain, tensile   The fractional extension of a sample given by the equation

$$\text{strain} = \frac{\text{extension}}{\text{original length}} \quad \text{or} \quad \varepsilon = \frac{\Delta l}{l}$$

Strength   The ability of a material to withstand an applied force without failing.

Stress, tensile   Unit: newton $metre^{-2}$ $(N\,m^{-2})$ or pascal (Pa). This is experienced by a sample under tension. It is defined as tensile force per unit cross-sectional area, i.e. $\sigma = F/A$.

Toughness   The ability of a material to absorb energy as it breaks. A tough material requires a lot of energy to break it. It is the opposite of brittleness.

Yield point   The value of stress on a stress–strain graph at which the sample undergoes substantial plastic extension for no increase (or even decrease) in stress.

Young modulus   Unit: pascal (Pa) or newton $metre^{-2}$ $(N\,m^{-2})$. A measure of the elasticity of a material. It is the ratio of tensile stress to strain evaluated within the linear part of the stress/strain graph for a particular material. The higher the value of the Young modulus, the stiffer (more rigid) the material. (Also called tensile modulus and modulus of elasticity.)

Ultimate tensile stress (uts)   The maximum tensile stress that a material can take before breaking, i.e. its breaking stress.

Answers to Ready to Study test

R1

See Figure 4.18.

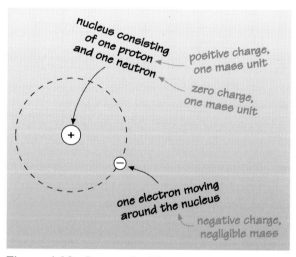

Figure 4.18   Answer for R1

R2

Six electrons orbit the nucleus.

R3

There are 13 protons.

R4

It will be most attracted to D^{--} and repelled most from C^{++}.

R5

The main ways are: (a) by ionic bonds, by charge attraction between oppositely charged ions; (b) by covalent bonds, by the sharing of an electron by two neighbouring atoms; (c) temporarily – an electron may depart from one atom to another, thus the atoms will be oppositely charged; (d) by metallic bonds, by interaction of atoms with 'free' electrons surrounding them; (e) by Van der Waals' bonds, by interaction between nuclei and the non-symmetrical charge distributions of electrons around them.

R6

The climber exerts a force of −1900 N on the rope (because the force is equal and opposite). The rope exerts a force of −1900 N on the rock face (for the same reason).

R7

Cross-sectional area is given by

$$A = \pi r^2$$

$$= \frac{\pi d^2}{4}$$

where r and d are radius and diameter respectively.

(a)

$$A = \frac{\pi (10.0\,\text{mm})^2}{4}$$

$$= 78.5\,\text{mm}^2 \text{ (to three significant figures)}$$

(b)

$$10\,\text{mm} = 0.010\,\text{m}$$

$$1\,\text{mm} = 10^{-3}\,\text{m}$$

$$(1\,\text{mm})^2 = 10^{-6}\,\text{m}^2$$

$$78.5\,\text{mm}^2 = 78.5 \times 10^{-6}\,\text{m}^2$$

$$= 7.85 \times 10^{-5}\,\text{m}^2$$

Therefore in m^2

$$A = 7.85 \times 10^{-5}\,\text{m}^2 \text{ (to three significant figures)}$$

R8

$$\text{Pressure} = \frac{\text{force}}{\text{area}}.$$ It is measured in pascals, symbol Pa.

Answers to questions in the text

Q1

The Bluewater rope produces the lowest impact forces and takes most falls in general.

Q2

The ropes aren't uniform throughout their length, and the drop towers are not quite the same. Drop tower 1 consistently seems to measure lower impact forces and the ropes take more drops before failing. This suggests that the results are being affected by the drop tower and not the rope in this case. It could be that the drop is slightly smaller.

Q3

(a) Nylon has a 2% strain and therefore extends $2/100 \times 10\,\text{m} = 0.2\,\text{m}$. Rubber has a 10% strain and therefore extends $10/100 \times 10\,\text{m} = 1\,\text{m}$. Steel, glass and aluminium have less than 0.5% strain and so extend less than $0.5/100 \times 10\,\text{m}$, i.e. less than 0.05 m.

(b) At 40 MPa nylon and rubber have broken.

	Strain/%	Extension/cm
Steel	0.05	0.5
Aluminium	0.1	1.0
Glass	0.1	1.0

(c) At 100 MPa, the glass will have broken. Steel has approximately 0.1% strain and therefore extends about 1 cm. Aluminium has approximately 0.2% strain and therefore extends about 2 cm.

Q4

Only stainless steel has a breaking stress over 127 MPa. The other materials would all break at this stress, so they should not be used for karabiners of *this shape and size*.

Q5

(a) Δl for the krab is 0.15 mm (0.015 cm), and the krab is 8.0 cm long. Therefore

$$\text{strain} = \frac{\Delta l}{l_o}$$

$$= \frac{0.015\,\text{cm}}{8.0\,\text{cm}}$$

$$= 1.88 \times 10^{-3}$$

(b) If the Young modulus of polyethylene is 1.0×10^9 Pa (and stress and strain are proportional)

$$E = \frac{\sigma}{\varepsilon}$$

so

$$\sigma = E \times \varepsilon$$

$$= 1.0 \times 10^9 \,\text{Pa} \times 1.88 \times 10^{-3}$$

$$= 1.88 \times 10^6 \,\text{Pa}$$

(This is much less than the uts of the polyethylene.)

(c) To limit the stress to this value the krab will need to be made with a large cross-sectional area.

Since $\sigma = \dfrac{F}{A}$, and the maximum force on each side is 1.0×10^4 N

$$A = \frac{F}{\sigma}$$

$$= \frac{1.0 \times 10^4 \,\text{N}}{1.88 \times 10^6 \,\text{N}\,\text{m}^{-2}}$$

$$= 5.32 \times 10^{-3} \,\text{m}^2$$

For this cross-sectional area the diameter of the krab material will be given by

$$A = \pi \left(\frac{d}{2} \right)^2$$

$$d^2 = \frac{4A}{\pi}$$

$$d = \sqrt{\frac{4A}{\pi}}$$

$$= \sqrt{\frac{4 \times 5.32 \times 10^{-3} \,\text{m}^2}{\pi}}$$

$$= 82 \times 10^{-3} \,\text{m}$$

or 8.2 cm!

(d) For a 8.0 cm long krab it would be *impossible* for it to have an 8.2 cm diameter!

Q6

Nylon is the material of choice. Rubber is too stretchy and the other materials are too stiff. With a rope made from rubber you might hit the ground. The other materials would produce such a high impact force that it would possibly kill you.

Q7

(a) stress = force/cross-sectional area

$$\text{stress} = \frac{\text{tension}}{\text{cross-sectional area}}$$

$$= \frac{22.5\,\text{kN}}{1.2 \times 10^{-4} \,\text{m}^2}$$

$$= 187.5\,\text{MPa}$$

$$= 190\,\text{MPa (to two significant figures)}$$

(b)

$$E = \frac{\text{stress}}{\text{strain}}$$

so

$$\text{strain} = \frac{\text{stress}}{E}$$

$$= \frac{187.5 \times 10^6 \text{ Pa}}{5.0 \times 10^9 \text{ Pa}}$$

$$= 3.75 \times 10^{-2}$$

(or 4%).

(c)

$$\text{strain} = \frac{\text{extension}}{\text{original length}}$$

so

$$\text{original length} = \frac{\text{extension}}{\text{strain}}$$

$$= \frac{0.15\,\text{m}}{0.0375}$$

$$= 4.0 \text{ m}$$

Q8

(a) Work done on sample while deforming it, in N m or J.

(b) Stiffness of a sample or spring-constant k of a spring, in N m^{-1}.

(c) Work done per unit original volume on the sample during deformation, in J m^{-3}.

(d) Young modulus (for the straight part through the origin only).

Q9

Energy per unit volume is given by area under a stress–strain graph. For glass-fibre

$$\text{area} = \frac{1}{2} \times 45\,\text{MPa} \times 0.1\%$$

$$= 22 \times 10^3 \text{ J m}^{-3}$$

For nylon

$$A = (\text{area under triangular part})$$
$$\quad + (\text{area under rectangular part})$$

$$= \left(\frac{1}{2} \times 30\,\text{MPa} \times 4\% \right) + \left(30\,\text{MPa} \times 6\% \right)$$

$$= \left(60 \times 10^4 + 180 \times 10^4 \right) \text{J m}^{-3}$$

$$= 2.4 \times 10^6 \text{ J m}^{-3}$$

Q10

(a) $E = \dfrac{\sigma}{\varepsilon}$

For rubber

$$E = \frac{4.5 \times 10^6}{2} \text{ N m}^{-2}$$

$$= 2.3 \times 10^6 \text{ N m}^{-2}$$

For steel

$$E = \frac{5.2 \times 10^8}{0.25 \times 10^{-2}} \text{ N m}^{-2}$$

$$= 2.1 \times 10^{11} \text{ N m}^{-2}$$

For tendon

$$E = \frac{7.5 \times 10^7}{5.0 \times 10^{-2}} \text{ N m}^{-2}$$

$$= 1.5 \times 10^9 \text{ N m}^{-2}$$

(b) For a linear relationship, energy stored per unit volume = area under stress/strain graph

For rubber

$$\text{energy} = \frac{1}{2} \times 4.5 \times 10^6 \text{ N m}^{-2} \times \frac{200}{100}$$

$$= 4.5 \times 10^6 \text{ J m}^{-3}$$

(to two significant figures)

For steel

$$\text{energy} = \frac{1}{2} \times 5.2 \times 10^8 \, \text{Nm}^{-2} \times \frac{0.25}{100}$$

$$= 6.5 \times 10^5 \, \text{Jm}^{-3}$$

(to two significant figures)

For tendon

$$\text{energy} = \frac{1}{2} \times 7.5 \times 10^7 \, \text{Nm}^{-2} \times \frac{5}{100}$$

$$= 1.9 \times 10^6 \, \text{Jm}^{-3}$$

(to two significant figures)

(c) The value for rubber is only approximate because rubber does not exhibit linear behaviour: it doesn't obey Hooke's law.

Q11

(a) The resultant force becomes repulsive. As the molecules get closer the repulsive force rises very rapidly.

(b) Energy is transferred *to* the particles, taking the form of electrical potential energy.

(c) Work is done by the external force against the attractive force pulling the molecules back together. Energy is transferred *to* the molecules, again as electrical potential energy.

(d) When the force is released the molecules move back to their equilibrium positions.

(e) If an external force is applied to a material to stretch it, or to compress it, then work is done on the material. Energy is stored because of the change in mean positions of the molecules relative to each other. When the force is removed the molecules return to their equilibrium [or original] positions. The strain energy may do external work and/or be transferred to internal [or thermal] energy.

Q12

(a) (i) This is probably the most dangerous, and is fairly useless for most climbs – the climber has no way to climb higher than the maximum length of rope. If they fell the fall would be very severe, with a potential fall factor of 2.

(ii) This offers good protection, but only if the other climbers are well placed to hold their fall. The leader must not fall, however. If they do, they could easily pull the second climber off the mountain. The two falling climbers could then pull off the third.

(iii) Lead climbing with well-placed karabiners holding the rope is the method used by most modern 'free' climbers.

(iv) Top-roping is the safest method of climbing used by novices. The climber doesn't have to carry any karabiners or equipment for attaching them to rock faces and the fall factor is always small.

(b) In (iii) the climber falls approximately 1 m on to about 3 m of rope.

$$\text{Fall factor} = \frac{1}{3}$$

In (iv) the climber falls maybe 1 m (if that, it depends on how much rope the belayer has pulled in), on to about 13 m of rope.

$$\text{Fall factor} = \frac{1}{13}$$

Your answers will depend on your estimates of the rope lengths.

Q13

A longer rope will stretch a longer distance at the same stress. Work done = force × distance. Since the work done by the rope stops the climber falling, the greater distance allows the climber to be stopped with less force.

Q14

The falling climber produces a very high force in the rope, but, because of friction at the karabiner, most of this is not transferred to the belayer.

If you have ever stood on a diving board and wondered how to get off it again without making a fool of yourself, you will appreciate something of the challenge of springboard diving. A perfectly executed dive has a thrill and beauty of its own. How physics affects the way the diver and the board behave is fixed and cannot be adjusted to allow a diver to correct even the smallest mistake, so the mechanics of the board and of human motion (biomechanics) from the board have a major effect on the outcome of the dive.

Each diver improves their diving techniques by fine-tuning their reflexes. There is very little time to think about anything during a dive, let alone applied physics! A diver must learn the correct techniques, so that the reflexes they develop will produce the best performances. Critical analysis is a vital factor in the development of a diver, and it is here that an understanding of physics is useful. It is also particularly useful for the coach.

BOB MORGAN

Bob Morgan, one of Britain's top divers, has been diving since he was 12. He says that he feels he needs to understand physics better, and that a better knowledge of physics would have helped him to avoid a lot of the bad habits he learned in his early years. Habits that have been difficult to change later.

'If you know that there is an ultimate way of doing it (you can't argue with physics if it's right can you?), if you believe in it, you can work toward it and know you are moving in the right direction.

'The pleasure of diving for me is getting the dive right mechanically and making it aesthetically pleasing for those watching. Both of these are needed in combination to get the dive exactly right and impress the judges.'

Basically the sport of diving as practised today requires taking off from a height, and aiming to remain free in the air for as long as possible. This height is obtained either by diving from a high platform or projecting oneself high into the air from a springboard. During the flight the body may be held in various positions at the choice of the diver whilst he [or she] performs either a graceful header or a more complicated dive consisting of a variety of somersaulting and/or twisting movements before entering the water.

Diving enables you to do something that can be achieved in few other sports, that is to fly through the air without any means of support and land safely without discomfort.

(Rackham, 1975)

PART II

PHYSICS FOR SPRINGBOARD DIVING

Springboard diving is a gymnastic sport in which the landing medium is water rather than a mat. Competition dives start with a take-off from either a rigid platform at a height of up to 10 m above the water surface (platform diving) or from a flexible springboard up to 3 m above the water (springboard diving).

There are about 70 dives listed, each with a number and for each one judges will mark the different stages in the dive: the starting position, take-off, flight and entry. Most dives start with the diver on their feet and end with a head-first entry, so the diver executes a half somersault. This can be forwards or backwards, and the diver may start facing away from the board or toward it. During flight the diver may also add a twist (rotating around an axis running from their head to their feet). Finally the diver will aim to hold a particular body shape during the dive – straight, piked or tucked.

Mark Lenzi, 1992 (Source: David Leah, Allsport)

Tracey Miles diving over Barcelona in 1992 (Source: Bob Martin, Allsport)

Each dive is given a tariff according to its difficulty. For example, a simple Forward Dive Tuck is rated at 1.2 from the 1 m springboard, whereas the Forward 3 1/2 Somersault Pike from the 3 m springboard is rated at 3.0.

A dive usually begins with a jump. The higher the jump, the more time the diver has to perform the dive before entering the water. Complicated dives such as two and a half somersaults take a relatively long time – so being able to jump high is essential for a successful diver. The diver must learn to control the forces that act on the body on take-off. The direction of the jump is crucial in determining the success of the dive, and the direction of the force on the diver's body determines the rotation that can be performed during the dive.

READY TO STUDY TEST

Before you begin this section you should be able to:

- define and calculate the moment of a force using $T = Fx \sin\theta$
- apply the principle of moments
- estimate the centre of gravity of a body
- explain what is meant by the weight of a body
- sketch and use diagrams that show the forces acting on a body
- define and use momentum as mass × velocity and impulse as force × time and explain how they are related
- state and use Newton's laws of motion
- explain the principle of conservation of momentum
- define energy, work and power and give their correct units
- use the equations of uniform acceleration

$$v = u + at$$

$$v^2 = u^2 + 2as$$

$$s = ut + \frac{1}{2}at^2$$

- use the formulae for kinetic energy:

$$E_k = \frac{mv^2}{2}$$

and for potential energy:

$$E_p = mgh$$

(the second formula is true for values of h near the Earth's surface)

- describe how energy is conserved in mechanical systems.

THE TAKE-OFF

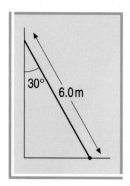

Figure 5.1
Ladder leaning
against a wall

R1 A 6.0 m ladder leans against a wall at an angle of 30° to the vertical (see Figure 5.1). If the ladder is perfectly uniform (i.e. it balances in the middle) and it has a mass of 20 kg, calculate the moment of the gravitational force on the ladder about the base of the ladder. (Use $g = 9.81$ N kg^{-1}.)

R2 A see-saw is balanced until a 50 kg girl sits on one end, 2.0 m from the fulcrum (see Figure 5.2). Where should her 55 kg friend sit in order to balance the see-saw again? (Use $g = 9.81$ N kg^{-1}.)

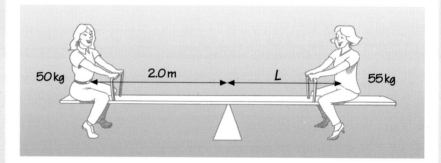

Figure 5.2
Balancing a see-saw

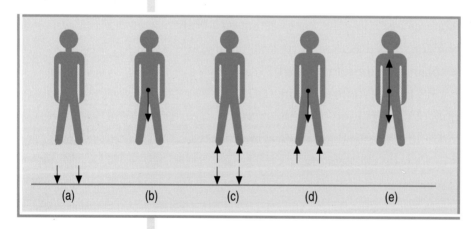

Figure 5.3
Free body diagrams
of a man standing on
the ground

R3 Which of the diagrams in Figure 5.3 correctly shows the forces that act on the man standing on the ground?

R4 A 0.70 kg ball initially at rest is pushed with a force of 300 N for 0.15 s. (a) Calculate the impulse that acts on the ball. (b) Calculate its velocity after 0.15 s.

R5 A 70 kg canoeist jumps horizontally into a 30 kg canoe at a speed of 4.0 m s^{-1}. The canoe is initially stationary, but is floating, untied, in a lake, so that very little friction acts on the boat. Use the principle of conservation of momentum to calculate the final speed of the canoe and the canoeist.

R6 A 55 kg diver climbs from the poolside to the top of a 3.0 m board (i.e. a vertical height of 3.0 m). (a) Calculate the work the diver did to climb up there. (b) If the climb took 5.0 s, calculate the diver's mean power output. (Use $g = 9.81$ N kg^{-1}.)

5.1 How to get high – the physics of jumping

 Exploration 5.1   How does the body generate the take-off forces?

Apparatus:

◆ *Multimedia Motion* CD-ROM package
◆ IBM compatible computer running MS Windows

The take-off forces are forces that push the body up, i.e. forces greater than gravity. These are generated by the legs pushing down.

1   Select the sequence 'Jump from stool' – either the man or the woman.

2   Use markers to plot the vertical movement of the jumper's centre of gravity (located just above their hips).

3   Plot graphs of the vertical displacement y, the vertical velocity $v(y)$ and the vertical acceleration $a(y)$.

4   Repeat steps 2 and 3 following the position of the balls of the feet of the man or the woman.

5   Compare the graphs: what do you notice about the timing of the forces (and hence the accelerations) of these body parts?

Q1   Why do you think that the centre of gravity starts to move before the feet? ◆

Analysis of forces

Q2   About 14% of the mass of the body is in the lower legs and the feet. The mass of the man is about 70 kg and the mass of the woman is about 50 kg. For the jumper you have analysed, calculate the mass of the lower legs and feet, and the mass of the rest of their body. ◆

There are two important phases during take-off: (1) when the feet are stationary, but the upper body is accelerating, (2) when the feet are accelerating to catch up with the upper body. However, we must first study the equilibrium of forces that act on the jumper before they begin to jump.

Phase 0 – before jumping

Consider the masses of the lower legs as if they were separate from the rest of the body. The rest of the body (ROB) rests on the lower legs (LL).

Q3   Using the mass of the ROB from Question 2, calculate the weight of the ROB, W_{ROB}, and draw a free body diagram of the ROB. (*Hint:* Assume ROB is in equilibrium and draw the ROB and LL as if cut off at the knees.) (Use $g = 10$ N kg^{-1}.) ◆

Q4   Using the mass of the LL from Question 2, calculate the weight of the LL, W_{LL}, and draw a free body diagram of the LL. (*Hint:* Remember that the LL hold up the ROB, and use the hint from Question 3 again.) (Use $g = 10$ N kg^{-1}.) ◆

Phase 1 – feet stationary

Use the graphs you plotted to estimate the maximum upward acceleration of the ROB when the person jumps.

Use the mass of the ROB calculated in Question 2 and Newton's second law to calculate the **net force** acting on the ROB.

Draw a labelled free body diagram of the ROB to show the forces acting on it in phase 1.

Phase 2 – feet moving

During phase 2 the feet accelerate upwards away from the stool. What gives rise to the force that accelerates the feet away from the stool? Discuss this with others in your group and check it with your teacher.

Use the graphs you have plotted to estimate the maximum upward acceleration of the LL when the person jumps. Estimate the size of this force.

Use the mass of the LL calculated in Question 2 and Newton's second law to calculate the net force acting on the LL.

Draw a labelled free body diagram of the LL to show the forces acting on it in phase 2.

What forces will act (i) on the stool, (ii) on the body during phase 2?

Discuss the answers to these questions with other students and your teacher.

Girl about to jump from the stool (Source: *Multimedia Motion* CD-ROM, Cambridge Science Media)

Exploration 5.2 How big are take-off forces?

30 MINUTES

Apparatus:

◆ bathroom scales ◆ metre rule

You need a partner to perform this experiment – don't try to do it on your own.

1 Stand on the scales, allowing them to become stationary, and make a note of the reading on the scales. Because you are not accelerating this will give an indication of your weight. (*Note:* Although bathroom scales are calibrated in terms of mass (in pounds or kilograms) they actually measure force, as you will see when you subject them to different accelerations using the same mass (i.e. you). In normal use the acceleration is a constant (*g*), so it can be ignored.)

2 Suddenly bend your knees. As your body accelerates down (i.e. when you start to move down) look at the reading on the scales.

3 When you finish dropping down, what happens to the reading on the scales?

4 From the stationary crouched position, jump up and off the scales. As your body accelerates upwards, what happens to the reading on the scales?

5 Now stand still on the scales and investigate the effect of swinging your arms (a) up and (b) down.

6 To jump to increasing vertical heights you need to increase your take-off velocity. This means increasing the take-off force (if the take-off time doesn't change.) Use the metre rule to investigate whether this is correct. Write down any assumptions you are making. Try not to exceed the maximum force allowed by the scales!

Analysis

Remember that your mass does not change during the experiment! The equal, but opposite force to your weight is the force you exert, pulling the Earth toward you! You are not in free fall, however, because of the ground (in this case the scales), which is pushing back with an equal, but opposite force to the force you exert from your feet.

Q5 Copy the diagrams in Figure 5.4 and sketch in the forces that act on your body in steps 1–4, then compare and discuss your answers with another student. (*Hint:* There are only two forces – your weight and the force from the scales.) ◆

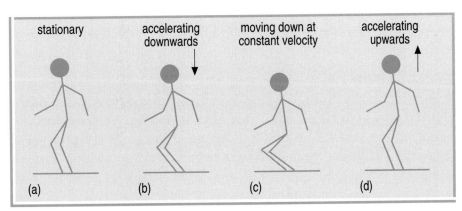

Figure 5.4
Pin diagrams to show the phases 1–4 of a take-off

Exploration 5.3   Techniques to increase vertical take-off velocity

Apparatus:

◆ metre rule   ◆ blackboard and chalk, or flip-chart   ◆ paper and pens

30 *MINUTES*

You need a partner to perform this experiment – don't try to do it on your own. Record all your results in a table like Table 5.1, but for analysis purposes the best jump is the one to consider.

Table 5.1   Sample table for Exploration 5.3

Type of jump	Height reached/m					
	1	2	3	4	5	Best
1 Basic						
2 Arm swing						
3						
4						
5						

1   The basic jump

Stand on the floor with your knees bent at about 90° with one arm above your head and the other arm pressed to your side. *Without bending your legs further*, see how high you can jump, reaching with your raised arm to touch the wall as high as possible. Make five attempts and record your highest reach using this technique. It is very important that you don't cheat and dip your knees or move your arms. Make sure that your partner checks your posture.

2   The effect of arm swing

Keeping the leg action the same as before, start with your arms low. Swing your arms upwards *just* before you extend your legs. With practice you should be able to reach higher than in 1. When you feel that you have mastered the technique, make a record of the heights obtained in your jumps and record the best five in a table similar to the sample Table 5.1.

3   The effect of dipping the knees

Go back to holding one arm above your head. Now start the jump with your knees only slightly bent. Dip to make your knees bend to 90°, and then spring up. With practice (you probably do this naturally) you will be able to reach much higher. When you feel that you have mastered the technique, record the heights achieved for your best five jumps.

4 The effect of jumping

Springing up from a preliminary jump magnifies the effect of dipping the knees. Hold one arm above your head as before, but this time do a preliminary jump. Jump, and as you land dip your knees and spring back up immediately for the main jump. When you feel that you have mastered the technique, record the heights achieved for your best five jumps.

5 Full arm swing and jump

Repeat 4, but this time jump with both arms above your head. As you land from the preliminary jump, drive your arms down hard as you dip. As you spring back up raise your arms. This may take a little practice, but it should get you higher even than 4. When you feel that you have mastered the technique, record the heights achieved for your best five jumps.

Analysis

Each adaptation of the basic jump should show an improvement in height – certainly in trained athletes it does. Explain why. Here are some hints to get you started.

- The vertical height reached by your centre of gravity depends only on the take-off velocity. Once you have left the floor gravity is the only force that acts on your centre of gravity, so it will accelerate you downwards at about 10 m s^{-2} (unless you can do the experiment on another planet!).

- Your take-off velocity is controlled by the **impulse** you receive. In all the jumps there will be an instant when your centre of gravity is stationary. The impulse (force × time) determines the increase in **momentum** from then on, and hence the take-off velocity.

- The impulse received by your body depends on both force and time for which the force acts. By using a similar angle of knee-bend we have made the time roughly the same. The impulse is therefore mostly determined by the size of the force. This force is called the **ground reaction force (grf)**. How do dipping, swinging the arms and jumping alter the ground reaction force?

- We can also analyse the jump in terms of energy. At the end of a dip or a jump the muscles and tendons in the back of your calf stretch like elastic. Why should that affect the height to which you can jump?

- Transfer of momentum. A well-known technique in sports science is called transfer of momentum. By swinging your arms up as you take off you can increase the height of your jump. This is an illustration of the transfer of momentum. Because your arms are joined to your body, when your arms slow down at the top of the swing, your body speeds up. (There are other complicating factors such as external forces, but the 'jolt' from your arms does speed up your body.) The principle of **conservation of momentum** can be applied within your body: your moving arms share their momentum with the rest of your body.

Summary

After working through the explorations above you should now understand the following principles of jumping.

- An upwards accelerating force is provided from the ground reaction force (grf) on the feet.

- The harder the feet push down, the larger the grf.

- The final take-off velocity is determined by the impulse (force × time) from the grf and the mass of the diver.

- The time for the impulse depends on the jumping technique, particularly on bending the knees.

- The size of the grf can be increased by driving the mass of the body down hard on the ground – by jumping down, dipping the knees and by swinging the arms down.

- Upon take-off, momentum is transferred through the body. First the arms, then the upper body and finally the legs and feet are accelerated away from the ground. (Not all the momentum of the body comes from the arms – but as the body takes off, the arms start off moving rapidly and are slowed down by the rest of the body – so they speed up the rest of the body!)

5.2 Getting into a spin

So far we have considered a vertical force, accelerating a diver upwards. A completely vertical take-off dive would not lead to a dive, since the diver would just land back on the board again. The direction of the force on the diver is crucial to determining the success of the dive, and we will be considering this later on, but the other factor that is crucial to the success of the dive is the **torque** generated on the body during take-off.

During a dive the diver is likely to somersault and/or twist (see Figure 5.5). A somersault is a rotation about a horizontal axis across the body, through the diver's centre of gravity. A twist is a rotation around an axis running from the head to the feet. Once the diver is in the air, because the only force acting on them is gravity, there is no way to set up a torque to rotate the body, but it is possible to slow the rotation down or speed it up by changing the shape of the body. Control of the forces that act on the body at take-off is crucial.

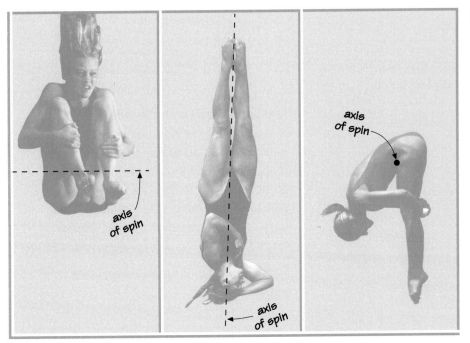

Figure 5.4
Divers twisting and somersaulting
(a) Erica Sorgi
(Source: Al Bello, Allsport)
(b) Cheril Santini
(Source: Jamie Squire, Allsport)
(c) Veroni Ribot
(Source: Sporting Pictures (UK) Ltd)

Over-balancing (lean)

Exploration 5.4 Investigating the relationship between angle of lean and rotation

Give the doll a 'landing area' (such as a cardboard box) away from the floor space required by other laboratory users.

40 MINUTES

Apparatus:

- ◆ Barbie doll, Action Man or other similar doll ◆ table or bench
- ◆ rule ◆ retort stand ◆ protractor

Develop a hypothesis based on the following scenario.

When a diver leans so that their centre of gravity no longer lies over the base of their support they will topple. This is because there is a net torque on their body produced by their weight and the ground reaction force acting on their feet.

How do you think the initial angle of lean of the doll will affect the number of rotations the doll makes before it hits the ground?

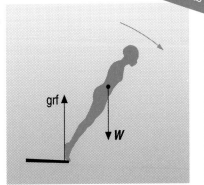

Figure 5.6 Forces acting on a doll to produce a torque

Test your hypothesis as follows.

Set up the retort stand and rule as shown in Figure 5.7 so that the angle of the rule to the vertical can be controlled easily.

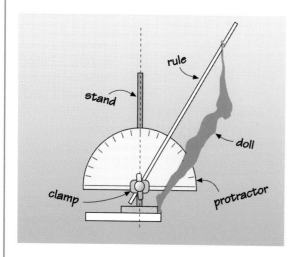

Line up the doll with the rule, holding it stationary by the head or hair. Release the head or hair and watch the doll tumble to the ground. Try to estimate the number of somersaults it completes between being released and hitting the ground. (Take care to count the number of complete rotations.)

Vary the angle of the ruler and test your hypothesis.

Figure 5.7 Apparatus for Exploration 5.4

Over-balancing (leaning) is the simplest method of creating rotation. Examples of dives performed entirely by this method are the elementary Sitting Dive, the Pike Fall, the Dead Drop and the Armstand Back Fall (see Figure 5.8). According to diving texts, the torque on the diver increases until the angle of lean is 48°, beyond which the diver loses effective contact with the board.

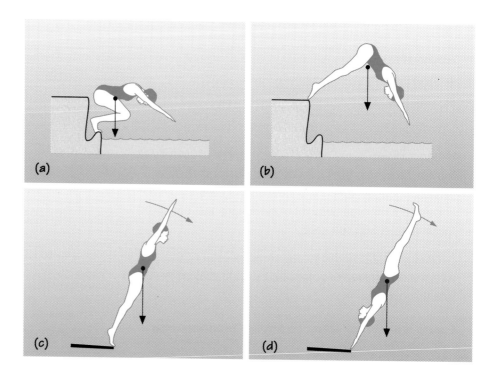

Figure 5.8
The four dives:
(a) Sitting Dive,
(b) Pike Fall,
(c) Dead Drop,
(d) Armstand Back Fall

Other methods of creating rotation

People are much more complicated than Barbie dolls, so we can't use dolls for biomechanical analysis, unfortunately! Divers rarely topple from a board with a stiff body. Springboard diving involves generating a large ground reaction force from the board in order to get height and also a controlled amount of spin.

 A greater lean at take-off may mean that greater rotational speed is created, but how will this lean affect the vertical velocity at take-off?

A greater lean makes the diver take off less vertically, so their vertical velocity is reduced, and the maximum height is lowered.

So, a greater angle of lean is at the expense of height and, therefore, time and style. Thus the angle of lean should be reduced to a minimum consistent with the requirements of safety and aesthetics. Biomechanical analysis of some of Britain's top divers, when compared with more successful international competitors, shows that the main difference in their take-off is in the angle of lean.

If lean were necessary for rotation, all dives would have to be in a forwards direction with the head moving over the feet, away from the board and Reverse and Inward Somersaults would not be possible.

So what other ways are there to create rotation? There are two further methods introduced in the following explorations.

Be careful as you swivel! Do not spin fast. Make sure you have plenty of room, and that the chair is on a firm floor.

 Exploration 5.5
Investigating momentum transfer

5 MINUTES

Apparatus:

◆ swivel chair

1 Sit on the chair with your feet on the floor. Move one arm out to the side and swing it quickly across your body. Just as your arm is completing its swing, raise your feet from the ground. Try it with the other arm. Explain this transfer of momentum.

2 Sit on the chair with your feet off the ground. Repeat the arm movements you used in 1. If you do not move very far, try again holding a heavy book in your extended hand. (Be particularly careful not to drop the book or hit anything with it!) Which direction do you move in, and why?

Momentum transfer

The swivel chair demonstrates a very important method divers use to gain rotation. It is known as momentum transfer and to some diving coaches as 'throwing' or 'blocking'. A diver uses the arms and/or the whole upper body to start a rotation, while the feet are still on the board. Because the upper body is now a rotating mass it has **angular momentum**. (*Note:* Angular momentum is considered in more detail in Section 6.) When the body leaves the board this angular momentum is shared with the entire body, and the whole body rotates.

 Because the feet have something to push on, the feet and body stay 'still' while the arms gain angular momentum – doesn't that break the law of conservation of momentum?

Conservation of momentum is maintained because the feet and body don't really stay still. When a canoeist jumps from a canoe the canoeist moves one way and the canoe moves in the opposite direction. When a diver executes a 'throw', the arms are thrown forward but the board, the feet and the body move in the opposite direction. However, because the board is firmly anchored to the Earth, the mass of this moving body (moving in the opposite direction) is so great that it has an equal, but opposite angular momentum, yet has an imperceptibly small velocity.

As the diver moves into the air the momentum of their upper body is shared with the whole body, so the whole body moves round – demonstrating the principle of conservation of momentum.

Transfer of angular momentum from the upper trunk in Forward and Inward Dives is obtained by moving the shoulder forward vigorously as the feet give their final push at take-off. For arm swing transfer the arms are swung forward at take-off in the same direction as the upper trunk, thereby giving combined transfer of angular momentum *from* the arms and upper trunk to the rest of the body (see Figure 5.9).

Visualize the diver's motion after the trunk transfer; arm swing transfer; eccentric leg thrust and board thrust. For each diagram in Figure 5.9 describe rotation as clockwise or anticlockwise.

Figure 5.9
Trunk transfer, forward rotation; arm swing transfer, forward rotation

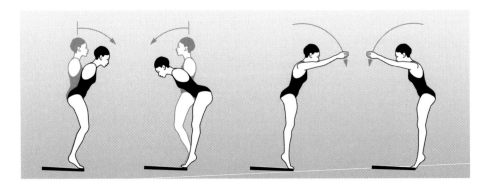

Eccentric leg thrust

As a diver straightens their legs and takes off, the reaction force from the board may well not pass through their centre of gravity. This could be due to friction off the board on their feet, or due to leaning. Whenever the reaction force does not pass through the centre of gravity, a torque is produced and the body will start to rotate (see Figure 5.10).

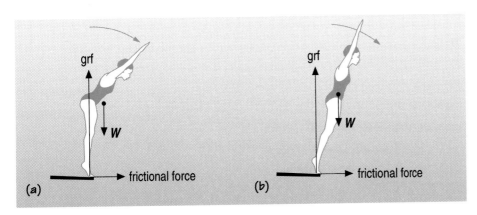

Figure 5.10   Eccentric leg thrust and board thrust

During take-off for a Forward or Inward Dive the body is bent forward at the hips so that the body's centre of gravity lies in front of the hip joint. When the legs push on the board, an off-centre or eccentric turning force will be applied, causing rotation of the body about its centre of gravity. As the distance between the hip joint and the centre of gravity increases, the torque, and consequently the angular momentum, increases. However, energy used to create rotational kinetic energy is not then available to project the body upwards, and the diver loses vertical height in their dive, and will then have less time in the air.

Novices attempting their first somersaults are sometimes so concerned to get sufficient rotation they jump upwards very little. They then have too little time in the air to complete the rotation. The expert diver is able to generate torque and push their body upwards so that they have a long flight time, and can therefore complete the requisite rotations.

As you will see in Section 6, the horizontal component of the force on the diver from the board is vital in projecting them safely away from the board.

 This horizontal force acts on the diver's feet and in a direction away from the board. In which direction will it tend to rotate the diver?

If the diver starts facing forward, the force, away from the board and below the diver's centre of gravity, will tend to move them in a backwards somersault.

Q6 A diver of mass 75 kg jumps upwards from a rigid surface.

(a) How fast must the diver leave the ground if they hope to raise their centre of gravity 1.2 m? Calculate their upwards velocity. (Use $g = 9.81$ m s^{-2}.)

(b) While their feet are in contact with the surface, their centre of gravity rises 0.45 m. What is their mean acceleration? (Assume that the centre of gravity is initially at rest and accelerates uniformly.)

(c) What accelerating force is required to provide acceleration in (b)? What force must the surface be exerting on the diver (i.e. the grf)? (Assume it is a constant force acting on the entire mass of the diver.)

(d) How much gravitational potential energy (relative to their starting position) does the diver have at the peak of their motion?

(e) Calculate their change in momentum and hence the impulse exerted on them when jumping.

(f) For how long did the grf act? ◆

Achievements

After studying this section you should be able to:

- describe how divers maximize their height attained during a dive
- define ground reaction force (grf)
- explain how height attained depends on grf and weight of the diver
- describe how divers initiate rotation during a dive
- explain how the combination of weight and grf can produce a torque
- apply the principle of conservation of energy to dynamic situations
- apply the principle of conservation of momentum to dynamic situations
- apply the equations of motion to dynamic situations.

Glossary

Angular momentum Unit: kilogram metre^2 radian^{-1} (kg m^2 rad^{-1}) The product of angular velocity and moment of inertia.

Conservation of momentum The total momentum of a system is constant, provided no external force acts on the system.

Ground reaction force (grf) Following Newton's third law, when a diver pushes down on a surface, the surface pushes up with an equal and opposite force (owing to fact that the surface deforms *and* on an atomic scale electrostatic interactions occur). This is often called a reaction force and if it is perpendicular to the surface, which it would be in the absence of friction, it is called a normal reaction. In the sport context, it is called the ground reaction force.

Impulse Unit: newton second (N s). The product of the mean force applied and the time for which that force is applied or, if force varies, the area beneath a force–time graph. Impulse is a vector quantity. Its value will be equal to the change of momentum produced.

Momentum Unit: kilogram metre per second (kg m s^{-1}) or newton second (N s). The product of mass and velocity. Momentum is a vector quantity.

Net force The total force that acts on a body: the sum of all the forces.

Torque Unit: newton metre (N m). The moment of a force that produces rotation.

Answers to Ready to Study test

R1

The moment of a force about a point a distance x away from its point of action is

$T = Fx \sin \theta$

where θ is the angle between x and F.

For the ladder

$$T = mgx \sin 30°$$
$$= 20 \, \text{kg} \times 9.81 \, \text{N kg}^{-1} \times 3.0 \, \text{m} \times 0.50$$
$$= 294.3 \, \text{N m}$$
$$= 2.9 \times 10^2 \, \text{N m} \text{ (to two significant figures)}$$

R2

One condition for equilibrium is that clockwise moments should equal anticlockwise moments. In this case

$$\text{clockwise moment} = 50 \, \text{kg} \times 9.81 \, \text{N kg}^{-1} \times 2.0 \, \text{m}$$
$$= 981 \, \text{N m}$$

and

anticlockwise moment $= 55\,\text{kg} \times 9.81\,\text{N}\,\text{kg}^{-1} \times L$

$$= 539.55\,\text{N} \times L$$

where L is distance between the fulcrum and the second girl. Therefore

$$539.55\,\text{N} \times L = 981\,\text{N}\,\text{m}$$

Rearranging gives

$$L = \frac{981\,\text{N}\,\text{m}}{539.55\,\text{N}}$$

$$= 1.8\,\text{m} \text{ (to two significant figures)}$$

R3

The correct diagram is (d).

R4

(a)

Impulse $= Ft$

$$= 300\,\text{N} \times 0.15\,\text{s}$$

$$= 45\,\text{N}\,\text{s} \text{ (to two significant figures)}$$

(b) Impulse of force = change in momentum of body. Since the body starts from rest

$$45\,\text{N}\,\text{s} = mv$$

So

$$v = \frac{45\,\text{N}\,\text{s}}{0.70\,\text{kg}}$$

$$= 64\,\text{m}\,\text{s}^{-1} \text{ (to two significant figures)}$$

R5

The principle of conservation of momentum states that, in an isolated system, the sum of the momentums of all the constituent parts of the system before an interaction will equal the sum afterwards; in this case we consider the canoe and canoeist as the system.

$m_{\text{canoeist}} \times v_{\text{canoeist}}$ before collision

$$= m_{\text{canoe and canoeist}}$$
$$\times v_{\text{canoe and canoeist}} \text{ after collision}$$

therefore

$$v_{\text{canoe and canoeist}} = \frac{m_{\text{canoeist}} \times v_{\text{canoeist}}}{m_{\text{canoe and canoeist}}}$$

$$v_{\text{canoe and canoeist}} = \frac{70\,\text{kg} \times 4.0\,\text{m}\,\text{s}^{-1}}{(70+30)\,\text{kg}}$$

$$= 2.8\,\text{m}\,\text{s}^{-1}$$

(to two significant figures)

R6

(a)

Work done = gain in potential energy

$$= mgh$$

$$= 55\,\text{kg} \times 9.81\,\text{N}\,\text{kg}^{-1} \times 3.0\,\text{m}$$

$$= 1619\,\text{J}$$

$$= 1.6\,\text{kJ} \text{ (to two significant figures)}$$

(b)

Mean power output $= \dfrac{\text{work done}}{\text{time taken}}$

$$= \frac{1619\,\text{J}}{5.0\,\text{s}}$$

$$= 323.8\,\text{W}$$

$$= 3.2 \times 10^{2}\,\text{W}$$

(to two significant figures)

Answers to questions in the text

Q1

The centre of gravity starts to move before the feet because it is accelerated by a force from the feet. The feet must be pushing on the floor (not accelerating up) to generate this force.

Q3

For the man:

$$W_{ROB} = 60.2\,kg \times 10\,N\,kg^{-1}$$
$$= 602\,N$$

(See Figure 5.11a.)

For the woman:

$$W_{ROB} = 43.0\,kg \times 10\,N\,kg^{-1}$$
$$= 430\,N$$

(See Figure 5.11b.)

The ROB is not accelerating, so an upwards reaction force R_L from the legs balances its weight.

Q2

	Mass/kg	Lower legs and feet/kg	Rest of body/kg
Man	70	$14\% \times 70 = 9.8$	$86\% \times 70 = 60.2$
Woman	50	$14\% \times 50 = 7.0$	$86\% \times 50 = 43.0$

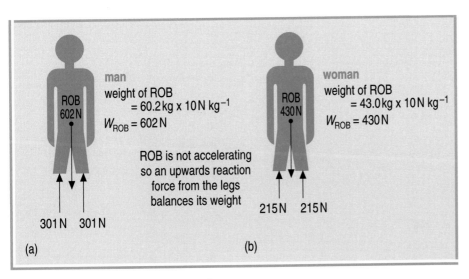

Figure 5.11 Answer for Question 3

Q4

For the man:

$$W_{LL} = 9.8\,\text{kg} \times 10\,\text{N}\,\text{kg}^{-1}$$
$$= 98\,\text{N}$$

Total downwards force $= W_{LL} + W_{ROB}$
$$= 98\,\text{N} + 602\,\text{N}$$
$$= 700\,\text{N}$$

For the woman:

$$W_{LL} = 7.0\,\text{kg} \times 10\,\text{N}\,\text{kg}^{-1}$$
$$= 70\,\text{N}$$

Total downwards force $= W_{LL} + W_{ROB}$
$$= 70\,\text{N} + 430\,\text{N}$$
$$= 500\,\text{N}$$

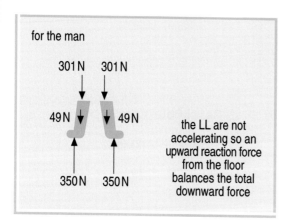

for the man

301 N   301 N

49 N   49 N

350 N   350 N

the LL are not accelerating so an upward reaction force from the floor balances the total downward force

Figure 5.12 Answer for Question 4

The LL are not accelerating so an upward reaction force from the floor balances the downward force.

Q5

See Figure 5.13

Q6

The diver is in free fall in a gravitation field, intensity g.

(a) Use

$$v^2 = u^2 + 2as$$

for path up to highest point. Therefore

$$0 = u^2 - 2 \times 9.81\,\text{N}\,\text{kg}^{-1} \times 1.2\,\text{m}$$

where 1.2 m is height above standing position (when feet leave ground). So

$$u^2 = 23.54\,\text{kg}\,\text{m}\,\text{s}^{-2}\,\text{kg}^{-1}\,\text{m}$$
$$= 23.54\,\text{m}^2\,\text{s}^{-2}$$
$$u = 4.9\,\text{m}\,\text{s}^{-1} \text{ (to two significant figures)}$$

Or use conservation of energy

$$\frac{1}{2}mu^2 = mgh$$

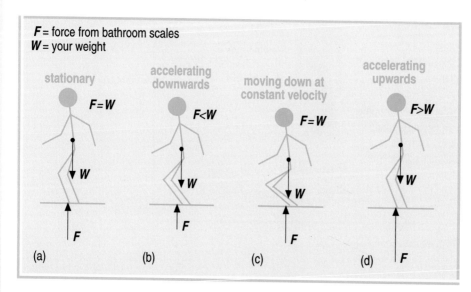

F = force from bathroom scales
W = your weight

stationary
$F = W$
W
F

accelerating downwards
$F < W$
W
F

moving down at constant velocity
$F = W$
W
F

accelerating upwards
$F > W$
W
F

(a)   (b)   (c)   (d)

Figure 5.13
Answer for Question 5

to give

$$u^2 = 2gb$$

$$= 2 \times 9.81 \text{ms}^{-2} \times 1.2$$

$$u = 4.9 \text{ms}^{-1}$$

(b) From rest, final speed attained (now v) is the value given above in distance 0.45 m.

$$v^2 = u^2 + 2as$$

so

$$v^2 = 2as$$

(a does not equal g!)

and

$$a = \frac{v^2}{2s}$$

Therefore

$$a = \frac{23.52 \text{m}^2 \text{s}^{-2}}{2 \times 0.45 \text{m}}$$

$$= 26.13 \text{ms}^{-2}$$

$$= 26 \text{ms}^{-2} \text{ (to two significant figures)}$$

(See Figure 5.14.)

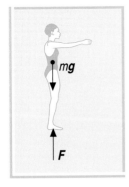

Figure 5.14
Answer for Question 6

(c) Accelerating force, $F = ma$. Therefore

$$F = 75 \text{kg} \times 26.16 \text{ms}^{-2}$$

$$= 1962 \text{N}$$

$$= 2.0 \times 10^3 \text{ N}$$

(to two significant figures)

$$\text{weight} = 75 \text{kg} \times 9.81 \text{ms}^{-2}$$

$$= 736 \text{N}$$

$$= 7.4 \times 10^2 \text{ N}$$

(to two significant figures)

$$\text{grf} = 1962 \text{N} + 736 \text{N}$$

$$= 2695 \text{N}$$

$$= 2.7 \times 10^3 \text{ N}$$

(to two significant figures)

(d) All their energy is gravitational potential energy, since there is no spin.

$$mgb = 75 \text{kg} \times 9.81 \text{Nkg}^{-1} \times 1.2 \text{m}$$

$$= 883 \text{Nm}$$

$$= 8.8 \times 10^2 \text{ J (to two significant figures)}$$

(e)

$$\text{Impulse} = \text{change in momentum}$$

$$= mv \text{ (since they start from rest)}$$

$$= 75 \text{kg} \times 4.9 \text{ms}^{-1}$$

$$= 368 \text{kgms}^{-1} (1 \text{kgms}^{-1} = 1 \text{Ns})$$

$$= 3.7 \times 10^2 \text{ N}$$

(to two significant figures)

(f)

$$\text{Impulse} = \text{accelerating force} \times \text{time}$$

$$= Ft$$

therefore

$$t = \frac{367.5 \text{Ns}}{1962 \text{N}}$$

$$= 0.19 \text{s (to two significant figures)}$$

6

When a diver leaves the board they have gone past the point of no return – the effect of gravity cannot be changed in mid-air. In this section you will learn how to predict the path of a diver from the instant they leave the board, and learn how divers can influence their dive by changing the shape their body makes in the air.

READY TO STUDY TEST

Before you begin this section you should be able to:

- decide whether a quantity is a vector or a scalar, and understand the difference between these two types of quantity
- use the usual ways of representing vectors
- add and subtract vectors
- resolve a vector into perpendicular components
- explain the difference between weight and mass of a body
- sketch and use diagrams that show the forces acting on a body
- define momentum and impulse and explain how they are related
- state and use Newton's laws of motion
- understand and explain the principle of conservation of momentum
- define energy, work and power and give their correct units
- use the equations of uniform acceleration

$$v = u + at$$

$$s = ut + \frac{1}{2}at^2$$

$$v^2 = u^2 + 2as$$

- locate the centre of gravity of a body
- use the formulae for kinetic energy:

$$E_k = \frac{mv^2}{2}$$

and for potential energy:

$$E_p = mgh$$

- describe how energy is conserved in a mechanical system
- relate frequency to period of oscillation of a wave.

IN THE AIR

QUESTIONS

Some of the concepts in this section were also used in Section 5 and tested in that section's Ready to Study test. You should therefore be able to answer the Ready to Study test questions for Section 5 before studying Section 6.

R1 A river 100 m wide runs from north to south, as shown in Figure 6.1. A group of students in a boat wish to cross the river and land 500 m downstream. The river is flowing at $1\ \text{m s}^{-1}$. The students want to aim their boat at 90° to the bank and let the river move them downstream. At what speed must they row if they are to be successful?

R2 During a sprint start a runner pushes vertically downwards with a total force of 1000 N (including her weight) and horizontally backwards with a force of 600 N.

(a) Sketch a diagram to show the forces that the runner exerts on the blocks.

(b) Calculate the size of the total force she exerts on the blocks.

(c) Calculate the direction of the force she exerts on the blocks.

(d) Given that the sprinter has mass 55 kg and she applies these forces for 0.15 s, calculate the horizontal and vertical impulses and velocities at which she leaves the blocks. (Use $g = 10\ \text{N kg}^{-1}$.)

R3 A parachutist, complete with kit, has a mass of 120 kg.

(a) (i) Calculate the change in the parachutist's gravitational potential energy when the parachutist has fallen, in free fall, the first 1.0 m. (ii) Applying the law of conservation of energy, discuss what happens to this energy during the fall.

(b) A few seconds later the parachutist has fallen 500 m. (i) After falling one more metre, what is the change in the parachutist's gravitational potential energy? (ii) Discuss what has happened to this energy during the fall.

(Use $g = 10\ \text{N kg}^{-1}$.)

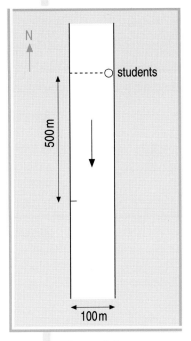

Figure 6.1
Rowing across the river

6.1 The human body as a projectile

When a diver has left the diving board, and before they enter the water, what force(s) act on them? Look at the stages on the dive shown in Figure 6.2. Where would you draw in forces acting on the diver at each stage?

From leaving the board, to entering the water, gravity is the only significant force acting on the diver. This should be shown as a vertical, downwards force through their centre of gravity. The size of the force does not change with the diver's position, and depends on their mass according to the equation $W = mg$.

Vertical motion

If you simply drop off a diving board, gravity will accelerate you downwards. All objects, whatever their mass, accelerate towards the Earth at roughly the same rate (unless air resistance, altitude or local variations in g become significant).

The gravitational field strength on the Earth is approximately 9.81 N kg^{-1}. Use Newton's second law to find out the acceleration of any mass m.

Newton's second law says that $F = ma$, where F is the force acting on mass m to produce acceleration a. So, the weight of a diver of mass m has a magnitude

$$mg = 9.81\,m\text{ N kg}^{-1}$$

This weight is the accelerating force, so

$$9.81\,m\text{ N kg}^{-1} = ma$$

By cancelling the ms we can see that
$$a = 9.81 \text{ m s}^{-2}$$

While gravity is the only force acting on a body we say that it is in **free fall**. Remember that a is a vector and in this example it is always directed downwards, even if the diver is moving upwards or sideways.

(*Note:* In the following questions you should ignore the fact that the diver's centre of gravity starts at about a metre above the board and assume that they do not rotate as they execute their dive. Use $g = 9.81 \text{ m s}^{-2}$.)

Q1 Calculate the time it takes the diver to fall to the water from the 10 m board. Assume that they start with zero vertical velocity, 10 m above the water. ◆

Q2 Assuming that the diver starts with zero vertical velocity, calculate the time it takes to fall from the 3.0 m board to the water. ◆

Q3 Instead of starting with zero vertical velocity, the diver takes off from the 3.0 m board with an upwards vertical velocity of 5.0 m s^{-1}.

(a) How high will the diver travel?

(b) How long will the diver take to reach their maximum height?

(c) How long will the diver take to fall from their maximum height to the water?

(d) How long will the dive last, in total? ◆

Q4 For a body leaving a board vertically upwards at velocity *u*, assuming no rotation (and ignoring the fact that they would hit the board!), sketch graphs of acceleration, velocity and position versus time for the subsequent motion. Arrange your graphs vertically above each other so that features on the graphs relate to each other. Explain the significance (if any) of the areas under and the gradients of each of your graphs. ◆

Q5 Why are there no boards higher than 10 m? (*Hint:* Calculate the time in the air and vertical entry speed for boards of 10 m, 15 m, 20 m and 25 m). (Use $g = 9.81$ m s^{-2}.) ◆

Q6 Copy Table 6.1, and fill in the missing details. (Use $g = 9.81$ m s^{-2}.) ◆

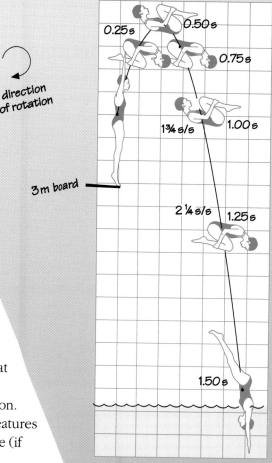

Figure 6.2
Stages in the dive
(s/s = somersault)

Table 6.1 Data for Question 6

Displacement, s/m	Time, t/s	Initial upwards velocity, u/m s^{-1}
0	0	0
(a)	0.50	4.6
−3.0	0.78	(c)
(b)	1.00	9.8
−10	(d)	14.0

Q7 What should your vertical take-off velocity be if you take off from a 1.0 m springboard and need a dive time of 1.0 s? ◆

Horizontal motion

Horizontal motion is essential to divers. If they go straight up, they will come straight down and hit the board. The actual distance required to clear the board depends on the position of the body as it passes board level. A diver who is travelling vertically as they pass the board needs only about 0.3 m between the board and their centre of gravity, whereas a diver who is horizontal as they pass the board needs at least 1.0 m (see Figure 6.3).

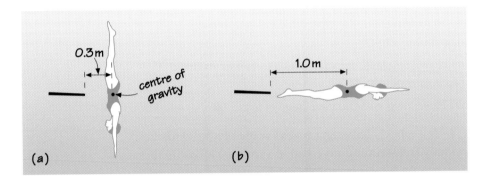

Figure 6.3
Distance between a diver's centre of gravity and the board

Vertical motion of a body will not affect its horizontal motion, and vice versa. So, even if a body is accelerating in the vertical direction, it remains at rest or moving at constant velocity in the horizontal direction, provided no unbalanced force acts on it in the horizontal direction.

 Which of Newton's laws is described in the last sentence?

Newton's first law of motion.

Because they are at right angles to each other, vertical and horizontal motion are independent of each other.

Q8 A diver leaves a board with a velocity of 3.0 m s^{-1} in a horizontal direction.

(a) What will their horizontal velocity be 2.0 s later?

(b) Would it make any difference if the diver were jumping from a spacecraft that had just landed on the moon? ◆

Minimum horizontal speed

In the time between taking off and passing the board on the way down a diver should travel a horizontal distance of at least 1 m, if they are to safely clear the board in any position. The horizontal velocity required for such a safe dive will depend on the time the diver spends in the air. Remember that the horizontal velocity of the diver in the air is constant.

displacement = velocity × time

thus the longer the time between take-off and returning to board level, the smaller the horizontal velocity needs to be.

Worked example

The example of a springboard dive illustrated in Figure 6.4 shows an angle of take off of 14° to the vertical. Knowing that the diver rises to a maximum height of about 1.3 m we can calculate their horizontal take-off velocity.

From Question 3 we know that a vertical take-off velocity of 5.0 m s^{-1}, is needed for a diver to rise by 1.3 m.

$$\tan 14° = \frac{v_x}{5.0 \,\mathrm{ms}^{-1}}$$

$$v_x = 5.0 \,\mathrm{ms}^{-1} \times \tan 14°$$

$$= 5.0 \,\mathrm{ms}^{-1} \times 0.249$$

$$= 1.3 \,\mathrm{ms}^{-1} \quad \blacklozenge$$

 What is the horizontal acceleration of the diver in free fall?

Zero. There is no significant force acting on the diver horizontally, so while they are in free fall, during the dive, they continue with their initial horizontal velocity until they hit the water.

Knowing the horizontal velocity of the diver, we can calculate the distance they will be from the board as they pass it on the way down.

Q9 For the ideal 3 m springboard dive under consideration in Question 3, is the diver safe to pass the board if their body is horizontal when they pass the board? (Remember that their centre of gravity should be at least 1 m horizontally from the board in order to clear it on the way down.) ◆

Parabolic paths

The centre of gravity of a diver (and any other object) under gravity makes an interestingly shaped curve. Mathematically we can prove that this fits the shape called a **parabola**. We always get this shape if an object moves at uniform velocity in the horizontal direction whilst accelerating uniformly in the perpendicular direction. Notice that the shape is not circular, it is parabolic: it is steeply curved when the body has a low vertical velocity, and becomes straighter as the body travels faster.

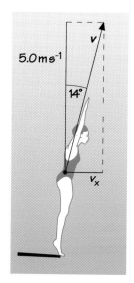

Figure 6.4
Resolving the velocity of the diver at take-off with a vector triangle

Figure 6.5
A parabola

Q10 Figure 6.6 shows a diagrammatic representation of a multiflash photo taken of a diver who is wearing a white spot near their centre of gravity. The flashes began as the diver left the board, when the board was horizontal. (Use $g = 10$ m s^{-2}.)

(a) How high is the diver's centre of gravity above the board?

(b) How high is the board above the water?

(c) What is the time interval between flashes?

(d) What is the frequency of the flashes?

(e) What was their x-component of initial speed?

(f) What was their y-component of initial speed?

(g) At what angle did the diver leave the board? ◆

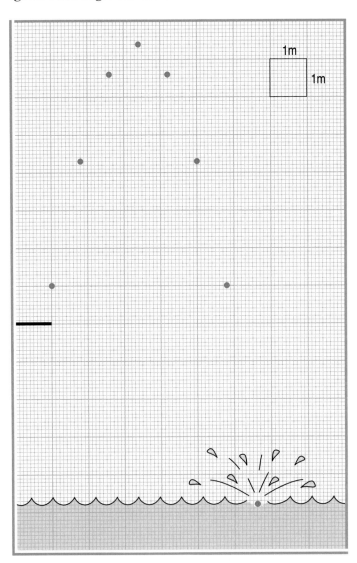

Figure 6.6
The path of a diver leaving the board wearing a white spot

6.2 Controlling rotation and spin

We mentioned earlier in Section 5 that somersaults are created at take-off; however, a diver can vary their rate of rotation by altering their body shape.

 Exploration 6.1 Rotating masses

Apparatus:

◆ two identical wooden metre rules (identical wooden sticks will do if you only have plastic metre rules) ◆ four fairly heavy G-clamps

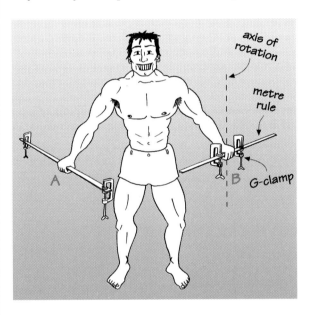

Clamp two G-clamps to each rule – on one rule (A) clamp them at either end, on the other rule (B) clamp them about 10 cm either side of the middle of the rule (see Figure 6.7). Now hold the rules in the middle, one in each hand. Rotate the rules backwards and forwards about an axis through the middle of the rule. Do the two rules feel the same? Which one is easier to start and stop rotating?

Figure 6.7 Rotating G-clamps

Give yourself plenty of space. Make sure you use strong wooden rules and not bendy plastic ones or any others that may break, and make sure that the clamps are tightened before rotating the rules.

5 MINUTES

If you had a chance to do Exploration 6.1 you should have noticed that although the rules had identical masses, rule A, the one with the masses at the ends, well away from the axis of rotation, felt 'heavier' than rule B. It couldn't have actually weighed more, and yet it was more difficult to start and stop rotating. This is because the behaviour of a rotating body depends crucially on the distance of the mass from the axis of rotation.

 If both the metre rules were spinning about the 50 cm mark, making one revolution per second, would both have the same kinetic energy?

No. The masses on rule A will have to move much faster than those on rule B, so the kinetic energy of A will be much greater that of than B.

This again illustrates that for a rotating body it is not only the size of the mass, but the distance of the mass from the axis, that is crucial in determining how it moves when we twist it.

Newton's second law, for linear motion, is often stated as $F = ma$. In Exploration 6.1, however, the centre of gravity of the body does not accelerate, but the masses rotate. Changing this speed of rotation (called **angular velocity, ω**) involves an **angular acceleration**, α, and this sort of acceleration is caused not by an ordinary linear force, but by a turning force or torque. So, when we are considering rotating bodies, the angular acceleration, α, is caused by a torque, T. (All these angular-type quantities must have their axis of rotation clearly defined. If you have done Exploration 6.1 you will have noticed a big difference between the metre rules when rotating them around an axis at right angles to the rules compared with rotating them about an axis along the length of the ruler, when they are easier to rotate and both rules behave identically.)

Exploration 6.1 illustrates clearly that the size of the acceleration is governed not just by the size of the mass but also by the distance of the mass from the axis. To make things simple when we are doing calculations involving angular motion, we define a new property of objects – their **moment of inertia**, I. Rotational motion about a certain axis can be treated very similarly to linear motion if we use the moment of inertia of the body around that axis instead of just mass. Newton's second law $F = ma$ becomes

$$T = I\alpha$$

Momentum = mass × velocity also has a rotational form:

angular momentum, $H = I\omega$

where ω is the angular velocity of the body.

 Which rule, A or B, has the larger moment of inertia?

Rule A. The mass is much further from the axis, and it is more difficult to start and stop rotating.

Moment of inertia of a rotating diver

During a dive a diver may change the shape of their body in the air. This is crucial to controlling their rate of rotation. The three basic diving positions are (a) straight, (b) piked and (c) tucked. These are illustrated in Figure 6.8.

 (a) Which position gives the diver the highest moment of inertia about the axis shown? (b) Which position gives the lowest?

(a) The straight position gives the diver their highest moment of inertia. (b) The tucked position gives the lowest.

If the straight position gives the diver a moment of inertia ($I = 1$) (on an arbitrary scale), the piked position gives $I = 0.5$ and the tucked position gives $I = 0.25$.

Conservation of angular momentum

We know that for linear motion, if no external forces act on a system, its momentum will be constant. The same is true for the angular momentum of a system: the angular momentum of system is constant if no external torque acts on it.

During a dive no torque acts on the diver, so

$$H = I\omega = \text{constant}$$

The mass of the diver is constant during the dive, of course, but, because their shape can change, the diver can control I by tucking or extending their body.

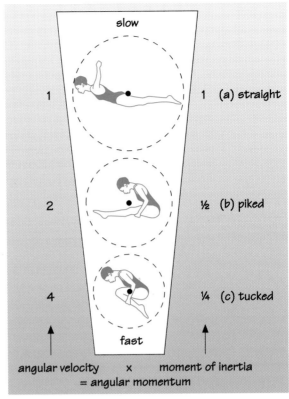

Figure 6.8
The basic diving positions

Suppose a diver takes off in the straight position with an angular velocity of 0.5 rad s^{-1}. ($I = 1$ in the straight position.)

$$H = I\omega = \text{constant} = I \times 0.5 = 0.5 \text{ (arbitrary units)}$$

If they tuck up, making $I = 0.25$,

$$\omega = \frac{H}{I}$$

$$= \frac{0.5}{0.25}$$

$$= 2 \text{ rad s}^{-1}$$

Because the moment of inertia has dropped to a quarter of its original value, the angular velocity has increased to four times its original value.

The tighter the tuck, the faster the rotation. If they need to slow the rotation they can extend their body.

You may have seen, or experienced, the same effect when ice-skaters spin. As they bring all their limbs in towards the spine the speed of the spin dramatically increases.

 Discuss which would be more difficult – a forward $2\frac{1}{2}$ somersault in a tucked position, or a forward $1\frac{1}{2}$ somersault pike.

In the tucked position the diver will rotate twice as fast as in the piked position, so they actually need less angular momentum to make the $2\frac{1}{2}$ turns involved in the tucked somersault than the $1\frac{1}{2}$ turns for the piked somersault.

Exploration 6.2 Demonstrating conservation of angular momentum

5 MINUTES

Apparatus:

◆ swivel chair

Work with a partner for this exploration. Sit in the chair with your feet and legs sticking out. Get your partner to push you around in the chair. Without touching the floor, pull your legs in close to the axis of rotation. What happens to your angular velocity? Why?

What happens if you stick your feet out again? Why?

Make sure that there is plenty of space around the chair and that you are not liable to fall off. Remember that you may be dizzy when you get off – so take your time and be careful! Don't allow your partner to push you too fast.

Note on angular terms

You will have noticed that $F = ma$ translated into $T = I\alpha$, where F is the force, m is the mass, a is the acceleration of a body, and T is the torque, I is the moment of inertia and α is the angular acceleration of a rotating body. This technique of translation can be extended to develop equations for rotational motion if some rules are remembered: terms representing quantities in joules, such as work, energy, etc., together with power and time do not change; F is replaced with T, m with I, a with α, v and u with ω_0 and ω_1, respectively, and s with θ. So, for example.

$$W = Fs$$

becomes

$$W = T\theta$$

where θ is the **angular displacement**;

$$s = ut + \frac{1}{2}at^2$$

becomes

$$\theta = \omega_0 t + \frac{1}{2}\alpha t^2$$

etc. (see Table 6.2).

Table 6.2 Translation of linear terms to angular terms

Linear form	Angular form
$F = ma$	$T = I\alpha$
u	ω_0
v	ω_1
s	θ
$W = Fs$	$W = T\theta$
$s = ut + \dfrac{1}{2}at^2$	$\theta = \omega_0 t + \dfrac{1}{2}\alpha t^2$
$p = mv$	$H = I\omega$

6.3 Belly-flops and board crashes – how to avoid some common diving mistakes

(*Note:* We strongly recommend that you watch some of the videos called *Progressive Steps in Diving* to illustrate some of the points below. See the Further Reading and Resources section at the end of the unit for details of how to obtain these videos.)

In the worked example on page 117, for the 'ideal' springboard dive with a take-off angle of 14° you would need a take-off velocity of about 5.2 m s^{-1} to achieve the vertical velocity of 5.0 m s^{-1}. We will look at the difficulty in obtaining this sort of take-off velocity in Section 7, but let's suppose that as a novice 3.0 m s^{-1} is the best take-off velocity you can do.

Q11 If you take off at 14° to the vertical, is a resultant initial speed of 3 m s^{-1} going to give you sufficient horizontal clearance to miss the board, if you come past it in a horizontal position? (*Hint:* Calculate (a) the vertical and horizontal velocities at take-off, (b) the time between leaving the board and passing it again, (c) the distance travelled horizontally in this time. Follow the calculations in the worked example given in Section 6.1, making the same assumptions as for Question 3, that the diver's centre of gravity takes off level with the board.) (Use $g = 9.81$ m s^{-2}.) ◆

Q12 A take-off angle of as little as 14° requires skill and confidence. Copy Table 6.3 and fill in the missing details for a novice who is learning to dive. Discuss the optimum angle of take-off for a novice springboard diver. (Use $g = 9.81$ m s^{-2}.) To keep things simple, ignore the diver's shape. Do the calculations for a ball leaving the board and arriving back at the board level. (Give all answers to two significant figures.)

(*Hint:* Halfway through the flight the vertical velocity is zero. $t_{1/2}$ can be calculated using $v_y = u_y + a_y t$.) ◆

Table 6.3 Data for Question 12

Take-off velocity v/m s^{-1}	θ/ °	u_x/m s^{-1}	u_y/m s^{-1}	$t_{1/2}$/s	t/s	Distance travelled horizontally/m
5.2	14	(a)	(d)	0.51	1.0	(j)
3.0	14	(b)	(e)	0.30	0.60	(k)
3.0	30	1.5	(f)	0.26	(h)	(l)
3.0	45	(c)	2.1	0.21	0.42	(m)
3.0	60	2.6	(g)		(i)	(n)

Fortunately for the novice diver, their centre of gravity will be some distance from the board at take-off. A take-off angle of 45° always gives maximum range, but good divers take off at smaller angles. By leaning at 30° during take-off, the diver's centre of gravity is already approximately 0.5 m from the end of the board, so a take-off angle of 30° is really quite safe. As the diver gains confidence they should quickly learn to minimize their take-off angle, since the more vertical the take-off the higher the peak of their dive, and the more time they will have in the air.

Belly-flops are caused by a combination of poor control of rotation at take-off, a lack of time in the air (due to insufficient vertical velocity at take-off) and coming out of tucked and piked somersaults too soon. If you have time, analyse some of the dives shown on the videos *Progressive Steps in Diving*, and work out why some of the novices do not make a vertical entry into the water.

Greg Louganis of the USA hit his head on the springboard during the preliminary dives at the 1988 Seoul Olympic Games. He was unhurt and was able to continue in the competition (Source: stf Associated Press)

Achievements

After you have studied this section you should be able to:

- apply equations of motion to two-dimensional free-fall situations

- resolve the vectors in the equations of motion into perpendicular components, exploiting the independence of vertical and horizontal motion

- explain the relevance of moment of inertia to rotational behaviour

- define angular displacement, velocity, acceleration and momentum

- 'translate' linear equations of motion into rotational ones.

Glossary

Angular acceleration, α   Unit: radian per second per second (rad s^{-2}). The rate of change of angular velocity with time. Angular acceleration is a vector quantity.

Angular displacement, θ   Unit: degree (°) or radian (rad). Change in angular position.

Angular momentum, H   Unit: kilogram metre^2 radian^{-1} (kg m^2 rad^{-1}) The product of angular velocity and moment of inertia.

Angular velocity, ω   Unit: radian per second (rad s^{-1}). The rate of change of angular position. Angular velocity is a vector quantity.

Free fall   Motion under gravity with no other forces acting.

Moment of inertia, I   Unit: kilogram metre^2 (kg m^2). A quantity involving both the mass and its distribution within an object about an axis of rotation. Moment of inertia is a scalar quantity. Unlike mass (a measure of linear inertia), moment of inertia depends on the axis about which rotation takes place.

Parabola   A curve obeying a quadratic relationship between y and x (e.g. $y = x^2$). In this context, an approximation to the path of an object in free fall, which assumes a flat Earth and constant g. For a spherical Earth and constant g, the path should technically be considered part of an ellipse with a focus at the Earth's centre.

Answers to Ready to Study test

R1

Time, t, taken to cross the river is given by

$$vt = 100 \text{ m}$$

where v is their rowing speed and t is also the time for the river to flow 500 m at 1.0 m s^{-1}, i.e. 500 s.

Rearranging gives

$$v = \frac{100 \text{ m}}{500 \text{ s}}$$

$$= 0.20 \text{ m s}^{-1}$$

R2

(a) See Figure 6.9

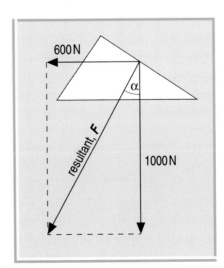

Figure 6.9

(b) F is given by

$$F^2 = (1000\,\text{N})^2 + (600\,\text{N})^2$$

$$= 1.36 \times 10^6\,\text{N}^2$$

so

$$F = 1166\,\text{N}$$

(c) In Figure 6.9, the direction of the force is α (in degrees) to the vertical, where

$$\tan\alpha = \frac{600\,\text{N}}{1000\,\text{N}}$$

so

$$\alpha = 31°$$

(d) Applying Newton's third law, the runner experiences a horizontal force of 600 N (to the right) and a vertical force of 1000 N (upwards).

Horizontal impulse $= 600\,\text{N} \times 0.15\,\text{s}$

$$= 90\,\text{N}\,\text{s}$$

Weight of runner $= 55\,\text{kg} \times 10\,\text{N}\,\text{kg}^{-1}$

$$= 550\,\text{N}$$

Hence

unbalanced upwards force on runner

$$= (1000 - 550)\,\text{N}$$

$$= 450\,\text{N}$$

net vertical impulse $= 450\,\text{N} \times 0.15\,\text{s}$

$$= 67.5\,\text{N}\,\text{s}$$

impulse = change in momentum from rest

$$= mv$$

Horizontal velocity is

$$v_x = \frac{90\,\text{N}\,\text{s}}{55\,\text{kg}}$$

$$= 1.6\,\text{ms}^{-1} \text{ (to two significant figures)}$$

Vertical velocity is

$$v_y = \frac{67.5\,\text{N}\,\text{s}}{55\,\text{kg}}$$

$$= 1.2\,\text{ms}^{-1} \text{ (to two significant figures)}$$

R3

(a) (i)

Change in gravitational potential energy

$$= -mgx \,(\text{change in height})$$

$$= -120\,\text{kg} \times 10\,\text{N}\,\text{kg}^{-1} \times 1.0\,\text{m}$$

$$= -1.2\,\text{kJ}$$

(ii) This loss in energy equals gain in kinetic energy plus the work done against drag forces.

(b) (i)

Change in gravitational potential energy

$$= -120\,\text{kg} \times 10\,\text{N}\,\text{kg}^{-1} \times 500\,\text{m}$$

$$= -6 \times 10^2\,\text{kJ}$$

After 501 m

change in potential energy

$$= -120\,\text{kg} \times 10\,\text{N}\,\text{kg}^{-1} \times 501\,\text{m}$$

$$= -6.012 \times 10^2\,\text{kJ}$$

Therefore change over 1 m $= -1.2$ kJ.

(ii) Again, the loss in energy equals gain in kinetic energy plus work done against drag forces, but this happens in a shorter time. Hence this time more work is done against drag forces and there is less gain in kinetic energy.

Answers to questions in the text

Q1

$$\boldsymbol{s} = \boldsymbol{u}t + \frac{1}{2}\boldsymbol{a}t^2$$

so

$$-10\,\text{m} = 0t - \frac{9.81}{2}\,\text{ms}^{-2}t^2$$

$$= 0t - 4.9\,\text{ms}^{-2}t^2$$

therefore

$$t = \pm\sqrt{2.0}$$

$$= 1.4\,s \text{ (to two significant figures)}$$

Q2

$$s = ut + \frac{1}{2}at^2$$

so

$$-3.0\,m = 0t - \frac{1}{2}9.81\,ms^{-2}t^2$$

s and a are downwards and assigned a negative value here.

Therefore

$$t = \sqrt{\frac{3.0\,m}{4.9\,ms^{-2}}}$$

$$= \pm 0.78\,s \text{ (to two significant figures)}$$

The positive square root is taken.

Q3

(a) At peak motion, $v = 0$, $u = 5.0\ m\ s^{-1}$.

$$v^2 = u^2 + 2as$$

so

$$s = \frac{-u^2}{2a}$$

$$= \frac{-(5.0\,ms^{-1})^2}{2 \times -9.81\,ms^{-2}}$$

$$= \frac{1.27\,m^2\,s^{-2}}{ms^{-2}}$$

$$= 1.3\,m \text{ (to two significant figures)}$$

(b) $v = u + at$, so time to rise is given by

$$t_1 = \frac{v - u}{a}$$

$$= \frac{0 - 5.0\,ms^{-1}}{-9.81\,ms^{-2}}$$

$$= 0.51\,s$$

(c) The diver falls 1.27 m + 3.0 m from rest at the peak of motion when initial velocity, u (not v this time) = 0.

$$s = \frac{1}{2}at_2^2$$

so time to fall is given by

$$t_2 = \sqrt{\frac{2s}{a}}$$

$$= \sqrt{\frac{-2 \times 4.27\,m}{-9.81\,ms^{-2}}}$$

$$= \sqrt{0.871\,s^2}$$

$$= 0.93\,s$$

(d)

$$\begin{aligned}\text{Total time} &= t_1 + t_2 \\ &= (0.51 + 0.93)\,s \\ &= 1.44\,s \\ &= 1.4\,s \text{ (to two significant figures)}\end{aligned}$$

Q4

See Figure 6.10 overleaf.

(a) The acceleration–time graph must follow this shape when a is constant at all times. $a = 9.8\ m\ s^{-2}$ if 'up' is positive.

(b) The equation linking the magnitudes of v, and t is $v = u + at$, which gives a straight line, gradient $a = -9.8\ m\ s^{-1}$

(c) The equation linking the magnitudes of s, and t is $s = ut + \frac{1}{2}at^2$, which is a parabola.

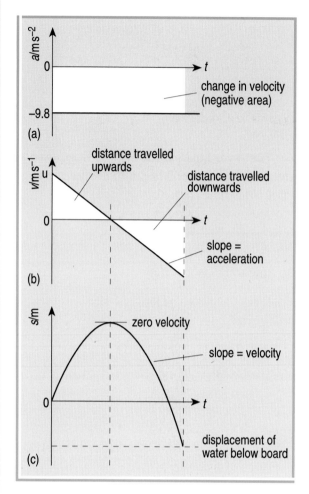

Figure 6.10 Answer for Question 4

(a) $s = ut + \frac{1}{2}at^2$

So, for $t = 0.50$ s and $u = 4.6$ m s^{-1}

$$s = 4.6\,\mathrm{ms}^{-1} \times 0.50\,\mathrm{s} - \frac{9.81\,\mathrm{ms}^{-2}}{2}(0.50\,\mathrm{s})^2$$

$$= 1.074\,\mathrm{m}$$

$$= 1.1\,\mathrm{m}\ \text{(to two significant figures)}$$

(b) For $t = 1.00$ and $u = 9.8$ m s^{-1}

$s = 4.9$ m

(c) $s = ut + \frac{1}{2}at^2$

Rearranging gives

$$ut = s - \frac{1}{2}at^2$$

therefore

$$u = \frac{s}{t} - \frac{1}{2}at$$

So, for $s = -3.00$ m and $t = 0.78$ s

$$u = \frac{-3.0\,\mathrm{m}}{0.78\,\mathrm{s}} - \frac{\left(-9.81\,\mathrm{ms}^{-2}\right) \times 0.78\,\mathrm{s}}{2}$$

$$= -0.02\,\mathrm{ms}^{-1}\ \text{(to two significant figures)}$$

(d) $s = ut + \frac{1}{2}at^2$

therefore

$$\frac{1}{2}at^2 + ut - s = 0$$

Substituting gives

$$0 = \frac{1}{2}\left(-9.81\,\mathrm{ms}^{-2}\right)t^2 + 14\,\mathrm{ms}^{-1}t - \left(-10\,\mathrm{m}\right)$$

$$= -4.9\,\mathrm{ms}^{-2}t^2 + 14\,\mathrm{ms}^{-1}t - \left(-10\,\mathrm{m}\right)$$

Q5

Height, h/m	Fall time, t/s	Entry velocity, v/m s^{-1}
10	1.41	14.0
15	1.73	17.2
20	2.00	19.8
25	2.24	22.2

Energy of the impact with the water is proportional to v^2 $\left(E_k = \frac{1}{2}mv^2\right)$, so higher boards present greater dangers to divers, but offer little extra time in the air.

Using

$$t = \frac{-b \pm \sqrt{b^2 - 4ac}}{2a}$$

gives

$$t = \frac{-\left(14\,\mathrm{ms}^{-1}\right) \pm \sqrt{\left(14\,\mathrm{ms}^{-1}\right)^2 - 4 \times \left(-4.9\,\mathrm{ms}^{-2}\right) \times 10\,\mathrm{m}}}{2 \times \left(-4.9\,\mathrm{ms}^{-2}\right)}$$

$$= \frac{-14\,\mathrm{ms}^{-1} \pm \sqrt{196\,\mathrm{m^2\,s^{-2}} + \left(4 \times 4.9\,\mathrm{ms}^{-2} \times 10\,\mathrm{m}\right)}}{-9.8\,\mathrm{ms}^{-2}}$$

$$= \frac{-14\,\mathrm{ms}^{-1} \pm \sqrt{196\,\mathrm{m^2\,s^{-2}} + 196\,\mathrm{m^2\,s^{-2}}}}{-9.8\,\mathrm{ms}^{-2}}$$

$$= \frac{-14\,\mathrm{ms}^{-1} \pm 19.8\,\mathrm{ms}^{-2}}{-9.8\,\mathrm{ms}^{-2}}$$

$$= 3.45\,\mathrm{s} \text{ or } -0.59\,\mathrm{s}$$

taking the positive value, $t = 3.5\,\mathrm{s}$ (to two significant figures).

Q7

$$s = ut + \frac{1}{2}at^2$$

Rearranging gives

$$u = \frac{s}{t} - \frac{1}{2}at$$

so

$$u = \frac{-1.0\,\mathrm{m}}{1.0\,\mathrm{s}} - \frac{\left(-9.81\,\mathrm{ms}^{-2}\right) \times \left(1.0\,\mathrm{s}\right)}{2}$$

$$= -1\,\mathrm{ms}^{-1} + 4.905\,\mathrm{ms}^{-1}$$

$$= 3.9\,\mathrm{ms}^{-1} \text{ (to two significant figures)}$$

Q8

(a) No forces act in the horizontal direction (if we ignore air resistance), so motion in this direction is uniform, i.e. a constant $3.0\,\mathrm{m\,s^{-1}}$.

(b) No, though they take longer to fall and therefore travel further sideways.

Q9

The time taken to travel up 1.3 m is 0.51 s

(see the answer to Question 3b) If we assume that the diver behaved like a point mass or like a ball bouncing off the board, because the motion is symmetric the time taken to travel the 1.3 m back down to board level is also 0.51 s.

Total time between leaving the board

and returning to board level $= 0.51\,\mathrm{s} + 0.51\,\mathrm{s}$

$$= 1.02\,\mathrm{s}$$

Horizontal distance travelled by the diver

$$= v \times t$$

$$= 1.3\,\mathrm{ms}^{-1} \times 1.02\,\mathrm{s}$$

$$= 1.3\,\mathrm{m} \text{ (to two significant figures)}$$

So, yes, 1.3 m is well over the 1 m minimum recommended.

(*Note:* As we mentioned earlier, the calculations in this section ignore the fact that the diver's centre of gravity starts at about a metre above the board, so if their centre of gravity climbs 1.3 m, it will fall about 2.3 m before passing board level, so it will travel even further than the 1.3 m calculated – so the diver is definitely safe.)

Q10

(a) 1.0 m.

(b) 4.8 m.

(c) From the peak, the diver descends 0.80 m vertically from rest during time interval t.

$$s = ut + \frac{1}{2}at^2$$

As $u = 0$

$$t = \sqrt{\frac{2s}{a}}$$

$$= \sqrt{\frac{2 \times -0.80\,\mathrm{m}}{-10\,\mathrm{ms}^{-2}}}$$

$$= 0.40\,\mathrm{s}$$

(d)

$$f = \frac{1}{\text{period}}$$

$$= \frac{1}{0.40\,\text{s}}$$

$$= 2.5\,\text{Hz or } 2.5\,\text{s}^{-1}$$

(e) u_x is constant and the diver travels 0.8 m in 0.40 s. So

$$u_x = \frac{0.80\,\text{m}}{0.40\,\text{s}}$$

$$= 2.0\,\text{ms}^{-1}$$

(f) Note that as the diver reaches the board level again they travel down at the same speed as the initial, speed six time intervals later, because of conservation of energy. Using

$$v = u + at$$

gives

$$-u_y = u_y + at$$

therefore

$$u_y = \frac{at}{-2}$$

$$= \frac{-10\,\text{ms}^{-2} \times 0.40\,\text{s} \times 6}{-2}$$

$$= 12.0\,\text{ms}^{-1}$$

(g) If α is angle to vertical

$$\tan\alpha = \frac{2.0\,\text{ms}^{-1}}{12.0\,\text{ms}^{-1}}$$

$$= 0.167$$

$$\alpha = 9.5° \text{ (to two significant figures)}$$

Q11

(a)

$$v_y = 3.0\,\text{ms}^{-1} \times \cos 14°$$

$$= 2.91\,\text{ms}^{-1}$$

$$v_x = 3.0\,\text{ms}^{-1} \times \sin 14°$$

$$= 0.73\,\text{ms}^{-1}$$

(b) If it accelerates at $-9.81\,\text{m s}^{-2}$, when it reaches maximum height

$$v = u + at$$

therefore

$$0 = 2.91\,\text{ms}^{-1} - 9.81\,\text{ms}^{-2}t$$

so

$$t = \frac{2.91\,\text{ms}^{-1}}{9.81\,\text{ms}^{-2}}$$

$$= 0.297\,\text{s}$$

If we assume that the diver's centre of gravity took off from board level, it will take the same length of time to fall down. Therefore

total time between leaving the board

and returning to board level $= 2 \times 0.297\,\text{s}$

$$= 0.59\,\text{s}$$

(to two significant figures)

(c) During this time

horizontal distance travelled

$$= v_x \times \text{total time}$$

$$= 3.0\,\text{ms}^{-1} \sin 14° \times 0.59\,\text{s}$$

$$= 0.43\,\text{m (to two significant figures)}$$

This is less than the 1 m horizontal clearance needed.

Q12

(a) The horizontal component of initial velocity is given by

$u_x = u\sin\theta$

$\quad = 5.2\,\mathrm{ms}^{-1}\sin14°$

$\quad = 1.258\,\mathrm{ms}^{-1}$

$\quad = 1.3\,\mathrm{ms}^{-1}$ (to two significant figures)

(b)

$u_x = 3.0\,\mathrm{ms}^{-1}\sin14°$

$\quad = 0.726\,\mathrm{ms}^{-1}$

$\quad = 0.73\,\mathrm{ms}^{-1}$ (to two significant figures)

(c)

$u_x = 3.0\,\mathrm{ms}^{-1}\sin45°$

$\quad = 2.121\,\mathrm{ms}^{-1}$

$\quad = 2.1\,\mathrm{ms}^{-1}$ (to two significant figures)

(d) The vertical component of initial velocity is given by

$u_y = u\cos\theta$

$\quad = 5.2\,\mathrm{ms}^{-1}\cos14° = 5.046\,\mathrm{ms}^{-1}$

$\quad = 5.0\,\mathrm{ms}^{-1}$ (to two significant figures)

(e)

$3.0\,\mathrm{ms}^{-1}\cos14° = 2.910\,\mathrm{ms}^{-1}$

$\quad\quad\quad\quad\quad = 2.9\,\mathrm{ms}^{-1}$

$\quad\quad\quad\quad\quad$ (to two significant figures)

(f)

$3.0\,\mathrm{ms}^{-1}\cos30° = 2.598\,\mathrm{ms}^{-1}$

$\quad\quad\quad\quad\quad = 2.6\,\mathrm{ms}^{-1}$

$\quad\quad\quad\quad\quad$ (to two significant figures)

(g)

$3.0\,\mathrm{ms}^{-1}\cos60° = 1.5\,\mathrm{ms}^{-1}$

(h)

$t = 2\times t_{1/2}$

$\quad = 2\times0.26\,\mathrm{s}$

$\quad = 0.52\,\mathrm{s}$

(i) To calculate $t_{1/2}$

$v_y = u_y + a_y t$

$0 = 1.5\,\mathrm{ms}^{-1} + \left(-9.81\,\mathrm{ms}^{-2}\right)t$

$t_{1/2} = \dfrac{1.5\,\mathrm{ms}^{-1}}{9.81\,\mathrm{ms}^{-2}}$

$\quad = 0.1529\,\mathrm{s}$

$t = 2\times t_{1/2}$

$\quad = 2\times0.1529\,\mathrm{s}$

$\quad = 0.30581\,\mathrm{s}$

$\quad = 0.31\,\mathrm{s}$ (to two significant figures)

(j) Horizontal distance travelled is given by

$x = u_x t$

$\quad = 1.258\,\mathrm{ms}^{-1}\times1.0\,\mathrm{s}$

$\quad = 1.3\,\mathrm{m}$ (to two significant figures)

(k) By the same method it follows that

$x = 0.726\,\mathrm{ms}^{-1}\times0.60\,\mathrm{s}$

$\quad = 0.44\,\mathrm{m}$ (to two significant figures)

(l) By the same method it follows that

$x = 1.5\,\mathrm{ms}^{-1}\times0.52\,\mathrm{s}$

$\quad = 0.78\,\mathrm{m}$ (to two significant figures)

(m) By the same method it follows that

$x = 2.121\,\mathrm{ms}^{-1}\times0.42\,\mathrm{s}$

$\quad = 0.89\,\mathrm{m}$ (to two significant figures)

(n) By the same method it follows that

$x = 2.6\,\mathrm{ms}^{-1}\times0.3058\,\mathrm{s}$

$\quad = 0.7951\,\mathrm{m}$

$\quad = 0.80\,\mathrm{m}$ (to two significant figures)

7

The techniques and the physics we have studied so far are matters of concern to all divers – whether they are diving from a high, firm platform or from a springboard. The difference between the two dives is obviously that the springboard diver has the added complication of the board, a device that has evolved, along with the techniques of springboard diving, to project the diver upwards as they take off. Accessing energy from the board is not simple – timing and strength are both demanded of the diver. It is a complex situation and is not totally understood even by diving coaches, but we can be sure that the laws of physics will apply. In this section we will be considering the physics of the bouncing and vibrating board and considering how the diver should use it to best effect.

READY TO STUDY TEST

Before you begin this section you should be able to:

- locate the centre of gravity of a body
- use the equations of uniform acceleration:

$$v = u + at$$

$$v^2 = u^2 + 2as$$

$$s = ut + \frac{1}{2}at^2$$

- use the formulae for kinetic energy:

$$E_k = \frac{mv^2}{2}$$

and for potential energy:

$$E_p = mgh$$

- understand how energy is conserved in mechanical systems
- recognize the common graphs of the trigonometry functions $\sin \theta$ versus θ and $\cos \theta$ versus θ
- describe the phase difference between two oscillations having the same frequency
- relate frequency and time period of an oscillation

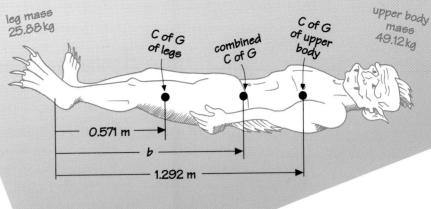

leg mass 25.88 kg

C of G of legs

combined C of G

C of G of upper body

upper body mass 49.12 kg

0.571 m

b

1.292 m

QUESTIONS

R1 Find the centre of gravity of the body shown in Figure 7.1 (*Hint:* Use the fact that weight of the body as a whole has no moment about the centre of gravity, so the moments of component parts of the body must balance about this point. Take the position of the centre of gravity as b from the foot end of the body.)

Figure 7.1
Creature from the Black Lagoon!

R2 A lemming plunges over a vertical cliff 45 m above a fjord by running horizontally over the edge at 15 m s^{-1}. Taking g as 10 m s^{-2} calculate (a) time of flight, (b) the velocity, including the angle at which the lemming hits the water, (c) how far out from the cliff the lemming hits the water. (*Hint:* Place an origin at the edge of the cliff, stick to a sign convention (up is positive, right is positive, etc.) and use y for vertical quantities and x for horizontal ones, e.g. x, y, v_x, v_y, etc.)

R3 (a) What kinetic energy does the lemming (mass 0.50 kg) in R2 have at the start of the flight? (b) What kinetic energy does it have at the end of the flight? (c) What is the potential energy lost? (d) How are these quantities related?

R4 (a) Which oscillators are in phase in Figure 7.2? (b) What is the phase difference between oscillator A and oscillator B?

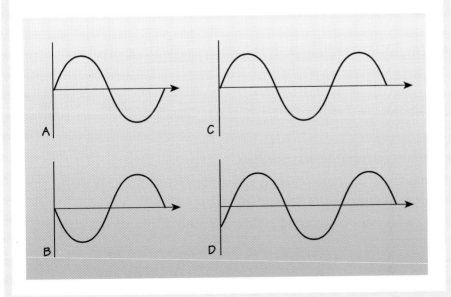

Figure 7.2 Which oscillators are in phase?

7.1 The development of the modern springboard

The first standard International Springboard was introduced at the Paris Olympic Games in 1924. Adopted from the USA, this wooden board featured a movable **fulcrum** and allowed the American divers who were trained on this board to make a clean sweep of the springboard medals. Each country used to have its own design of springboards, considerably disadvantaging visiting teams; so nowadays all international diving pools use the same type of board, generally produced by the same manufacturer.

The modern springboard resembles an aircraft wing more closely than the planks of wood that were used up to 20 years ago. Made of aluminium, it combines stiffness, flexibility and strength, allowing an expert to rise more than 1.5 m above the board during a dive. Regulations require that boards are installed at heights of 1 m and 3 m above the water level, they are at least 4.8 m long and 0.5 m wide, and are covered in a non-slip surface. Fixed rigidly into the poolside at one end, the board rests on a freely movable fulcrum, which allows the diver to adjust the board to suit their mass, their technique and the dive they wish to perform.

7.2 Masses and springs – the ingredients for vibrations

For a springboard diver, one of the most difficult skills to learn is to use the board to gain maximum height. The movement of the board is extremely complicated, and it is not fully understood – however, by studying the physics of vibrations we are able to identify key principles for successful springboard diving.

 Exploration 7.1 Examining some natural oscillating systems

Apparatus:

◆ set up as many of the oscillating systems shown in Figure 7.3 as possible

For each system:

1 Identify the rest position, or **equilibrium position**.
2 Move the oscillation point (P on the diagrams) in one of the directions shown, producing a small **displacement** from the equilibrium position.
3 Release P and watch what happens carefully. How does the displacement vary with time?
4 Match each system to one of the graphs shown in Figure 7.4. Try to estimate a scale for each axis (displacement and time).

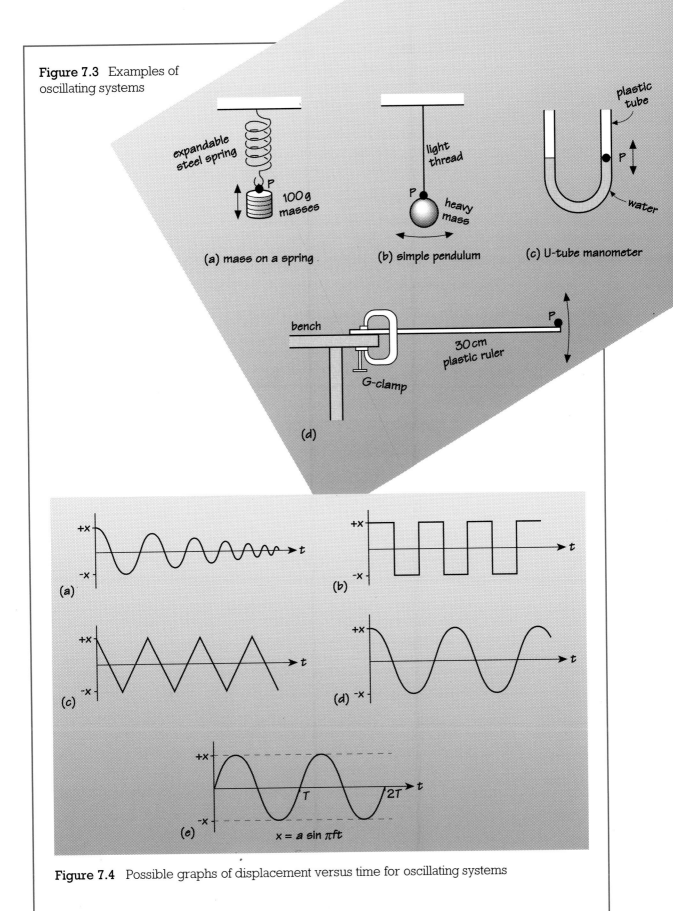

Figure 7.3 Examples of oscillating systems

(a) mass on a spring

(b) simple pendulum

(c) U-tube manometer

(d)

Figure 7.4 Possible graphs of displacement versus time for oscillating systems

$x = a \sin \pi f t$

135

You should have noticed that all the systems in the exploration oscillate with a similar pattern. The time period for a given oscillator is constant and the displacement varies regularly with time. When not heavily damped, this type of motion is called **simple harmonic motion (shm)**.

When a particle is undergoing shm it is always accelerating towards the equilibrium position with an acceleration that increases in proportion to the displacement from the equilibrium position.

For a point moving with shm:

$$\text{acceleration} = -\text{constant} \times s \qquad\qquad (7.1)$$

where s is the displacement of the point. This relationship defines shm. If the acceleration of an oscillator does not fit this condition the motion is not true shm.

Another form of this equation is force, $F = -ks$ (where k is another constant).

 What does the minus sign in these equations tell us?

The acceleration is always in the opposite direction to the displacement – i.e. the acceleration is always directed towards the equilibrium position.

7.3 Building an equation to relate displacement and time for simple harmonic motion

So far we have looked at the equations that are considered a definition of simple harmonic motion;

$$F = -\text{constant} \times s$$

and

$$a = -\text{constant} \times s$$

(*Note:* The two constants are different.)

However, these do not help us to predict where the object undergoing shm will be at any particular time. To do this we need an equation that contains both s and t. We are unable to get to this from the equations above, so we must look for another way, based on what we already know and can readily test.

We know that a mass on the end of a spring undergoes shm when it is displaced and allowed to move freely.

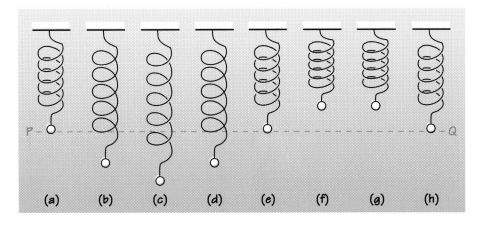

Figure 7.5
A mass oscillating on a spring (PQ is the level of the equilibrium position of the oscillating mass)

Q1 Copy Figure 7.5 and add arrows to represent displacement and acceleration of the mass on the spring for each position. Indicate the size of each quantity by the length of your arrow. ◆

Something else that undergoes simple harmonic motion is the shadow of a marker placed on a rotating turntable when lit by a parallel beam of light (see Figure 7.6).

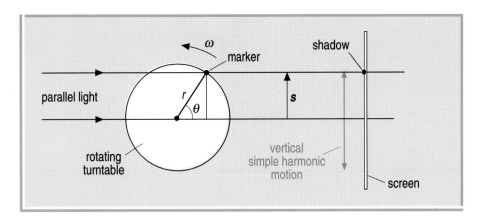

Figure 7.6
The simple harmonic motion of the shadow of a marker fixed to a rotating turntable

The figure shows the marker on a turntable at a radius r having rotated through an angle θ from the zero (equilibrium) position. The turntable is rotating with an angular velocity of magnitude ω, and the displacement of the shadow from the zero position is given by s.

 How could you easily show that the shadow is undergoing simple harmonic motion?

The easiest way to do this is by trial and error. Select a suitable combination of a spring and a mass and start them oscillating with the same amplitude as the shadow of the object on the turntable, and in phase with it (see Figure 7.7 overleaf). The shadow and the mass will move together if the shadow is moving with simple harmonic motion. (*Note:* If the radius is quite large you may need to connect two or more springs.)

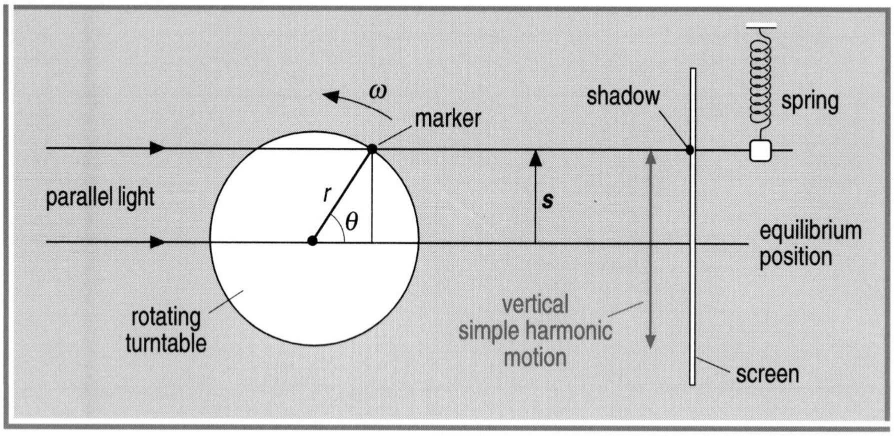

Figure 7.7
Comparing the motion of the shadow of the marker on the turntable with that of a mass on a spring

So, we have found something that we are already familiar with and that we can use to model shm. If we can use this model to find an equation that links the displacement of the shadow with time we should also be able to apply this to the mass on the spring.

By cutting the diagram to the bones we can see what we are doing more clearly (see Figure 7.8).

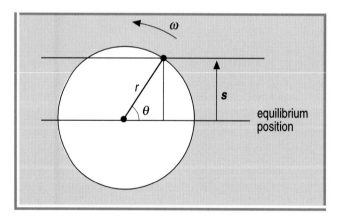

Figure 7.8
Looking more closely at the motion of the shadow

Using trigonometry

$$s = r\sin\theta$$

Since r is the maximum value of s we can replace it with s_{max}, or more simply s_0. We call this maximum displacement of the motion the **amplitude**.

$$s = s_0\sin\theta$$

This is a snapshot taken at a particular time but the position of the marker is constantly changing owing to the rotation of the turntable. The turntable is rotating with angular velocity ω and at a time t it will have passed through an angle

$$\theta = \omega t$$

To make our equation take account of this motion we need to replace θ.

$$s = s_0\sin(\omega t)$$

As we now have an equation relating the displacement of the shadow of the rotating marker with time there are no more changes that we need to make. We could, though, substitute for ω using ideas from your work on circular motion.

$$\omega = 2\pi f$$

or

$$\omega = \frac{2\pi}{T}$$

since

$$f = \frac{1}{T}$$

We could therefore use any of these three forms:

$$s = s_0 \sin(\omega t)$$

$$s = s_0 \sin(2\pi f t)$$

$$s = s_0 \sin\left(\frac{2\pi t}{T}\right)$$

as they are all the same equation.

We most often see the middle one of these, so we will continue to use this version; but remember that, if you prefer, you can use either of the other two instead.

This is an unusual looking equation so let's take a closer look at it:

$$s = s_0 \sin(2\pi f t)$$

For any particular instance of shm, s and t are the only variables. s_0 is the amplitude and was determined when the motion was initiated, f is the **frequency** of the motion and is determined by the system itself.

The equation can be thought of as having two parts on the right-hand side:

$$s = \underset{B}{[s_0]} \ \underset{A}{[\sin(2\pi f t)]}$$

Part A looks quite complicated, but it is the familiar sine function, with $2\pi f t$ as the angle, in radians, to be converted. A has a maximum value of 1 and a minimum value of -1

Part B is the amplitude of the motion and is a scaling factor to make the maximum and minimum displacements predicted by the equation match the actual motion.

A graph of displacement versus time therefore gives a sine curve with upper and lower limits not of 1 and -1 but of the amplitude of the motion. It also has a **period of oscillation** dependent on f.

Another point to note is that we have assumed that our initial value of θ was zero, i.e. that the shadow (and the mass) began their motion from the equilibrium position. This does not always happen. In practice, the motion often begins from the maximum displacement position, s_0. For this we should add $\dfrac{\pi}{2}$ radians to all the angles; have another look at Figure 7.7. The simple way to do this is to switch from using sines to cosines.

> Objects that oscillate with shm can be started from the equilibrium position with a timed force that gradually builds up the motion: for example, a child on a swing. They can also be started by being taken to their maximum displacement, the amplitude, and released: for example, playing a double bass or starting a pendulum swinging.

$$s = s_0 \sin\left(2\pi f t\right)$$

becomes

$$s = s_0 \cos\left(2\pi f t\right)$$

In any discussion about shm you may see either of these as the form of the equation used.

The two functions sine and cosine are really graphically the same – the only difference being where you define the zero of angle, and there is no absolute definition of where 0 radians is. This is shown in Figure 7.9.

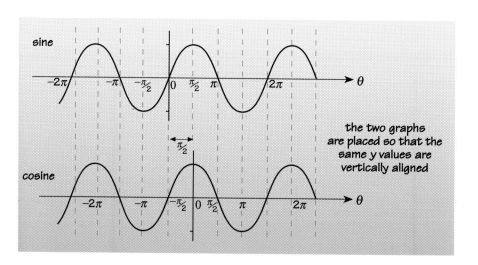

Figure 7.9
Comparing sine and cosine

7.4 Forming equations to relate velocity versus time and acceleration versus time

There are two ways in which we can form these equations. The first is graphically, using ideas from your GCSE science course. The second involves a process called differentiation, which you will cover if you are studying A-level mathematics. We will not consider differentiation here but will look at the graphical method.

Figure 7.10(a) shows how s changes with time. From your GCSE work you should remember that the gradient at any point on a displacement–time graph gives the instantaneous velocity. We can use this idea to construct a velocity–time graph, as shown in Figure 7.10(b).

Again, the gradient at any point on the velocity–time graph gives the instantaneous acceleration. The acceleration–time graph can also be easily constructed and is shown in Figure 7.10(c).

If you have covered differentiation in mathematics you will see how we arrived at the maximum and minimum values for velocity and acceleration. If you have not studied differentiation and really want to check these values you will need to draw accurate graphs having chosen values for f and s_0.

From these graphs we can put together equations for the velocity and acceleration of an object undergoing shm.

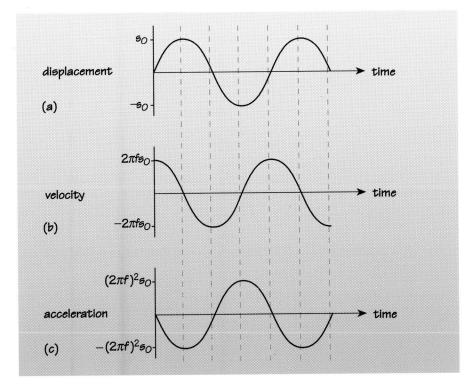

Figure 7.10
Graphs of displacement, velocity and acceleration against time for shm

$$v = 2\pi f s_0 \cos(2\pi f t)$$
$$a = -(2\pi f)^2 s_0 \sin(2\pi f t)$$

The minus at the front tells us that the acceleration is opposite in direction to the displacement.

Remember that the maximum value of the trigonometric part of each of these equations is one. This enables us to write down equations that will give the maximum values for the velocity and the acceleration, v_0 and a_0.

$$v_0 = 2\pi f s_0$$
$$a_0 = -(2\pi f)^2 s_0$$

It will help if we put all the equations for shm together (see Table 7.1). They might seem like a bewildering array, but remember that in each row of the table the equations are the same, but with a substitution based on your work on circular motion. It is always good to memorize the equations that you need to use as it saves a lot of time, particularly in examinations. As the equations are most often written in terms of f, this is probably the best choice to make for memorizing, along with the two substitution equations given underneath the table.

There is one more useful equation that we can add to the table. It comes from combining our equations for displacement and acceleration.

We have found that

$$a = -(2\pi f)^2 s_0 \sin(2\pi f t)$$

but we also know that

$$s_0 = \frac{s}{\sin\left(2\pi f t\right)}$$

from rearranging

$$s = s_0 \sin\left(2\pi f t\right)$$

Now we can replace s_0 in our equation for acceleration

$$a = -(2\pi f)^2 \frac{s}{\sin(2\pi f t)} \sin(2\pi f t)$$

Which reduces to

$$a = -(2\pi f)^2 s$$

(If you look again at Equation (7.1) you can see that the constant in the equation for shm must be equal to $(2\pi f)^2$.)

Now do the following data analysis exercise to confirm the equations of simple harmonic motion.

Table 7.1 Equations for simple harmonic motion

Subject	ω	In terms of f	T
s	$s = s_0 \sin(\omega t)$	$s = s_0 \sin(2\pi f t)$	$s = s_0 \sin\left(\frac{2\pi t}{T}\right)$
v	$v = \omega s_0 \cos(\omega t)$	$v = 2\pi f s_0 \cos(2\pi f t)$	$v = \left(\frac{2\pi}{T}\right) s_0 \cos\left(\frac{2\pi t}{T}\right)$
a	$a = -\omega^2 s_0 \sin(\omega t)$	$a = -(2\pi f)^2 s_0 \sin(2\pi f t)$	$a = -\left(\frac{2\pi}{T}\right)^2 s_0 \sin\left(\frac{2\pi t}{T}\right)$
a	$a = -\omega^2 s$	$a = -(2\pi f)^2 s$	$a = -\left(\frac{2\pi}{T}\right)^2 s$
v_0	$v_0 = \omega s_0$	$v_0 = 2\pi f s_0$	$v_0 = \left(\frac{2\pi}{T}\right) s_0$
a_0	$a_0 = -\omega^2 s_0$	$a_0 = -(2\pi f)^2 s_0$	$a_0 = -\left(\frac{2\pi}{T}\right)^2 s_0$

Substitution equations: $\omega = 2\pi f$ and $\omega = \dfrac{2\pi}{T}$

Data analysis

The data in Table 7.2 overleaf was collected from an oscillatory system (in this case a mass on a spring) being scanned with an ultrasonic sensor attached to a computer via an interface. The computer software calculates values of position h (distance from the sensor), time, velocity and acceleration from the computer's clock. The mass's equilibrium position was found to be 0.30 m from the sensor by scanning it while it was stationary. Unfortunately the resolution of the system is only ± 0.25 cm. Work through the following questions (the answers are given at the end of this section after the answers to the questions in the text).

Table 7.2 Data for simple harmonic motion exercise

h/m	t/s	v/m s^{-1}	a/m s^{-2}
0.440	0.000	0.000	−1.260
0.434	0.100	−0.124	−1.204
0.416	0.200	−0.237	−1.040
0.387	0.300	−0.329	−0.783
0.351	0.400	−0.391	−0.457
0.310	0.500	−0.419	−0.089
0.268	0.600	−0.409	0.286
0.229	0.700	−0.363	0.636
0.197	0.800	−0.284	0.929
0.173	0.900	−0.179	1.139
0.161	1.000	−0.059	1.247
0.162	1.100	0.066	1.244
0.174	1.200	0.186	1.130
0.198	1.300	0.289	0.915
0.231	1.400	0.366	0.618
0.270	1.500	0.411	0.266
0.312	1.600	0.418	−0.110
0.353	1.700	0.389	−0.476
0.389	1.800	0.325	−0.800
0.417	1.900	0.231	−1.052
0.434	2.000	0.117	−1.210
0.440	2.100	−0.007	−1.260

(a) Either using a spreadsheet program, or by copying the table and data-processing manually, evaluate the displacement (change in position), s, from equilibrium position, when $h = 0.30$ m, with time.

(b) Plot three graphs using the same time scale: s versus t; v versus t; a versus t. Draw best-fit lines, which may be up to 0.0025 m above or below any value of s.

(c) What kinds of curve do you get? What is the period T?

In this idealized exercise the clock had started when $s = s_0$, $v = 0$ and $a = a_0$.

Consequently, your graphs can be represented by these equations:

$$s = s_0 \cos(2\pi f t)$$ (7.2)

$$v = -v_0 \sin(2\pi f t) \tag{7.3}$$

$$a = -a_0 \cos(2\pi f t) \tag{7.4}$$

or at another time

$$s = s_0 \sin(2\pi f t) \tag{7.5}$$

$$v = v_0 \cos(2\pi f t) \tag{7.6}$$

$$a = -a_0 \sin(2\pi f t) \tag{7.7}$$

Divide Equation (7.4) by Equation (7.2) (or Equation (7.7) by Equation (7.5)) and simplify. You should obtain:

$$a = -\frac{a_0}{s_0} s \tag{7.8}$$

The term $\dfrac{a_0}{s_0}$ is a constant of proportionality, which we gave earlier as

$$(2\pi f)^2$$

This is again the equation for shm, i.e.

$$\boldsymbol{a} = -\text{constant} \times \boldsymbol{s}$$

(d) Plot a graph of a against s. We have just shown that

$$a = -(2\pi f)^2 s$$

for shm. Is this confirmed by your graph?

(e) Measure the gradient. Put your value of gradient equal to $-(2\pi f)^2$ and find f.

(f) Find period T.

(g) Does this correspond with T measured from each of your s, v, a graphs?

(h) Now plot v against s.

It is pretty clear from this that both s and v have positive and negative maximum values. Record these. We are now going to try to turn this into a straight-line graph. Look at Equations (7.6) and (7.7); rearranging them gives:

$$\frac{s}{s_0} = \cos 2\pi f t$$

and

$$\frac{v}{v_0} = -\sin 2\pi f t$$

squaring them both gives

$$\frac{s^2}{s_0^2} = \cos^2 2\pi f t$$

and

$$\frac{v^2}{v_0^2} = \sin^2 2\pi f t$$

Now, if you add $\sin^2\theta$ and $\cos^2\theta$, whatever the value of θ, you will get 1 – try it on your calculator! So if you add $\dfrac{s^2}{s_0^2} + \dfrac{v^2}{v_0^2}$ you should get 1.

There is a better way to check this than all that arithmetic even if you have got a spreadsheet. If

$$\frac{s^2}{s_0^2} + \frac{v^2}{v_0^2} = 1$$

then

$$\frac{v_0^2 \times s^2}{s_0^2} + v^2 = v_0^2$$

$$v^2 = \frac{-\left(v_0^2 \times s^2\right)}{s_0^2} + v_0^2$$

$$= \left(\frac{-v_0^2}{s_0^2}\right) s^2 + v_0^2$$

Compare this to the standard form of an equation of a straight line

$$y = mx + c$$

 If we plot v^2 as y and s^2 as x, what should we get?

A straight line with gradient $-\left(\dfrac{v_0}{s_0}\right)^2$ and an intercept $c = v_0^2$.

(i) Plot v^2 versus s^2 and find the gradient.

(j) Does the intercept $c = v_0^2$? What is its value from your graph?

It turns out that $\dfrac{v_0}{s_0} = 2\pi f$ so check again that this is consistent with your slope; i.e. does the value of f from your slope yield $T = \dfrac{1}{f}$ from your first graphs? This leads to another version of our equations:

$$s = s_0 \cos 2\pi f t$$

$$v = -(2\pi f)s_0 \sin 2\pi f t$$

$$a = -(2\pi f)^2 s_0 \cos 2\pi f t$$

If so, you've confirmed (though not proven or derived) the three time-dependent shm equations. These, along with $T = \dfrac{1}{f}$, enable us to find out any value of s, v or a at any time, given f and s_0, if the clock starts at maximum displacement. ◆

What makes these systems oscillate?

Consider the mass on a spring.

 When the mass is pulled down slightly and released, why does it accelerate back towards its equilibrium position?

The spring produces tensions that are greater than the weight of the spring, so the spring accelerates upwards.

 When the mass subsequently reaches its equilibrium position, why doesn't it stop?

At the equilibrium position there is no net force on the mass, so, according to Newton's first law, it will not change its velocity, and so it carries on moving.

For a system to oscillate two conditions have to be satisfied:

- there must be a restoring force, which will pull the particle back towards its equilibrium position
- the particle must have mass, so that when it gets back to its equilibrium position it doesn't stop.

 In the case of simple harmonic motion, how does the restoring force vary with displacement?

The force must be proportional to the displacement, and directed towards the equilibrium position. This will make the acceleration proportional to the displacement – i.e. it will make it fulfil the definition of shm.

7.5 Resonance and waves in boards

There are two ways that divers take off from springboards – standing and running. Like novice divers, we will start by considering the standing take-off. (Standing take-offs are used by experts for back take-offs.)

The diver stands at the end of the board and moves their body to oscillate the board so that it pushes them upwards at take-off.

The movement has two phases, as illustrated in Figure 7.11.

The diver must time their movements so that they oscillate the board with its natural frequency. The energy of the oscillating board will build up only if the driving frequency is about the same as the natural frequency of the board.

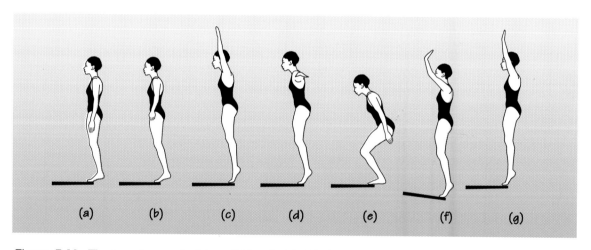

Figure 7.11 The two stages of a take-off. Part 1: (a)–(c); Part 2: (d)–(g)

Exploration 7.2 What factors control the natural frequency of a springboard?

2 HOURS including presentation

Apparatus:

◆ 30 cm plastic rule to use as a model springboard ◆ slotted masses and Sellotape, or Blu-Tack, to represent the diver ◆ stopclock ◆ G-clamp ◆ wooden block ◆ pencil

Make a list of factors that may affect the period of oscillation of the board, assuming that the diver is standing on the end of the board.

Select one of these variables and design an experiment to determine how this variable controls the period of oscillation – if it does. Check your proposal with your teacher – it might be interesting to choose different variables amongst different groups in your class.

Design suitable apparatus for timing the period and measuring your chosen variable. Use a standard 30 cm plastic ruler to model the board (see Figure 7.12). You can use clamps, masses, Sellotape, Blu-Tack, stopclocks and other standard lab apparatus. Make sure that you get a large enough set of data, covering a suitable range of time periods.

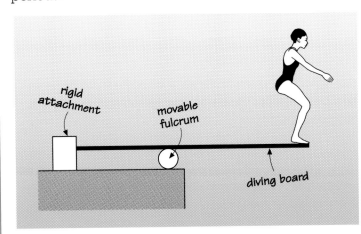

Work out how to analyse and present your data. Try to display your data so that you can see a pattern in your results. To be sure of a mathematical relationship between the period and your variable you should find a straight line you can plot.

Figure 7.12
The construction of a springboard

Carry out your experiment then present your findings to the rest of the class in the form of a spoken presentation, or design a poster to describe your experiment and give the results of your conclusions.

The vibration of the ruler, like all the oscillations we have looked at in this section so far, is a **free vibration**: it is caused by the system itself, moving with no other external forces interfering. In the next exploration we look at a situation where we have **forced vibrations** – vibrations that are driven by an external oscillator.

Exploration 7.3 How does the amplitude of oscillation vary with driving frequency?

Apparatus:

◆ signal generator, capable of producing frequencies as low as 1 Hz, connected to a vibration generator ◆ 10 g slotted masses and holder ◆ two expendable steel springs ◆ 30 cm rule ◆ clamps and stands

Set up the apparatus as shown in Figure 7.13.

1 With the signal generator turned off, and 30 g of masses suspended between the springs, measure the natural frequency of the masses in a vertical oscillation. If this is less than 1.5 Hz, remove masses until the frequency is greater than 1.5 Hz.

2 Stop the oscillation of the masses, and adjust the signal generator so that it produces vibrations at a frequency of 1 Hz.

   Observe the movement of the masses carefully, seeing how they change with time. Measure the maximum amplitude of the oscillation. (This is done most easily by measuring the distance between the two extremes of the oscillation and dividing by 2.)

3 Repeat step 2 for increasing frequencies, covering a range from 1 Hz to well above the natural frequency of the mass and spring. Pay particular attention to frequencies close to the natural frequency – take more measurements here. Remember to make room in your results table for comments about the movement of the masses. (Watch for erratic amplitudes, and for bouncing of the masses.)

4 Plot a graph of amplitude versus driving frequency. Draw a smooth curve between the points. What link can you see between the shape of your graph and the natural frequency of the mass and spring system?

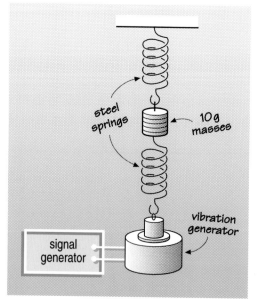

Figure 7.13 Apparatus to show how driving frequency and amplitude are related for an oscillating system.

If you did the above exploration you should have noticed that the amplitude is a maximum at around the natural frequency of the oscillation. This is an example of **resonance**. A system resonates when there is a regular driving force that works in time with the natural oscillation of the system, and so builds up the oscillation energy of the system to a maximum (see Figure 7.14).

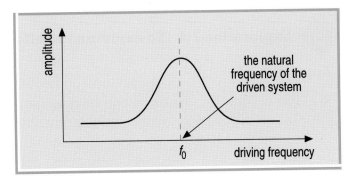

An everyday example of resonance occurs when you push a child on a swing. You push, regularly, at the right moment, and the child gradually swings higher and higher, even if you are pushing only fairly gently.

Figure 7.14
Graph of amplitude versus driving frequency

 When you push a child on a swing, if you keep pushing gently, the amplitude of the swing will settle at a maximum value, why?

As the swing moves faster and further the frictional drag on the swing increases, so more energy is converted to thermal energy in each swing. Eventually the rate at which energy is put into the system from your pushing is equal to the rate of energy loss as it is transferred to thermal energy, so the energy, and hence the amplitude, of the system no longer increases.

All oscillating systems lose some energy somewhere: friction transfers kinetic energy into thermal energy; thermal energy may also be released in materials as they are stretched and squashed. Some systems may also lose energy electromagnetically. This energy loss will eventually cause the oscillator to stop, unless we put more energy in to keep it moving. The process by which energy is lost from an oscillating system is called **damping**. Resonance and damping are important areas of study for instrument manufacturers and sound engineers. If you would like to learn more about this you should study the SLIPP unit *Physics, Jazz and Pop,* which looks at resonance and damping in the context of oscillations of strings in musical instruments.

Exploration 7.4   To examine the effect of damping on resonance

Apparatus:

◆ 2 sets of Barton's pendulums: one set made with polystyrene spheres for pendulums, the other set with slightly heavier weights (e.g. curtain rings on the spheres)

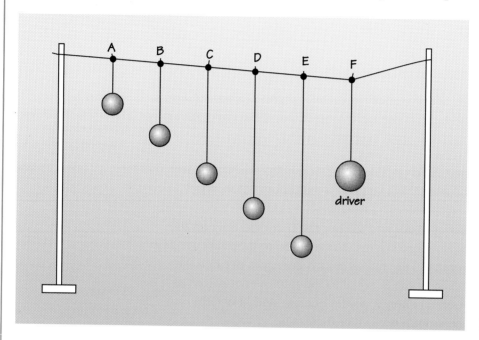

Figure 7.15
Barton's pendulums with driver pendulum labelled

Set up the apparatus as shown in Figure 7.15. (*Note:* Be gentle with this apparatus. The largest amplitudes should be less than about 30°.)

For each set of pendulums, set the driver pendulum moving and watch carefully. First look at the amplitudes of the pendulums. Copy the axes in Figure 7.16(a) on to graph paper and estimate the data for the two sets of pendula.

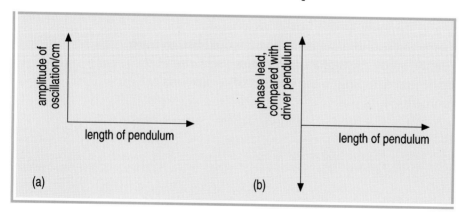

Figure 7.16
Graph for Exploration 7.4

Then, if you have time, look at the phase of the pendulums – are they in step? If not, what is the phase difference?

Copy Figure 7.16(b) on to graph paper and fill in the data for the pendulums.

7.6 Accessing the hidden forces

A diver on a springboard can be likened to a mass on a spring. The system has a natural period of oscillation. If the diver can shake the end of the board at this natural frequency, the amplitude of oscillation builds up, and hence the impulse available to propel the diver into the air is increased. There are many factors that make the real world of diving much more subtle and complex than this; in this section we consider some of the techniques of using a springboard.

The Running Take-off

The Running Take-off from the springboard consists of a three-step walk followed by a jump upwards from one foot to land on the end of the board. Coaches divide the Running Take-off into five parts (see Figure 7.17).

The aim in the springboard take-off is to deflect the board as much as possible but at the same time ensure that when it reaches the bottom of

Figure 7.17 The Running Take-off: 1 The Walk (a, b) – a minimum of three steps; 2 The Hurdle (c, d, e) – the jump upwards from one foot; 3 The Crouch (f, g) – the soft landing on the end of the board; 4 The Drive Down (h, i) – the depressing of the board, during which the board pushes up hard on the diver's feet; 5 The Push Up (j, k) – the acceleration of the body upwards during the recoil as the board relaxes and pushes less and less hard on the diver

its swing the diver's heels are down with the legs still bent slightly at the knees, ready for their final extension as the board recoils.

Q2 Tony is 14 stone. He sets the fulcrum of the springboard so that the free end is fairly short, otherwise, when he takes off, the board hits the water because of the high forces he generates upon take-off. Bob is 10 stone. All other factors being equal: (a) Will Bob's lower mass affect the deflection of the board? (b) How should Bob move the fulcrum? ◆

Q3 The natural frequency of the board when Tony is diving is 2.0 Hz. (a) How many steps per second must Tony make to use resonance to help his dive? (b) If he wants to walk faster how can he adjust the board to suit his style of diving? ◆

Until fairly recently, divers learned their by instinct. They simply kept trying until their coaches told them that it was right. Divers learn to get the feel of a board, and do not necessarily understand what the board and their body are doing at every instant of the dive. With modern sport science, coaches are looking to physics and engineering to help them work out what is right and wrong in diving technique, but when it comes to the interaction between the springboard and the diver, there is still a lot of uncertainty. The points raised below are, at the time of writing, still real issues of interest to coaches and divers. You may like to work together with two or three other students and discuss some of these points.

- According to Russian diving coaches, a diver must relate the timing of their run to the free oscillation period of the springboard *without* the diver. Does the mass of the diver have any influence on the resonant frequency of the board during the running take-off?

- Can a heavy diver get more energy out of a board? What sort of diver do you expect to be able to gain most height from a springboard?

- At the moment of contact with the board, should the muscles of the legs be tense?

- Kinematic analysis shows that expert divers make contact with the support in a squatting position. Why? How does this affect the time in contact with the support?

- During a perfectly timed dive, when a diver has landed on the board really hard before take-off and given it a large deflection, they say that they feel the 'kip' – the board reaches a 'maximum' deflection. Has the board really reached its elastic limit?

 Suggested further exploration

Develop a hypothesis and test it by designing and carrying out an experiment to find out what controls the height reached by a rigid object when it is propelled into the air by a flexed board (or plastic ruler).

Achievements

After you have studied this section you should be able to:

- understand and define the terms associated with shm, especially 'period', 'frequency' and 'amplitude', and use the basic relationships between them
- explain resonance and its relevance to springboard diving
- realize that simple physics models are sometimes insufficient to discuss the nuances of some phenomena, e.g. the run-up in springboard diving
- explain the difference between free and forced vibrations.

Glossary

Amplitude Maximum displacement in shm.

Damping The process leading to the loss of energy by a vibrating system.

Displacement The change in position of a particle from its equilibrium position or from the centre of its vibrating path.

Equilibrium position The position in which a body experiences no resultant force and obeys Newton's first law.

Forced vibration Vibration produced in a system by external forces acting on that system and controlling its frequency.

Free vibration Vibration of a system when no external forces control its frequency.

Frequency The number of complete vibrations in a unit time interval.

Fulcrum The point about which a lever rotates.

Period of oscillation The duration of one cycle of an oscillation or rotation or orbit of a body

Resonance Vibration of a system at maximum amplitude at its natural frequency as a result of energy being supplied to the system at that frequency.

Simple harmonic motion (shm) Oscillatory motion in which the acceleration (or force acting) is always towards the equilibrium position (position of zero net force), and its magnitude is proportional to the displacement of the oscillating body from this position.

Answers to Ready to Study test

R1

See Figure 7.18.

Let the distance from the centre of gravity of the legs to the centre of gravity of the body be x. Let the distance from the centre of gravity of the upper body to the centre of gravity of the body be y.

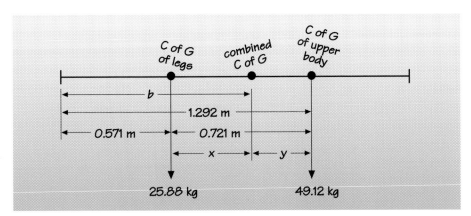

Figure 7.18

Taking moments about the centre of gravity of the body gives:

$$25.88\,\text{kg} \times x = 49.12\,\text{kg} \times y$$

Since

$$y = (0.721\text{m} - x)$$

substituting for y gives

$$25.88\,\text{kg}\, x = 49.12\,\text{kg}\, (0.721\text{m} - x)$$

$$25.88\,\text{kg}\, x = 49.12\,\text{kg} \times 0.721\text{m} - 49.12\,\text{kg}\, x$$

$$x(25.88\,\text{kg} + 49.12\,\text{kg}) = 35.41552\,\text{kg}\,\text{m}$$

Therefore
$$x = 0.4722\text{m}$$

so

$$b = 0.571\text{m} + 0.4722\text{m}$$
$$= 1.0432\text{m}$$
$$= 1.04\,\text{m} \text{ (to three significant figures)}$$

R2

(a) Time of flight is time to fall 45 m vertically, given by

$$s = ut + \frac{1}{2}at^2$$

$$(u_y = 0)$$

So it follows that

$$t = \sqrt{\frac{2s}{a}}$$

$$= \sqrt{\frac{2 \times -45\text{m}}{-10\text{ms}^{-2}}}$$

$$= \sqrt{9.0\text{s}^2}$$

$$= 3.0\text{s}$$

(b) Horizontal (conserved) velocity = 15 m s^{-1}

vertical velocity is given by

$$v_y = u_y + at$$

$$(u_y = 0)$$

Therefore

$$v_y = at$$

$$= -10\text{ms}^{-2} \times 3.0\text{s}$$

$$= -30\text{ms}^{-1}$$

So total velocity is

$$v = \sqrt{\left(15\text{ms}^{-1}\right)^2 + \left(30\text{ms}^{-1}\right)^2}$$

$$= 33.54\text{ms}^{-1}$$

$$= 34\text{ms}^{-1} \text{(to two significant figures)}$$

The angle, α, to the horizontal is given by

$$\tan\alpha = \frac{33.54}{15}$$

$$= 2.236$$

$$\alpha = 65.9°$$

$$= 66° \text{ (to two significant figures)}$$

(c) In 3.0 s, at 15 m s^{-1} sideways the lemming travels 45.0 m.

R3

(a)

$$\frac{1}{2}mu^2 = \frac{1}{2} \times 0.50\text{kg}\,\left(15\text{ms}^{-1}\right)^2$$

$$= 56.25\text{J}$$

(b)

$$\frac{1}{2}mv^2 = \frac{1}{2} \times 0.50\text{kg}\,\left(33.54\text{ms}^{-1}\right)^2$$

$$= 281.23\text{J}$$

(c)

PE lost $= mgb$

$$= 0.50\text{kg} \times 10\text{ms}^{-2} \times 45\text{m}$$

$$= 225\text{J}$$

(d)

$$225\text{J} \approx (281.23 - 56.25)\text{J}$$

by the conservation of energy

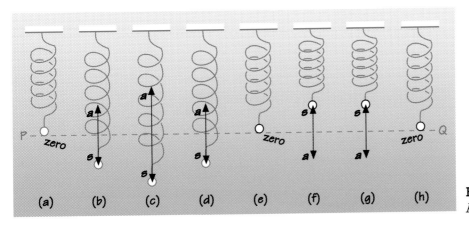

Figure 7.19
Answer for Question 1

R4

(a) A and C are in phase.

(b) 180° phase difference.

Answers to questions in the text

Q1

See Figure 7.19

Q2

(a) Bob's lower mass will mean that the forces on the board are smaller, so the board will not deflect as far at the same setting.

(b) Bob can move the fulcrum to a higher setting giving him a longer free end of board.

Q3

(a) He must step at the natural frequency of the board – i.e. 2 steps per second.

(b) If he wants to walk faster he needs the board to oscillate at a higher frequency. This will require a shorter free end – the fulcrum should be moved to a lower setting.

Data analysis solutions for shm exercise

(a) s column.

(b) s, v, a versus t graphs (Figure 7.20(a), (b) and (c)).

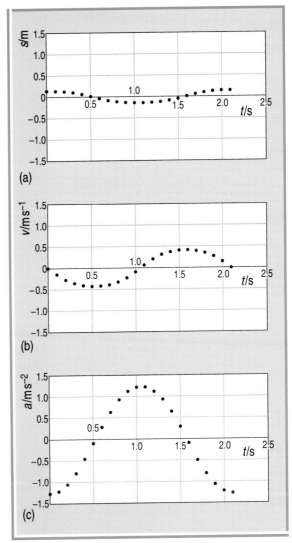

Figure 7.20 Data analysis (b)

(c) Sinusoidal, $T = 2.2$ s.

(d) a versus s graph (Figure 7.21 overleaf). Equation (7.1) says that a is directly proportional to s, so a graph of a against s should be a straight line passing through the origin. Is yours?

(e)

Gradient = −0.11

$$f = \sqrt{\frac{-\text{gradient}}{2\pi}}$$

$$= 0.478\,9\,\text{Hz}$$

$$= 0.48\,\text{Hz (to two significant figures)}$$

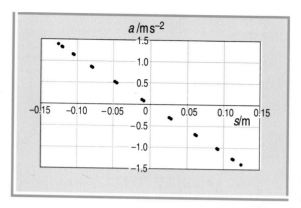

Figure 7.21 Data analysis (d)

(f) Remember f cycles occupy one second, then each occupies $\dfrac{1}{f}$ seconds, so period is given by

$$T = \frac{1}{f}$$

$$= 2.088\,\text{s}$$

$$= 2.1\,\text{s (to two significant figures)}$$

(g) It's close!

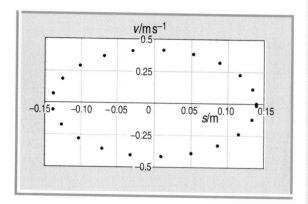

Figure 7.22 Data analysis (h)

(h) See Figure 7.22, $s_0 \approx 0.14$ m, $v_0 = 0.42$ m s^{-1}.

(i) See Figure 7.23.

$$\text{Gradient} = -\left(\frac{v_0}{s_0}\right)^2$$

$$\approx -9.0$$

(j) $c = 0.175\,\text{m}^2\,\text{s}^{-2}$

and

$$v_0^2 = 0.176\,\text{m}^2\,\text{s}^{-2}$$

It's close!

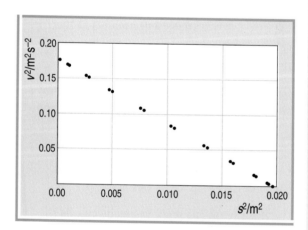

Figure 7.23 Data analysis (i)

Imagine yourself exploring the underwater world – floating in water watching colourful fish feed on a fertile coral reef. It might seem just like a dream, but underwater diving using **s**elf-**c**ontained **u**nderwater **b**reathing **a**pparatus (scuba) is a rapidly growing sport, and many students are finding room in their budgets to finance diving lessons and holidays.

Some people enjoy the beauty of the underwater world from their armchairs, watching wildlife programmes on television, and do not even consider diving themselves. However, with the improvements in training and safety that have taken place over the last 20 years, diving is becoming one of the safest sports. Many disabled people are successful divers – people with limited mobility can enjoy an independence of movement under water that they do not have on land. Others who are trained in special skills, such as sign language, may have an advantage over people who have not needed to acquire those skills.

One reason for the popularity of diving is that it is now so safe. Nowadays dive centres will not hire dive equipment to just anyone – divers, just like car drivers, have to pass exams before they are allowed to use potentially dangerous equipment. And just like driving, if everyone follows the guidelines diving is very safe.

But to understand diving, and to pass diving exams, you need to understand the physics of diving. By working through Part III, you will learn about the physics of gases (their pressure, volumes and densities), liquids (buoyancy and pressure), sound and light, motion and energy loss, and you will also learn about diving safety.

More information about diving schools, holidays and licensing is contained in the Further Reading and Resources section at the end of this unit.

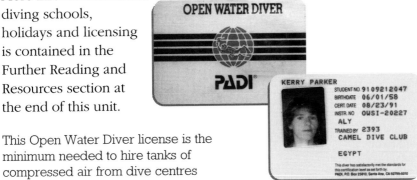

This Open Water Diver license is the minimum needed to hire tanks of compressed air from dive centres

PART III

PHYSICS FOR SCUBA DIVING

8

Modern diving may be a very safe sport, but it has not always been so. Many people have died or received terrible injuries when trying to dive – often because they did not understand the physics of what they were doing.

Humans have been diving since primitive peoples foraged for food in the sea. The main impetus for deeper diving may have been the recovery of valuables from shipwrecks. Diving as a sport probably began with the development of an independent or 'autonomous' diving apparatus, which did not require lines and air hoses up to the surface. William James, an Englishman, invented a compressed air system in 1825, but the first record of diving using breathing apparatus is of the American Charles Condert, who used a waist-mounted reservoir to provide air to a flexible helmet. He successfully dived many times in New York's East River before suffocating to death in 1832 because of a broken air tube.

Modern masks, fins and snorkel tubes were developed by a group of breath-holding fishermen in the south of France in the 1920s and 1930s, but it was Georges Commeinhes who developed the first fully automatic aqualung, which was approved by the French Navy in 1937. Finally, Jacques Cousteau, another French Navy officer, collaborated with engineer Emile Gagnan to produce a mouth-held regulator with an inlet and exhaust tube that was fully automatic – the modern aqualung was born. Cousteau and his team made numerous underwater films, and these inspired the first generation of scuba divers.

There is something exceedingly impressive about a person who can walk down a beach into the sea, disappear for 40 minutes, and then walk back out. We learn from an early age that we cannot breathe under water, we need to keep our faces surrounded by air, and yet a scuba diver can survive surrounded in water with no connection to the life-giving air above. Without an understanding of physics, the development of scuba diving would not have been possible. In this section we will look at the physics of making gases flow, and of storing and releasing compressed air safely.

William James's autonomous diving apparatus (Source: *Sport Diving*, BSAC, 1985)

READY TO STUDY TEST

Before you begin this section you should be able to:

■ define pressure, P, as $\dfrac{\text{force}}{\text{area}}$, $\quad P = \dfrac{F}{A}$

■ remember that the SI unit of pressure is the pascal ($1\ \text{Pa} = 1\ \text{N m}^{-2}$)

■ understand that the atmosphere exerts a pressure

■ calculate the weight, $\boldsymbol{W}$, of an object, knowing its mass, m, and the gravitational field strength, g ($\boldsymbol{W} = m\boldsymbol{g}$)

■ draw and interpret force diagrams, including representing the weight of a body as a vertical force that acts from a single point known as the centre of gravity

■ define density, ρ, as $\dfrac{\text{mass}}{\text{volume}}$, $\quad \rho = \dfrac{m}{V}$

■ remember and be able to use Newton's laws of motion

■ state the conditions for equilibrium of a body.

QUESTIONS

R1 A diver with a weight of 600 N stands on the ground with their weight spread evenly over both feet, each of area 200 cm². Calculate the pressure they exert on the ground. (Remember, $1\ \text{cm} = 10^{-2}\ \text{m}$, so $(1\ \text{cm})^2 = (10^{-2}\ \text{m})^2 = 10^{-4}\ \text{m}^2$).

R2 Why does a steel can crumple if you take the air out of it? Is it because:

(a) The suction pulls the walls of the can in?

(b) Atmospheric pressure is no longer balanced by the pressure of air inside the can, so the can is pushed in by the atmosphere?

(c) The air that is removed from the can produces an increase in atmospheric pressure, which then pushes the can in?

R3 A 60 kg diver carries 20 kg of scuba gear and a 3.0 kg weight belt. What is her total weight? (Use $g = 9.81\ \text{N kg}^{-1}$.)

R4 A diver, with all his gear, has a weight of 1000 N. If he is floating perfectly still under the water, what is the total upwards force of the water on him?

R5 Draw a simplified diagrammatic copy of the diver in Figure 8.1 and (a) draw the line along which the upwards buoyancy force must act, (b) mark the point of action of the buoyancy force.

R6 If the diver in the last question began to float slowly to the surface, even though she hadn't lost any gear, what could you say had happened (a) to her weight, (b) to the buoyancy force?

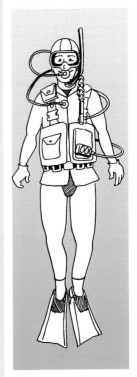

Figure 8.1
A diver under water

8.1 The biological problem

The most obvious problem for someone who wants to spend any amount of time under water is how to breathe. Inhaling oxygen and exhaling carbon dioxide are vital to life. Fish are naturally adapted to remove oxygen from water and some mammals, such as sperm whales, can dive to 1000 m and stay under for 50 minutes or more. Humans, however, even with training, can stay under water no more than a couple of minutes, and untrained people can manage just a few seconds. So, for longer dives:

- the lungs must be connected to a supply of oxygen
- the oxygen must move into the lungs throughout the dive.

8.2 The mechanics of breathing

Normal breathing

Breathing is controlled by signals from the nerve centre in the brain stem. Breathing in (inspiration) is brought about by signals causing the muscles between the ribs to contract, pushing the ribs upwards and outwards, while the diaphragm, which is below the lungs, pulls downwards, further increasing the volume of the chest cavity. As the chest expands, air pressure in the lungs is reduced, and so air immediately flows into the lungs to equalize the pressure with that of the atmosphere outside the body.

 Explain, in terms of gas pressure, how we breathe out (expiration).

When we breathe out, air moves from our lungs through our nose and mouth into the atmosphere. This occurs because the lung volume is decreased by contraction of the ribs and the diaphragm. The pressure inside the lungs rises slightly above **atmospheric pressure**, and this pressure difference causes the air to flow out.

E ⬥ Exploration 8.1   Investigating the physics of breathing

Apparatus:

◆ bell jar ◆ rubber diaphragm ◆ two balloons ◆ T-junction and tube

10
MINUTES
plus
report writing

Set up the apparatus as shown in Figure 8.2. Push the rubber diaphragm in and observe the movement of the balloon 'lungs'. Allow the diaphragm to drop back down.

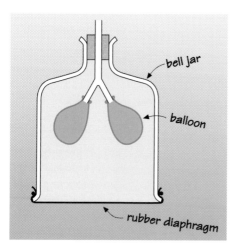

What happens to the balloons now? Why does the movement of the diaphragm control the passage of air in and out of the balloons? If the diaphragm could not move, would there be any way to inflate or deflate the balloons?

Write a report of this experiment relating the movement of the rubber diaphragm and balloons to the mechanisms we use in breathing.

Figure 8.2   Balloon 'lungs'

8.3   The physics of making gases flow

There are two important physics principles that explain breathing:

1   Fluids flow from high pressure to low pressure until the pressure in both places is equal.

2   For a fixed mass of gas, if volume increases, pressure decreases, and vice versa (if the temperature doesn't change). In other words, pressure and volume are inversely proportional.

If P = pressure and V = volume

$$P \propto \frac{1}{V}$$

so

$$PV = \text{constant}$$

or

$$P_1V_1 = P_2V_2$$

this is called **Boyle's law**.

Experiments to demonstrate Boyle's law

 Exploration 8.2   Exerting a force on air in a bicycle pump or syringe

Apparatus:

◆ bicycle pump or plastic syringe (without its needle)

10 MINUTES

Pull out the plunger of a bicycle pump or plastic syringe. Seal the end with your finger and press down the plunger, as in Figure 8.3. How is the position of the plunger related to the force you exert on it?

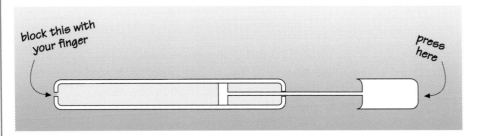

Figure 8.3
Pressing on a bicycle pump

 As you push harder, what are you doing to the air pressure inside the pump or syringe?

As the force increases the pressure increases.

 As the plunger moves further down the syringe, what is happening to the volume of gas?

As the plunger moves further down, the volume of gas decreases.

 Exploration 8.3   Boyle's law

Check that the tube is firmly fixed and restricted before starting.

Apparatus: ◆ Boyle's law apparatus as shown in Figure 8.4

Using special apparatus such as that shown in Figure 8.4, you can gradually increase the pressure on some air trapped in a glass tube. It is important that the increase is slow, so that the temperature of the gas doesn't rise when you squash it. Open the tap before pumping and close the tap afterwards. After closing the tap *wait* for some time before taking readings. This allows the gas temperature to return to that of the surroundings if it has risen.

60 MINUTES

Readings

Press the foot pump to alter the pressure of the trapped air. Use the level of the liquid to determine the *length* of tube occupied by the trapped air. The volume of the air will be proportional to this reading.

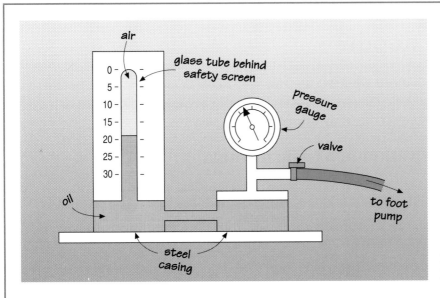

Figure 8.4
Boyle's law apparatus

Record this *length* and the pressure indicated on the gauge.

(*Note:* This pressure (an absolute pressure) includes the contribution from atmospheric pressure, as opposed to the confusingly named gauge pressure, which doesn't. Hence this apparatus gives you the total pressure you need.)

Alter the pressure several times so that you can collect at least six pairs of readings. Plot a graph to see how closely the real gas matches Boyle's prediction. Temperature, as we will see later, affects pressure too.

 If Boyle's law works perfectly, what will be the shape of a graph of *V* versus *P*?

Neither the volume nor the pressure can ever reach zero, because the other quantity would have to be infinitely large, so we have a curve that tends to infinity along both axes (see Figure 8.5). It is difficult to prove that the plot of *V* versus *P* obtained from our experiments really has this precise mathematical shape because of the limited range and accuracy of our results.

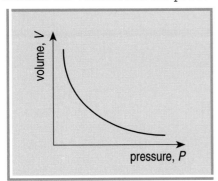

Figure 8.5 A graph of *V* versus *P* for an ideal gas

 If the data matches Boyle's law exactly, what should you use for your *x*- and *y*-axes if you are to get a straight line?

Rearranging PV = constant we get V = constant/P. This is similar to the equation of a straight line, $y = mx$, so, using V as the *y*-axis and $1/P$ as the *x*-axis, we should get a straight line, passing through the origin.

8.4 How does fluid pressure depend on depth?

Breathing air while we are surrounded by air is no problem. But there are many difficulties associated with diving because of the additional pressure on the body caused by the water.

Derivation of a basic formula

When we derive a formula we prove, mathematically, that it must be true, if certain starting-points are valid. In this case we know four things:

1. liquids are virtually incompressible; thus, even as the pressure in a liquid increases its density will remain constant

2. $\text{density} = \dfrac{\text{mass}}{\text{volume}}, \; \rho = \dfrac{m}{V}$

3. $\text{weight} = \text{mass} \times g, \; \boldsymbol{W} = m\boldsymbol{g}$

4. $\text{pressure} = \dfrac{\text{force}}{\text{area}}, \; P = \dfrac{F}{A}$

If these four facts are true, the equation we are to derive from these *must* be true. The logic goes as follows:

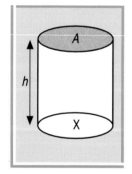

Figure 8.6
A cylinder of height h full of liquid

Consider a cylinder of liquid, like the one shown in Figure 8.6. The vertical height of the liquid from the surface to point X is distance h. The cylinder has a cross-sectional area A. X must be under pressure, due to the liquid, because all the weight of the fluid between A and X is pressing on X. The liquid has density ρ.

Volume of fluid above X = hA

Since

mass = volume × density

it follows that

mass of fluid = ρhA

and as

$\boldsymbol{W} = \text{mass} \times \boldsymbol{g}$

it follows that

magnitude of weight of fluid = ρhAg

Now, pressure, P, is defined as $\dfrac{\text{force}}{\text{area}}$.

The pressure at X must be the force acting on it (i.e. the weight of the fluid) divided by the cross-sectional area of the cylinder:

$$P = \frac{W}{A}$$

$$= \frac{\rho h A g}{A}$$

so

$$P = h\rho g$$

Worked example

Calculate the pressure due to 5.0 m depth of water and the total pressure at a depth of 5.0 m.

(The density of water is about 1 000 kg m^{-3}; use $g = 9.81$ N kg^{-1}).

Pressure due to the water:

$$P = h\rho g$$

$$= 5.0\,\text{m} \times 1000\,\text{kg}\,\text{m}^{-3} \times 9.81\,\text{N}\,\text{kg}^{-1}$$

$$= 49\,050\,\text{Pa}$$

$$= 49\,\text{kPa}$$

This is not the total pressure, however, because the atmosphere is also pressing down on the top of the water, adding to the pressure. At sea level the atmospheric pressure is about 110 kPa.

Total pressure = water pressure + atmospheric pressure

$$= 49\,\text{kPa} + 110\,\text{kPa}$$

$$= 159\,\text{kPa} \quad \blacklozenge$$

Q1 Copy Table 8.1 and fill in the missing pressures. (Use $g = 9.81$ N kg^{-1} and quote answers to three significant figures.) ◆

Table 8.1 Fill in the missing pressures

Depth/m	Pressure in freshwater (density = 1000 kg m^{-3})/kPa	Pressure in seawater (density = 1100 kg m^{-3})/kPa
0	110	110
5.00	159	(b)
10.0	(a)	218
15.0	257	272
20.0	(c)	326
25.0	355	(d)

8.5 Never hold your breath

Never hold your breath – this is the simplest and the most important rule a novice diver learns. If you have access to a deep swimming pool and you are a good underwater swimmer you might try the following experiment, or you could watch the video made by PADI (Professional Association of Diving Instructors), *PADI Open Water Diver Video – module one, the underwater world*, or just use your imagination. Details of how to obtain the PADI video are given in the Further Reading and Resources section at the end of the unit.

Take an ordinary balloon and inflate it by the poolside. Then pull the balloon under the water. Use your knowledge of Boyle's law to answer the next two questions.

Q2 What will happen to the volume of the balloon as it is pulled down 10.0 m? ◆

Q3 Imagine taking a similar balloon to a depth of 10 m, inflating it with air using a cylinder of compressed air, sealing it and then allowing it to rise slowly to the surface. What would happen to the balloon? ◆

This experiment is not so impressive until you realize that the balloon behaves in an identical way to your lungs. If you hold your breath and dive whilst snorkelling the squashing of your lungs is not a problem. Lungs, like the balloon, are not damaged by being squashed gently. However, if you fill your lungs with air at a depth of 10 m and then return to the surface whilst holding your breath, your lungs suffer the same fate as the ascending balloon. Lung rupture is the most serious injury a diver can suffer, but it is the easiest to prevent by breathing continuously and never holding your breath. Divers are trained to sing when they ascend in an emergency to allow the air to expand and escape from their lungs.

8.6 Air supply under water

Being able to breathe under water involves more than just connecting yourself to an air supply. The mechanics of breathing require that the pressure of the air supply must always be slightly greater than the pressure of air in the expanding lungs.

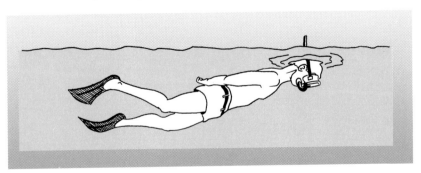

Figure 8.7
Snorkelling

A snorkel is an easy to use, convenient way of supplying air when you are just under the surface of the water (see Figure 8.7), but have you ever wondered why divers do not use longer snorkels in order to dive more deeply?

The problem is that if you dive with a tube to depths of 3 m or more, the air just won't go into your lungs any more. This is because your lungs, along with the rest of your body are being pressurized by the water around you. The air pressure in your lungs is therefore greater than that in the atmosphere above, so even when you expand your lungs you can't get air to enter. In order to dive at depths of, say, 25 m, people have devised two different solutions.

Figure 8.8
A rigid suit and air tube (Source: *Illustrated London News*, vol. 72, p. 389, 1878)

The first involves protecting the body from the extra fluid pressure by wearing a rigid suit and breathing air at atmospheric pressure through a tube (see Figure 8.8). The second involves letting the person breathe air that is at a pressure slightly greater than the pressure around them.

If you want to be free to explore caves, wrecks and generally have fun under water, the second solution, using scuba apparatus, is much better than being confined to a bulky, awkward suit. Scuba uses pressurized air, held in tanks on the diver's back, which is released into the diver's mouth at a pressure matching that of the surrounding water.

(There is, in fact, a third solution. Commercial divers, such as those who work for long periods on the North Sea pipelines, use pressurized gas supplied through a pipe from the surface.)

An aqualung is apparatus designed to supply pressurized gas to the diver's mouthpiece. It consists of a set of valves allowing the release of air from a cylinder of compressed air to the mouthpiece (see Figure 8.9 overleaf). When the user inhales through the mouthpiece, air is drawn through the regulator at a pressure just above that of the surrounding water pressure. When they exhale, the valves close and the exhaled air leaves the regulator as bubbles in the water. One of the most important instruments that is always fitted is a pressure gauge. This tells the diver the pressure of the air in their tank. A full tank is normally pressurized to around 20 MPa, but as they use the air this pressure falls.

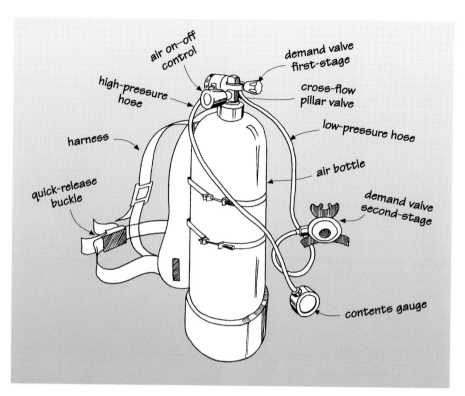

Figure 8.9
The aqualung or scuba apparatus

 If a diver was at a depth of 25 m in seawater, what would be the absolute minimum pressure they would need in their tank to be able to breathe? (*Hint:* To find the pressure on a diver at a depth of 25 m, look back to your answers to Question 1.)

380 kPa, the same as for Question 1(d).

To avoid the risk of seawater entering the tank and causing corrosion, divers are advised to allow a substantial margin of error. Many divers aim to finish diving with about 5 MPa air pressure in their tanks.

8.7 Equalizing – a critical diving technique

When considering the effect of pressure on the human body, we can think of the body as a bag of liquid containing a few pockets of air (see Figure 8.10). (The skeleton does not protect us from pressure because it is on the inside of the soft tissue.) When the outside pressure on the body increases, for example when a diver descends, the pressure on the whole body increases. There is little noticeable effect on the fluid-filled parts of the body, but the air-filled pockets decrease in volume.

The ears and the sinuses in particular can be painfully crushed by the water pressure, so divers have to blow air from their lungs into these spaces. This technique, known as equalizing, is a vital skill to avoid terrible injuries such as burst eardrums. You may have experienced the uncomfortable feeling in your ears due to pressure changes when you have flown in an aeroplane or driven up a mountain road. By chewing, blowing your nose or wiggling your jaw you can encourage air to move into the ears and sinuses – it is this movement of air that makes your ears pop. Gas in the stomach is rarely a problem, but some divers get indigestion or may just feel hungry.

The middle ear is sealed from the outer ear by the eardrum. It is only connected to the outside atmosphere by a soft, flexible tube called the Eustachian tube, which runs from the ear to the throat. As pressure increases on a diver, air must move up the Eustachian tube to equalize the pressure difference between the middle ear and the outer ear. If a diver forgets to equalize as they begin to descend, they experience pains in their ears. They may then find it impossible to equalize. This is because the pressure difference between the middle ear and outer ear becomes too great and pressure on the eardrum causes intense pain. Wiggling the jaw, blowing the nose, etc. – techniques that normally encourage air to move up the Eustachian tube – may no longer work because the Eustachian tube has been compressed by the high external pressure. To solve the problem the diver should slowly ascend, with their buddy (diving partner), until they are able to equalize.

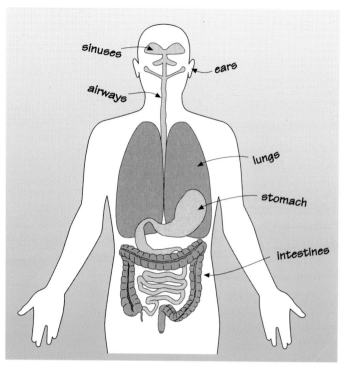

Figure 8.10
The air-filled spaces in the body

 What happens to the air in the middle ear when a diver ascends?

As they ascend the pressure in the outer ear decreases. Eventually the greater air pressure in the middle ear pushes air out, down the Eustachian tube. This is rarely a problem.

 Divers sometimes can't equalize when they have a cold. Why do you think this is?

Their sinuses become blocked and air cannot enter the Eustachian tube.

Achievements

After studying this section you should be able to:

- calculate pressure at various depths
- recall and verify Boyle's law
- explain why air enters the lungs during breathing.

Glossary

Atmospheric pressure   The pressure exerted by the atmosphere at any place because of the weight of atmosphere above the place in question. At sea level atmospheric pressure is approximately equal to 1×10^5 Pa.

Boyle's law   The law that outlines the mathematical relationship between temperature and volume of a gas. It states that the product of pressure and volume of a fixed mass of gas at uniform temperature remains constant. Or, put another way, the pressure of a fixed mass of gas at constant temperature is inversely proportional to volume

$$P \propto \frac{1}{V}$$

or

$$PV = \text{constant}$$

Answers to Ready to Study test

R1

$$P = \frac{F}{A}$$
$$= \frac{600\,\text{N}}{2 \times 200 \times 10^{-4}\,\text{m}^2}$$
$$= 1.5 \times 10^4 \text{ Pa or 15kPa}$$

R2

(b)

R3

$$\text{Weight} = \text{mass} \times g$$
$$= (60 + 20 + 3.0)\,\text{kg} \times 9.81\,\text{N}\,\text{kg}^{-1}$$
$$= 814.23\,\text{N}$$
$$= 8.1 \times 10^2 \text{ N (to two significant figures)}$$

R4

Newton's first law applies, so the net force on the diver must be zero if he is not accelerating. This means that the upwards force equals the downwards force. So the total upwards force of the water on the diver is 1000 N.

R5

(a) The buoyancy force must act vertically upwards through the centre of the body and head.

(b) The point of action (centre of buoyancy) must be above the centre of gravity, otherwise the slightest disturbance will flip the diver over.

R6

(a) Her weight had reduced.

(b) The buoyancy force had increased (e.g. caused by the diver expanding her lungs).

Answers to questions in the text

Q1

From the worked example

total pressure = water pressure
                         + atmospheric pressure

$P = P_{\text{w}} + P_{\text{At}}$ and $P_{\text{w}} = \rho_{\text{w}} g h$, where h is the depth of water, ρ_{w} its density and $P_{\text{At}} = 110$ KPa.

(a) For freshwater, $\rho = 1000$ kg m^{-3}, so

$$P = \left(1000\,\text{kgm}^{-3} \times 9.81\,\text{Nkg}^{-1} \times 10.0\,\text{m}\right)$$
$$+ 110 \times 10^3\,\text{Pa}$$
$$= 2.08 \times 10^5\,\text{Pa}$$
$$= 208\,\text{kPa}$$

(b) Method as for (a) but $\rho = 1100$ kg m^{-3}, therefore

$$P = \left(1100\,\text{kgm}^{-3} \times 9.81\,\text{Nkg}^{-1} \times 5.00\,\text{m}\right)$$
$$+ 110 \times 10^3\,\text{Pa}$$
$$= 1.64 \times 10^5\,\text{Pa}$$
$$= 164\,\text{kPa}$$

(c) Method as for (a)

$$P = \left(1000\,\text{kgm}^{-3} \times 9.81\,\text{Nkg}^{-1} \times 20.0\,\text{m}\right)$$
$$+ 110 \times 10^3\,\text{Pa}$$
$$= 3.06 \times 10^5\,\text{Pa}$$
$$= 306\,\text{kPa}$$

(d) Method as for (a) but $\rho = 1100$ kg m^{-3}, therefore

$$P = \left(1100\,\text{kgm}^{-3} \times 9.81\,\text{Nkg}^{-1} \times 25.0\,\text{m}\right)$$
$$+ 110 \times 10^3\,\text{Pa}$$
$$= 3.80 \times 10^5\,\text{Pa}$$
$$= 380\,\text{kPa}$$

Q2

Dropping 10 m roughly doubles the pressure on the balloon, so its volume will halve.

Q3

As it rose, the pressure on the air in the balloon would be reduced, so the gas would expand. The pressure roughly halves, so the volume would double – if the balloon didn't explode first.

9

In the early days of diving there were many fatalities. Divers were allowed to hire equipment and dive without any checks being made on their competence to do so safely. There is something deceptively simple about diving with good scuba gear. You can breathe under water – and suddenly you feel invincible. Unfortunately, the human body is not designed to operate under water, and solving the immediate problem of air supply is not the end of the story. In this section we will look at the laws of gases that allow us to predict and therefore avoid dangerous situations.

READY TO STUDY TEST

Before you begin this section you should be able to:

- state and use Boyle's law
- recall and use the equation momentum = mass × velocity
- recall and use Newton's laws of motion
- use the equations of uniformly accelerated motion
  $$v = u + at$$

  $$v^2 = u^2 + 2as$$

  $$s = ut + \frac{1}{2}at^2$$
- state and use Pythagoras' theorem
- work with vectors.

QUESTIONS

R1 A scuba tank containing 11.5 litres of compressed gas at 20 MPa slowly leaks into the atmosphere. How much volume will the gas occupy at atmospheric pressure of 1.0×10^5 Pa? (Assume for now that Boyle's law is obeyed.)

R2 The diver, annoyed at the expense of refilling his tank, throws a lead weight 1.2 m downwards on to his foot at 2.0 m s^{-1}. How fast will it strike his foot? (Use $g = 9.81$ m s^{-1})

R3 If the lead weight has mass 1.5 kg, what is its momentum when striking his foot?

R4 If it takes 0.10 s to come to a halt, what mean force is exerted on the foot?

R5 The diver thinks better of his impetuous outburst and moves his foot out of the way 0.50 s after throwing the weight. Is this quick enough to avoid injury?

R6   To add insult to injury, the weight bounces into the harbour and falls so deep that it attains terminal velocity of 4.1 m s^{-1}. What is the net force acting on the weight then?

R7   An inquisitive fish, seeing the weight descending some distance away, swims at 2.4 m s^{-1} horizontally to intercept it. What is the closing speed and direction of weight toward fish?

9.1 Running out of air

Dives need to be planned very carefully to avoid the danger of running out of air. Every diver carries a submersible pressure gauge (SPG) attached to their tank, so you might think that when a diver notices that they are low on air they should simply float up to the surface. This could, however, put the diver in a life-threatening situation. A rapid ascent could put them at risk of decompression sickness (you can learn more about that in Section 9.2) or of surfacing in difficult seas, so that they are a long way from a pick-up point, which could be dangerous. Also, a direct ascent may not be an option for some divers who are exploring wrecks or caves. Dives must therefore be planned so that at the end of the dive every diver has plenty of air remaining in their tank. (Diver training also teaches divers how to share breathing equipment, but this is an emergency procedure and should not used routinely.)

Calculating how long a tank of air will last is a very difficult business. Different people use air at different rates. Not only are their lungs different sizes, but the frequency and depth of their breathing are related to the amount of energy they use under water and how relaxed they are. As divers become more experienced and more relaxed in the water they learn to move slowly and efficiently in the water and to breath slow, deep breaths, which use their air most effectively.

One factor that is the same for all divers, however, is that they use air more rapidly when they dive deeper. Their lung capacity is not altered by depth – a lung full of air contains the same volume of air on the surface as it does at a depth of 10 m. However, at 10 m the pressure on the air is approximately double that at the surface.

 If the pressure on the air is doubled, what will have happened to the density of the air?

If the pressure is doubled, the air that originally occupied the full lung will now occupy just half that volume. The density of this air is calculated using the equation density = mass/volume. So, if the original volume halves, the density must double.

If the density of the air is doubled, what will have happened to the mass of air in one lung full?

Since the lung volume has not changed, and
mass = density × volume, doubling the density means doubling the mass of air.

 So, if a diver keeps breathing full lungs of air at the same rate, how will the time to empty the tank alter?

Each breath at 10 m uses twice as much air as surface breathing, so it should take half the time to empty the tank. However, they will not be able to breathe the air from the tank when it drops to the pressure of the surrounding water. So the time to empty the tank is even less than half.

At a depth of 30 m, air is twice as dense as at 10 m, so at 30 m you will get through your air very quickly, and from 30 to 70 m depth the pressure doubles again. Diving to 70 m is very dangerous, because one tank of air is not enough to allow the very slow ascent that is needed from such a depth to remove the risk of decompression sickness. Also, at 70 m the air is significantly denser and more difficult to inhale. Many sport divers who have gone down to such a depth have not survived. For recreational diving 30 m is considered deep, and divers are not allowed to dive in water deeper than 10 m until they have proved to their instructor that they can control their movement well and understand emergency procedures.

The effect of temperature

Temperature plays an important part in determining the pressure of a gas, and this should not be forgotten when using scuba equipment. Between the time when the tank is filled at the dive centre and when the diver breathes from it under water, the air in the tank may have been cooled or heated, depending on local circumstances. For example, the tank may have been filled in a warm shop, and then used in sub-zero seawater for a diver under ice, or it may have been filled in a cool store room and then left in a car in direct sunlight.

The **pressure law** (discovered by Amontons in 1699) provides the mathematical relationship between pressure and temperature. It states that if the temperature is measured on the absolute scale, pressure and temperature are directly proportional for a fixed mass and volume of gas, so if the temperature doubles, the pressure doubles. This won't work if temperature is measured on the Celsius (°C) or Fahrenheit (°F) scales – it works only for the absolute scale, the **Kelvin scale**.

Exploration 9.1
To demonstrate the pressure law

Apparatus:

◆ 250 cm³ round-bottomed flask with connection to thick rubber tubing ◆ Bourdon gauge ◆ can or beaker, big enough to hold the flask with at least 1 cm all around it ◆ thermometer (0–100°C) ◆ tripod and gauze ◆ Bunsen burner and heat-proof mat, or similar means for heating the can of water

Do not heat the round-bottomed flask with a Bunsen burner, always use the water bath. Take care when heating the water bath – use a low flame to avoid scorching the rubber tubing or the clamps. Securely clamp all the apparatus before you start heating. Do not try to lift the beaker of water while the water is still hot – let it cool down. Wear eye protection.

60 MINUTES

The pressure law can be checked in the laboratory using apparatus such as that shown in Figure 9.1. The temperature of the water is raised by the Bunsen burner and the water heats the air in the flask. It takes quite a while for the air in the flask to reach the temperature of the water, so the water must be heated very slowly. The pressure of the air should be measured at a variety of temperatures. You should then plot a graph of pressure versus temperature.

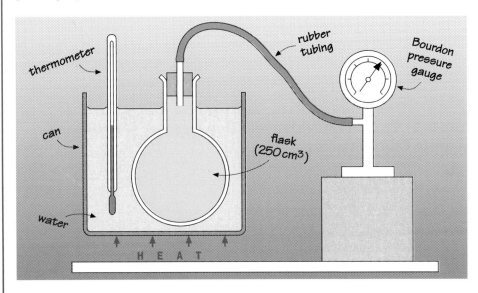

Figure 9.1
Apparatus to demonstrate the pressure law

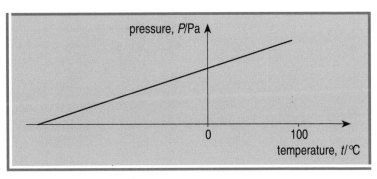

Figure 9.2 A typical pressure versus temperature graph

Your data should form a straight line, like Figure 9.2. Extend the line to the left to find the temperature at which the pressure would be zero. This is **absolute zero**. It should be between –200° and –300°C.

This is an example of the sort of graph you should get when you plot pressure against temperature in degrees Celsius. Although the data forms a straight line, it does not pass through the origin, so pressure is *not* directly proportional to temperature measured on the Celsius scale. However, the line does hit the *x*-axis, and if a new zero temperature scale was invented starting at this intercept, then pressure would be proportional to temperature.

The Kelvin scale of temperature was designed for that very reason. The zero (0 K) was chosen to fit the behaviour of gases such as air, so that if pressure continued to drop as it does when the gas cools from 100° to 0°C, by the time the gas had been cooled to 0 K it would exert no pressure. Of course, the gases that make up air would liquefy before it got that cold, but there is a lot of evidence to suggest that at this absolute zero atoms stop their normal vibrations and cannot lose any more **internal energy**: at 0 K a material has practically no kinetic energy, so it has no energy to lose. Unlike zero on the Fahrenheit or Celsius scales, the zero on the Kelvin scale is not an arbitrary point chosen for convenience – nothing can get colder than 0 K.

Boyle's law relates pressure and volume. The pressure law relates pressure and temperature. It should come as no surprise that volume is also related to temperature. This relationship is known as **Charles's law**.

Exploration 9.2 To find the value of 0 K in degrees Celsius and to demonstrate Charles's law

Apparatus:

◆ 1 litre can or beaker of water ◆ 30 cm rule (heat resistant) ◆ thermometer (0–100°C) ◆ capillary tube containing a concentrated sulphuric acid or mercury index ◆ rubber bands ◆ clamp stands ◆ tripod and gauze ◆ Bunsen burner and heat-proof mat, or similar heating device

This experiment involves working with two long glass tubes: a thermometer and a capillary tube. If any liquid is spilt from the capillary tube seek advice on how to clear it up, as it may be sulphuric acid, which is corrosive, or mercury, which is toxic. Don't try to lift the beaker of water while the water is still hot – let it cool down.

90 MINUTES

This apparatus, shown in Figure 9.3, allows us to study how the volume of a fixed mass of air varies as it is heated, the pressure of the gas being kept constant.

When you set up this experiment, make sure that the rule and the thermometer are designed to cope with temperatures up to 100°C. The liquid index in the capillary tube is free to move up the tube if the gas below it starts to expand, so the position of the index is a measure of the volume of the gas.

 The length of the air column is related to the volume of air trapped below the liquid index. What equation will relate the two?

Volume = length × cross-sectional area.

The aim of the experiment is to show that the volume of the gas is proportional to its temperature. The units of volume are therefore unimportant.

 If the cross-sectional area of the capillary tube is constant, do you need to know the actual size of the capillary?

No, because the length is proportional to the volume, if the volume doubles the length must double. The length of the air trapped in the capillary tube can be used as a measure of volume.

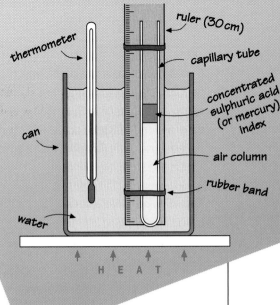

Figure 9.3
Apparatus to demonstrate Charles's law

Heat the water slowly and measure the length of trapped air at regular temperature intervals. Because the temperature of the trapped air may not be the same as the temperature of the water, it is important to heat slowly, but it is also useful to take a second set of results as the apparatus cools.

 Why will the second set of results make the graph more reliable?

As the apparatus is heated the temperature of the water will always be greater than that of the trapped air – because it takes time for the air to heat up from the water. When the apparatus cools the temperature of the water will always be less than that of the trapped air. By taking results during both heating and cooling, we should get data that average to the true value.

Make a table of results following the example given in Table 9.1. Use your data to plot a graph to find the value of absolute zero in °C.

Finally, compare your result with the accepted value of −273°C. Discuss with others in your group why your value might be slightly different from the accepted value.

Temperature/°C	Length of capillary/cm	
	When heating	When cooling

Table 9.1 Example table for Exploration 9.2

If you now plot a graph of length against temperature in kelvins you should be able to find the relationship between temperature and volume. This is Charles's law. It is important to remember that a straight line is not proof of proportionality unless it goes through the origin, that is why you need to convert from degrees Celsius to kelvins to find the relationship between temperature and volume.

Table 9.2 will help you convert from °C to K and vice versa.

Table 9.2 Conversion chart for degrees Celsius and kelvins

Temperature/°C	−273	−200	−100	0	100	200
Temperature/K	0	73	173	273	373	473

Just think of the x-axis of the graphs you have plotted as a number line, and the conversion is very easy. The temperature interval of 1 K has been fixed to be the same as 1°C.

Temperature in kelvins = (temperature in °C) + 273

(*Note:* To be more precise, add 273.15.)

The equation of state of an ideal gas

Putting the equations from Boyle's law, Charles's law and the pressure law together we can show that for a fixed mass of gas

$$\frac{PV}{T} = \text{constant}$$

or

$$\frac{P_1 V_1}{T_1} = \frac{P_2 V_2}{T_2} \tag{9.1}$$

where P = pressure, V = volume and T = temperature in kelvins.

This turns out to be true for most gases that are not on the point of liquefying. The constant is the same for all gases if the samples contain the same number of molecules. A gas that obeys this law perfectly is called an **ideal gas**. For one **mole** of gas the constant is 8.31 Pa m^3 K^{-1}. This constant is called the **universal molar gas constant** and it is given the symbol R in most textbooks. (The number of molecules in one mole of any substance is always 6.02×10^{23} – this is called **Avogadro's number**.)

 If pressure is measured in pascals, volume in metres cubed and temperature in kelvins, and 1 Pa = 1 N m^{-2}, simplify the units of the constant in Equation (9.1).

$$1\,\mathrm{Pa\,m^3\,K^{-1}} = 1\,\mathrm{N\,m^{-2}\,m^3\,K^{-1}}$$

$$= 1\,\mathrm{N\,m\,K^{-1}}$$

$$= 1\,\mathrm{J\,K^{-1}}$$

because the joule, the unit of work and energy, is defined so that $1\,\mathrm{J} = 1\,\mathrm{N\,m}$.

For an ideal gas, Equation (9.1) is then normally written:

$PV = RT$ for one mole of gas

 What would happen to the pressure if the number of molecules of gas in a given volume, at a given temperature, was doubled?

The pressure would double.

For n moles of gas the pressure would be n times bigger, so

$PV = nRT$

This is called the equation of state for an ideal gas.

> Equation of state for an ideal gas
> $PV = nRT$

Q1 An 11.5 litre tank is filled in an air-conditioned hire shop, temperature 15°C, to a pressure of 20 MPa. The tank is left in a car in the sun and the temperature rises to 40°C. Answer the following questions using the data given in Table 9.3. (Assume the ideal gas equation holds.)

(a) What is the new pressure?

(b) How many moles of gas are in the tank?

(c) What is the density of the gas in the tank if it is 20% oxygen, mass $32\ \mathrm{g\ mol^{-1}}$, and 80% nitrogen, mass $28\ \mathrm{g\ mol^{-1}}$? ◆

Table 9.3 Data for Question 1

Gas	Relative molecular mass
Oxygen	32
Nitrogen	28
Helium	4

Worked example

A standard scuba tank has a volume of 11.5 litres and is normally filled with compressed air at a pressure of 20 MPa. Smaller tanks are also available with a volume of 8.0 litres (1 litre = 1000 cm³ = 10^{-3} m³).

(a) If a diver has enough air for a one hour dive using the standard tank, how long would the smaller tank last if it were filled with air at the same temperature and pressure? (b) If the smaller tanks were to be filled with the same mass of gas as the standard tank, what would be the pressure of air in the tank?

(a) $PV = nRT$

Rearranging this we get

$$\frac{P}{RT} = \frac{n}{V}$$

Because P, R and T are the same for both cylinders

$$\frac{n_1}{V_1} = \frac{n_2}{V_2}$$

$$\frac{n_1}{n_2} = \frac{V_1}{V_2}$$

$$= \frac{11.5 \text{ litres}}{8.0 \text{ litres}}$$

$$= 1.44$$

So we know that the larger cylinder contains 1.44 times as many molecules as the smaller one, and it should therefore last 1.44 times as long. If the large tank lasts an hour, the smaller one will last about

$$\frac{1 \text{ hour}}{1.44} = 0.70 \text{ hour}$$

i.e.

$$0.70 \times 60 \text{ minutes} = 42 \text{ minutes}$$

(b) For one hour we need $\dfrac{60}{42}$ as much gas, therefore the pressure will be

$\dfrac{60}{42}$ times higher.

$$\text{New pressure} = \frac{60}{42} \times 20 \text{ MPa}$$

$$= 29 \text{ MPa} \quad \blacklozenge$$

 In one breath a diver inhales 1 litre of air. If the air is at a pressure of 10 MPa and a temperature of 13°C, calculate (a) the number of moles he breathes in and (b) the number of molecules he breathes in. (*Note:* Remember 1 mole of gas contains 6.02×10^{23} molecules.)

(a) Using the equation $PV = nRT$, where $P =$ pressure, $V =$ volume, $n =$ number of moles, $R =$ universal molar gas constant, and $T =$ temperature in kelvins, gives

$$1 \times 10^7 \text{ Pa} \times 10^{-3} \text{ m}^3 = n \times 8.31 \text{ Pa m}^3 \text{ K}^{-1} \text{ mol}^{-1} \times (273 + 13) \text{ K}$$

so

$$n = \frac{1 \times 10^7 \, \text{Pa} \times 10^{-3} \, \text{m}^3}{8.31 \, \text{Pa} \, \text{m}^3 \, \text{K}^{-1} \text{mol}^{-1} \times (273 + 13) \text{K}}$$

$$= \frac{1 \times 10^4 \, \text{mol}}{2376.66}$$

$$= 4.2 \, \text{mol (to two significant figures)}$$

So the diver breathes in 4.2 moles of air.

(b) 4.2 moles of air contains $4.2 \times 6.02 \times 10^{23} = 2.5 \times 10^{24}$ molecules.

Explaining ideal gases – a qualitative approach

It is easiest to explain why gases usually have *ideal* properties (behaving according to the ideal gas equations) if we imagine them to be composed of very tiny, fast-moving particles moving at random in all directions (see Figure 9.4). The collisions of the particles with each other and with solid objects, such as the wall of a gas cylinder, explain the movement and pressure of gases. An elastic collision (in which no kinetic energy is lost) of a fast-moving particle with a wall will exert a force on the wall. Lots of such forces on an area of wall will produce an even pressure.

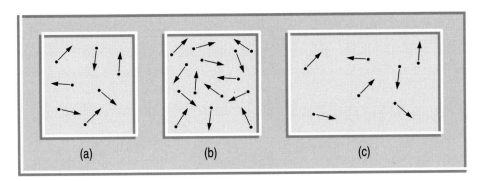

(a) (b) (c)

Figure 9.4
The moving-particles model for a gas

 Consider a box of fast-moving particles – gas molecules. In a given time, what will happen to the number of collisions experienced by the walls: (i) if more particles are added to the box (Figure 9.4b), (ii) if the volume of the box is increased (without adding any particles) (Figure 9.4c)?

(i) If more particles are added to the box there will be more collisions in any given time and so the pressure inside the box will increase. (ii) If the box is made bigger, a given area of wall will have fewer collisions in any given time and so the pressure inside the box will decrease. More collisions inside the box therefore result in higher pressure; fewer collisions mean lower pressure.

The moving-particles model for a gas also explains the effect of temperature changes on gas pressure. A higher temperature corresponds to molecules with more kinetic energy. We know that to increase the temperature of a gas we have to increase its energy, either by heating it or compressing it. So it makes sense that this energy could, in the gas, take the form of kinetic energy in faster-moving molecules.

Increasing the temperature of a gas increases its pressure.

 Use the particle model to explain why particles with more kinetic energy will exert more pressure on the wall of a container.

Particles with more kinetic energy move faster, so they have harder collisions with the walls of the container, exerting more force. Also there will be more collisions per second with the walls of the container.

Explaining ideal gases – a quantitative approach

The qualitative approach in the last section explains how a moving-particle theory, a **kinetic theory**, can explain the behaviour of ideal gases. The tiny particles that make up gases are usually molecules – a few atoms bound tightly together by chemical bonds. The kinetic theory suggests that gas molecules behave just like tiny particles. If we make sensible assumptions about these particles we should be able to apply Newton's laws of motion to the collisions of the particles with the walls of the container and develop an equation that will agree with experimental measurements. (See Figure 9.5.)

In this section we show the derivation of a very important equation.

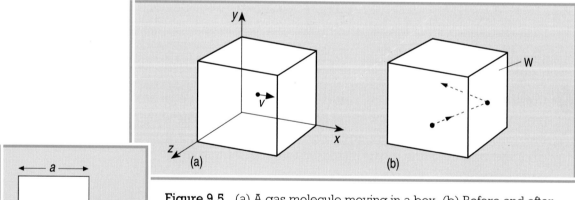

Figure 9.5 (a) A gas molecule moving in a box. (b) Before and after collision with the wall, W

This is a very long derivation, so it is best to break it down into stages.

Figure 9.6
A gas molecule moving in the x-direction in a box to hit wall W of area a^2

Stage 1: the force of one molecule

Consider one gas molecule moving at velocity c. If we put it in a box it will eventually hit wall W. But W will affect its movement only in the x-direction, so we really only need to think about its movement in the x-direction. (See Figure 9.6.)

We think that gas pressure is caused by collisions between the molecule and the walls of the box. To find the pressure exerted by this one molecule we have to make some assumptions:

I   The molecule moves at constant velocity unless it is involved in a collision.

II The collisions are perfectly elastic, so an isolated molecule loses no speed as a result of the collision with the walls of the container.

III The molecule moves very fast and is unaffected by external forces except during collisions, which take an insignificant time compared with time spent between collisions.

IV The molecules are very tiny. The volume of the molecules themselves is negligible compared with the space between them.

Newton's second law tells us that

$$\text{force} = \text{rate of change in momentum} \qquad (9.2)$$

The third law tells us that the force on the particle must be equal and opposite to the force on the wall.

If the mass of the molecule is m and the component of its velocity in the x-direction is v, its momentum in the x-direction is therefore mv. After colliding with the wall its velocity must be $-v$, because it is travelling at the same speed in the opposite direction (assumption II), so its momentum is $-mv$.

$$\begin{aligned}
\text{Change in momentum during collision} &= \text{final momentum} \\
&\quad - \text{initial momentum} \\
&= -mv - mv \\
&= -2mv \qquad (9.3)
\end{aligned}$$

If we apply assumption III we can assume that lots of collisions occur with wall W in one second, so

$$\begin{aligned}
\text{rate of change of momentum for particle on wall} \\
= (\text{number of collisions per second}) \\
\times (\text{change of momentum on each collision})
\end{aligned}$$

$$(9.4)$$

Since

$$\text{speed} = \frac{\text{distance}}{\text{time}}$$

$$\text{time between collisions} = \frac{\text{distance travelled between collisions}}{\text{speed}}$$

$$= \frac{2a}{v}$$

$$\text{Number of collisions per second} = \frac{1}{\text{time between collisions}}$$

$$= \frac{v}{2a} \qquad\qquad (9.5)$$

So, if we rewrite Equation (9.4), substituting in the terms we have developed from Equations (9.3) and (9.5) we get:

$$\text{rate of change of momentum for particle on wall} = \frac{v}{2a} \times (-2mv)$$

$$= -\frac{mv^2}{a}$$

Newton's second law tells us that this is the force on the particle, while Newton's third law tells us that the force on the wall, caused by the particle, is equal and opposite, so the minus sign disappears, telling us that the force is in the other direction, i.e.

$$\text{force on the wall, } F = \frac{mv^2}{a}$$

Stage 2: the force of n molecules

If there are n times as many molecules, they will produce n times as many collisions and therefore n times as much force. But we have no reason to suppose that they will all be moving at the same speed.

For one molecule we know that the force on the wall is

$$F = \frac{mv^2}{a}$$

For the n molecules

$$F = \left(\frac{mv_1^2}{a}\right) + \left(\frac{mv_2^2}{a}\right) + \left(\frac{mv_3^2}{a}\right) + \cdots + \left(\frac{mv_n^2}{a}\right)$$

And if all the molecules have the same mass:

$$F = \frac{m}{a}\left(v_1^2 + v_2^2 + v_3^2 + \cdots + v_n^2\right)$$

We are not interested in the speed of every single molecule, but we are interested in the effect of the speed of the molecules – since this determines how hard the collisions will be, and therefore how high the pressure will be. We can't use the mean speed of the molecules, because it is the squares of their speeds that determine the size of the force. So, we use the mean square speed or the **mean square velocity**, as it is usually known. As its name implies, the mean square velocity is the mean of the squares of the velocities:

The symbol for mean square velocity is $\langle v^2 \rangle$.

$$\langle v^2 \rangle = \frac{\left(v_1^2 + v_2^2 + v_3^2 + \ldots + v_n^2\right)}{n}$$

so

$$\left(v_1^2 + v_2^2 + v_3^2 + \ldots + v_n^2\right) = n\langle v^2 \rangle$$

and the total force on the wall is

$$F = \frac{mn\langle v^2 \rangle}{a}$$

We also have to allow for the fact that the molecules will be moving in all three dimensions, so we make some more assumptions:

V   The number of molecules in a typical laboratory sample of gas is very, very large.

VI The molecules move at random.

If the mean square speed in real space, allowing for movement in all three directions, is c_{mean}^2, the mean square speed in any one direction is one-third of this:

$$v_{mean}^2 = \frac{\langle c^2 \rangle}{3}$$

(This can be proved mathematically using Pythagoras' theorem.)

Total force on wall W is now given by:

$$F = \frac{mn\langle c^2 \rangle}{3a}$$

Stage 3: the pressure of n molecules

The last stage of the derivation is to convert the force into a pressure.

The pressure, P, exerted by the gas must be:

$$P = \frac{F}{\text{area of wall W}}$$

$$= \frac{F}{a^2}$$

where a is the length of the square-sided wall W

Substituting for F we get:

$$P = \frac{mn\langle c^2 \rangle}{\left(3a \times a^2\right)}$$

But a^3 = the volume of the box, V

so

$$P = \frac{mn\langle c^2 \rangle}{3V}$$

This equation is very important in physics because it helps us to explain many of the properties of gases, and to make predictions about what they will do. If you are a diver, you may need to use those predictions to save your life!

Q2 Given that 1 mole of gas occupies 22.4 litres at a pressure of 103 kPa, find the mean kinetic energy of one molecule. ◆

Q3 The density of a gas is 1.1 kg m^{-3} at a pressure of 1.0×10^5 Pa. What is the r.m.s. velocity of its molecules? ◆

Q4 Five gas molecules have speeds of 500.00, 520.00, 540.00, 560.00 and 580.00 m s^{-1} respectively. Find (a) their mean velocity, (b) their r.m.s. velocity. For this exercise, work to five significant figures. ◆

9.2 Decompression sickness: how divers avoid it

Decompression sickness (or the bends as it is commonly known) is caused when a diver surfaces rapidly and bubbles of gas form inside their body. The effect is similar to that of opening a bottle of fizzy drink. While the top is tightly on the bottle, the bottle is pressurized, and few, if any, bubbles are visible because the gas is dissolved in the water. However, if the top is unscrewed, releasing the pressure, bubbles immediately appear in the liquid. The gas moves out of solution when the pressure drops.

The symptoms

Few divers suffer from the effects of decompression sickness during their underwater ascent. The symptoms may not show up for as long as 24 hours after they have surfaced, by which time it may be too late. It is therefore important that divers avoid rapid decompression, and that they know the warning signs and first-aid treatment. Bubbles of gas forming in the body are very bad news.

The symptoms are numerous. In mild cases joints such as the elbows, shoulders and knees start to ache, and the pain may increase to become intense. Bubbles of gas forming in the skin produce an itchy rash – not dangerous in itself, but a serious indicator that other symptoms may be emerging. In more severe cases the diver may become confused, dizzy and finally paralysed as their nervous system is affected. Bubbles forming near the lungs may restrict blood supply and cause the 'chokes', which can be fatal. A diver might also die if bubbles become lodged in vital organs such as the brain.

Understanding the physics of decompression sickness

In order to dive safely, without risking decompression sickness, divers follow strict codes of practice regarding the depth, duration and frequency of dives. To understand these codes it is important to understand the limitations imposed on the human body by the physical properties of gases. Avoiding decompression sickness requires the ability to predict when bubbles are likely to form in the body as gases move out of solution. The solubility of a gas depends on the chemical properties of the gas and the liquid, and also on the pressure exerted by the gas on the liquid surface. If the pressure of the gas increases, more gas is dissolved in the liquid. This is known as **Henry's law**: at constant temperature, the amount of gas that dissolves in a liquid with which it is in contact is proportional to the pressure of that gas. (See Figure 9.7.)

The kinetic theory provides an explanation for this law. If the gas is kept at a constant temperature the mean square speed of the molecules won't change, so if the pressure is doubled the gas molecules must hit the liquid surface twice as frequently. Twice as many molecules move into solution, because twice as many are hitting the surface of the solution each second. Oxygen and nitrogen dissolve into the blood capillaries from air in the lungs (oxygen is also carried by haemoglobin molecules). If the air pressure in the lungs increases, the amount of oxygen and nitrogen dissolved in the blood increases.

Diffusion

Although Henry's law ultimately controls the amount of gas that moves into a diver when they are breathing air at a certain pressure, the rate at which this saturated state is reached depends on the rate at which the gas molecules move into the body cells. This movement occurs principally by **diffusion** – the process by which substances spread because of their random molecular movement. The rate of diffusion of gases depends on the speed of

Figure 9.7
Illustration of Henry's law

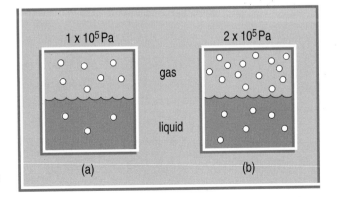

their molecules – faster molecules diffuse faster. Diffusion in aqueous (watery) and adipose (fatty) human tissues is more complex, but so far as decompression sickness is concerned, it is important to realize that diffusion is much slower in adipose tissue.

When a diver descends to a depth of 30 m, the increased gas pressure causes gas to dissolve into the tissues of the human body, into aqueous and, more slowly, into adipose tissue. If they are subjected to the higher pressure for a short time the extra gas will be principally in their aqueous tissue, and, after an hour or so, there will be little excess air dissolved in their body. However, if they spend an hour or more at 30 m, a considerable amount of air will have diffused into adipose tissue. When the diver ascends, the air pressure in their lungs reduces and oxygen and nitrogen move out of solution. Gradually the body cells lose the excess dissolved gases, again by diffusion. If they have been under water for a short time they will not take long to recover, but after a long dive it will be many hours before the excess nitrogen leaves their body.

Recreational divers are taught to dive within no decompression limits – they limit the time of their dive so that they can at any moment end the dive and ascend to the surface without risking decompression sickness. (A safety stop, a pause of a few minutes during the ascent, usually about 5 m from the surface, is still normal practice to avoid stressing the body.) Part of all divers' training is learning to read dive tables (which give the maximum safe time at the bottom of the dive and at different depths) so that if they make more than one dive in a day they don't build up dangerous levels of dissolved air in their bodies.

Divers suffering from decompression sickness cannot be flown to hospital, and divers are strongly advised to wait for 6 hours after diving before flying. Why?

The reduced air pressure in an aircraft during a flight is likely to cause bubbles to form in the body, even if they would not have formed at normal atmospheric (sea-level) pressure.

Analysing air

Air is not a pure gas. It is a mixture comprising, by volume, 78% nitrogen (N_2) and 21% oxygen (O_2), with traces of other gases such as argon and carbon dioxide (totalling about 1%).

In one litre of air (1000 cm^3), nitrogen accounts for 780 cm^3 of the volume, oxygen takes up 210 cm^3 and the other gases occupy about 10 cm^3. The equation of state, $pV = nRT$ tells us that in a gas at a fixed temperature and pressure, the number of moles of gas, n, depends on the volume.

Out of every 100 molecules of gas in air, how many must be nitrogen and how many oxygen?

78 nitrogen, 21 oxygen.

Partial pressure

The **partial pressure** of a gas is the pressure that would be exerted by that gas alone if all other types of gas molecule were removed while keeping other conditions constant. It is a useful concept to use when gases are in mixtures, as they are in air. If gas pressure is due to particles of gas continuously hitting the walls of the container, each type of particle would cause pressure, so the total pressure would equal the sum of the partial pressures. We know this to be true from experimental tests. Looking again at the equation $pV = nRT$ we can see that for any given volume of gas the pressure is proportional to the number of moles of gas. This is also true for the partial pressures, so the partial pressure of nitrogen from a 100 kPa tank is 78 kPa, whilst the partial pressure of oxygen is 21 kPa.

At very high pressures oxygen acts as a poison in the body. Diving with 21% oxygen at depths of 60 m or more is dangerous because of the amount of oxygen that dissolves in the body. To avoid this danger commercial divers use a lower proportion of oxygen in their tanks, keeping the partial pressure of oxygen, even during deep dives, to safe limits.

Q5 Calculate the partial pressure of oxygen in air at sea level. (Normal atmospheric pressure is 110 kPa.) ◆

Q6 Calculate the pressure on a diver 100 m under the sea. (Assume that the density of seawater is 1.1×10^3 kg m^{-3} and use $g = 9.81$ N kg^{-1}.) ◆

Q7 For a diver to breathe the normal, sea-level, partial pressure of oxygen at 100 m depth, what percentage of oxygen is needed in their tank? ◆

9.3 Nitrogen – a dangerous drug!

Diving to depths below about 30 m with compressed air leads to an effect called nitrogen narcosis. The excess nitrogen in the body affects the brain, and divers exhibit a variety of symptoms. Some may be mildly impaired, as if they had drunk one or two units of alcohol, but at increasing depths, divers may hallucinate and behave totally irrationally. Divers have been known to remove their scuba gear because they believe they have become fish! Others have dived deeper still, forgetting their diver training. To avoid the risks of this narcosis, commercial divers who routinely dive to depths below 30 m (to as deep as 200 m) breathe a mixture of helium and oxygen – heliox. Helium, like nitrogen, is an inert gas, so it does not affect their breathing, it simply dilutes the oxygen. However, it has a much lower molecular mass than nitrogen, and that makes people talk in a strange squeaky voice after breathing a heliox mixture.

Sounding like Mickey Mouse

To understand why the funny voice is produced when breathing helium we must first revise sound. The **pitch** (i.e. the **frequency**) of a sound we hear is determined by the frequency of the sound wave arriving at our ears. The higher the frequency, the higher the pitch. When someone has breathed helium they still move their larynx in the normal way to produce the sound – so why do we hear a higher pitch?

Although the sound of someone talking mostly *originates* in the larynx the sound we hear is produced by resonance of gas in the air cavities of the head. The head acts as a sort of **acoustic amplifier**. (The precise shape of the air cavities gives you your distinctive voice – have you ever wondered why holding your nose changes the sound of your voice?) The **resonant wavelengths** are fixed by the size of your head, and it is sound at these wavelengths that is amplified.

The frequency at which the air in the cavities in the head vibrates is determined according to the wave equation:

wave speed = frequency × wavelength

$$v = f\lambda$$

The speed of sound in helium is much greater than that in nitrogen so, with the wavelength being fixed, if the speed increases, so does the frequency of the sound that is amplified.

Q8 Use the equations and the information below to calculate the root of the mean square speed of nitrogen and of helium at 20°C. Is there any connection between the random speed of gas molecules and the speed at which sound travels through the gas?

Use the following information in your answer.

For one mole of gas

$$P = \frac{mn \left\langle c^2 \right\rangle}{3V}$$

and

$$PV = RT$$

Combining these equations we get

$$RT = \frac{mn \left\langle c^2 \right\rangle}{3}$$

$$R = 8.31 \, \mathrm{J\,K^{-1}}$$

$$n = 6.0 \times 10^{23}$$

mass of one mole of nitrogen molecules $= 28.0 \times 10^{-3}$ kg

mass of one mole of helium molecules $= 4.0 \times 10^{-3}$ kg ◆

Achievements

After studying this section you should be able to:

- state the gas laws and apply them to diving situations
- use the equation $P = \rho g h$
- use the law of partial pressures
- apply Henry's law about dissolved gasses
- derive and apply the equations associated with the kinetic theory, especially

$$PV = \frac{1}{3} mn \langle c^2 \rangle$$

- describe the assumptions and limitations of the kinetic theory.

Glossary

Absolute zero The temperature at which the kinetic energy of ideal gas molecules would be zero. It is 0 K on the Kelvin scale, which is equivalent to $-273°C$.

Acoustic amplifier A mechanical (as opposed to electronic) device to make a sound louder. In an acoustic guitar the vibration of the string is amplified by vibration of the guitar body. Electric guitars are extremely quiet unless the vibration of the string is detected and amplified electronically before being fed to loudspeakers.

Avogadro's number, N_A The number of molecules in a mole of substance: $N_A = 6.02 \times 10^{23}$ molecules mol^{-1}. This is agreed, internationally, to be the number of carbon atoms in 12.00×10^{-3} kg of carbon-12.

Boyle's law The law that outlines the mathematical relationship between pressure and volume of a gas. It states that the product of pressure and volume of a fixed mass of gas at uniform temperature remains constant. Or, put another way, the pressure of a fixed mass of gas at constant temperature is inversely proportional to volume

$$P \propto \frac{1}{V}$$

or

$$PV = \text{constant}$$

Charles's law The law that outlines the mathematical relationship between volume and temperature of a gas. It states that, for a given sample of an ideal gas, held at fixed pressure, the volume of the gas is proportional to temperature measured on the absolute (Kelvin) scale. So, for example, if the temperature doubles, the volume doubles. Temperature must be measured on the Kelvin scale; the relationship is not demonstrated if temperature is measured on the Celsius (°C) or Fahrenheit (°F) scales.

Diffusion The process by which substances spread out because of their random molecular movement. They move from a region of high concentration into a region where the molecules are less concentrated.

Frequency The number of complete vibrations in a given time interval.

Henry's law For a gas in contact with a liquid at constant temperature, the amount of gas that dissolves in the liquid is proportional to the pressure of that gas.

Ideal gas A theoretical gas that obeys the equation of state $PV = nRT$. (No gases do at all values of P, V or T, but many do to a high level of accuracy within limited ranges of these parameters.)

Internal energy In a gas, the random kinetic energy of the molecules that is manifested outwardly as its thermal energy. In solids and liquids, the molecules are close enough for internal energy to be in the form of potential energy too, associated with intermolecular bonds.

Kelvin scale   A temperature scale employing the same intervals of temperature as the Celsius scale, but with its zero at absolute zero. So temperature expressed in kelvins is directly proportional to kinetic energy of the gas.

Kinetic theory   A simple theory used to explain the behaviour of gases. It assumes that gas molecules have no volume and move randomly without losing kinetic energy as they collide with each other or the walls of their container.

Mean square velocity   In a gas, the mean of the squares of individual molecular velocities. Since high velocities contribute more to the value than low ones, the square root of this value, the r.m.s. velocity, is somewhat higher than the mean velocity.

Mole   A mole is defined as the amount of a substance that contains the same number of entities as there are carbon atoms in 12.00 g of carbon-12. This number is a fixed quantity and is known as Avogadro's number – rather like a dozen means 12, Avogadro's number means 6.02×10^{23}. So, one mole of any gas, or mixture of gases, always contains 6.02×10^{23} molecules. Such an amount of gas molecules occupies 22.4 litres at standard temperature and pressure.

Partial pressure   The pressure that would be exerted by a gas from a mixture of gases if all the other types of molecule were removed from the mixture while keeping other conditions the same.

Pitch   The musical term describing whether a note sounds 'high' or 'low', i.e. whether it has a high or low frequency.

Pressure law   The law that outlines the mathematical relationship between pressure and temperature of a gas. It states that the pressure of a fixed mass of gas at constant volume is directly proportional to temperature measured on the absolute (Kelvin) scale. So, for example, if the temperature doubles, the pressure doubles. Temperature must be measured on the Kelvin scale; the relationship is not demonstrated if temperature is measured on the Celsius (°C) or Fahrenheit (°F) scales.

Resonant wavelength   The wavelength of a sound that exactly matches the length of a gas-filled cavity so that it reflects and produces a strong vibration.

Universal molar gas constant   A constant, which equals 8.31 J K^{-1} mol^{-1}. It is given the symbol R in most textbooks.

Answers to Ready to Study test

R1

Boyle's law applies since the change in state of the gas occurs isothermally (at constant temperature).

$$P_1 V_1 = P_2 V_2$$

therefore

$$V_2 = \frac{P_1 V_1}{P_2}$$

$$= \frac{20 \times 10^6 \, \text{Pa} \times 11.5 \, \text{litres}}{1.0 \times 10^5 \, \text{Pa}}$$

$$= 2300 \, \text{litres}$$

R2

If down is negative then displacement of weight is −1.2 m. So, from

$$v^2 = u^2 + 2as$$

we have

$$v = \left\{\left(-2.0\,\text{ms}^{-1}\right)^2 + 2\times\left(-9.81\,\text{ms}^{-2}\right)\times\left(-1.2\,\text{m}\right)\right\}$$

$$= \sqrt{27.54\,\text{m}^2\,\text{s}^{-2}}$$

$$= \pm 5.3\,\text{ms}^{-1}\ (\text{to two significant figures})$$

So the weight will hit his foot at -5.25 m s^{-1} (taking the negative root as downwards).

R3

$$\text{Momentum} = \text{mass}\times\text{velocity}$$

$$= 1.5\,\text{kg}\times 5.25\,\text{ms}^{-1}$$

$$= 7.88\,\text{kgms}^{-1}$$

$$(\text{to three significant figures})$$

R4

From Newton's second law

$$F = \frac{m\boldsymbol{v} - m\boldsymbol{u}}{t}$$

so

$$F = \frac{0 - \left(-7.88\,\text{kgms}^{-1}\right)}{0.10\,\text{s}}$$

$$= 78.8\,\text{N}$$

This is the upwards force on the lead weight. The force on his foot is therefore -79 N (i.e. downwards), from Newton's third law.

R5

The time, t, for the weight to reach his foot is given by

$$\boldsymbol{v} = \boldsymbol{u} + \boldsymbol{a}t$$

so

$$-5.25\,\text{ms}^{-1} = -2.0\,\text{ms}^{-1} - 9.81\,\text{ms}^2 t$$

$$t = \frac{3.25\,\text{ms}^{-1}}{9.81\,\text{ms}^{-2}}$$

$$= 0.3\,\text{s}\ (\text{to two significant figures})$$

The weight will therefore hit his foot.

R6

From Newton's first law, for uniform velocity resultant force equals zero.

R7

See Figure 9.8.

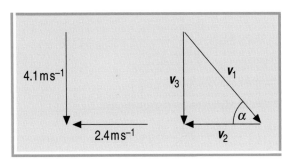

Figure 9.8 Answer for R7

Velocity of weight relative to fish ($\boldsymbol{v}_1$)

+ velocity of fish relative to seabed ($\boldsymbol{v}_2$)

= velocity of weight relative to seabed ($\boldsymbol{v}_3$)

(Note how these phrases are constructed!)

From Pythagoras' theorem

$$v_1^2 = \left(2.4\,\text{ms}^{-1}\right)^2 + \left(4.1\,\text{ms}^{-1}\right)^2$$

so

$$v_1 = 4.8\text{ m s}^{-1}$$

$$\alpha = \tan^{-1}\left(\frac{4.1}{2.4}\right)$$

$$= 60°\ (\text{to two significant figures})$$

Answers to questions in the text

Q1

(a)

$$\frac{P_1V_1}{T_1} = \frac{P_2V_2}{T_2}$$

so

$$P_2 = \frac{P_1 V_1}{V_2} \frac{T_2}{T_1}$$

There is no change in volume, therefore $V_1 = V_2$ and so

$$P_2 = \frac{P_1 T_2}{T_1}$$

$$= 20\,\text{MPa} \frac{(273+40)\,\text{K}}{(273+15)\,\text{K}}$$

$$= 21.736\,\text{MPa}$$

$$= 22\,\text{MPa (to two significant figures)}$$

(b) $PV = nRT$, where n is the number of moles. Therefore

$$n = \frac{PV}{RT}$$

$$= \frac{20 \times 10^6\,\text{Pa} \times 11.5 \times 10^{-3}\,\text{m}^3}{8.31\,\text{J K}^{-1}\,\text{mol}^{-1} \times 288\,\text{K}}$$

$$= 96.10\,\text{mol}$$

$$= 96\,\text{mol (to two significant figures)}$$

(c) For 20% oxygen:

$$20\% \times 96\,\text{mol} = 19.2\,\text{mol}$$

$$\text{mass} = 19.2\,\text{mol} \times 32\,\text{g mol}^{-1}$$

$$= 614\,\text{g}$$

For 80% nitrogen:

$$80\% \times 96\,\text{mol} = 76.8\,\text{mol}$$

$$\text{mass} = 76.8\,\text{mol} \times 28\,\text{g mol}^{-1}$$

$$= 2150\,\text{g}$$

$$\text{total mass} = 614\,\text{g} + 2150\,\text{g}$$

$$= 2764\,\text{g}$$

$$\text{density} = \frac{2764 \times 10^{-3}\,\text{kg}}{11.5 \times 10^{-3}\,\text{m}^{-3}}$$

$$= 240\,\text{kg m}^{-3}$$

$$= 2.4 \times 10^2\,\text{kg m}^{-3}$$

$$\text{(to two significant figures)}$$

Q2

$$PV = \frac{1}{3} mn \langle c^2 \rangle$$

and for 1 mole, $n = 6.02 \times 10^{23}$

$$3PV = mn \langle c^2 \rangle$$

so

$$\frac{3}{2} \frac{PV}{n} = \frac{1}{2} m \langle c^2 \rangle$$

The right-hand term is the mean kinetic energy

$$\text{KE} = \frac{3}{2} \frac{PV}{n}$$

$$= \frac{3 \times 103 \times 10^3\,\text{Pa} \times 22.4 \times 10^{-3}\,\text{m}^3}{2 \times 6.02 \times 10^{23}}$$

$$= 5.75 \times 10^{-21}\,\text{J (to three significant figures)}$$

Q3

$$\rho = \frac{mn}{V}$$

and

$$PV = \frac{1}{3} mn \langle c^2 \rangle$$

so

$$3P = \frac{mn}{V} \langle c^2 \rangle$$

$$= \rho \langle c^2 \rangle$$

$$\text{r.m.s. speed} = \sqrt{\frac{3P}{\rho}}$$

$$= \sqrt{\left(\frac{3 \times 1.0 \times 10^5\,\text{Pa}}{1.1\,\text{kg m}^{-3}} \right)}$$

$$= 522\,\text{ms}^{-1}$$

$$= 5.2 \times 10^2\,\text{ms}^{-1}$$

$$\text{(to two significant figures)}$$

Q4

(a)

$$\frac{500.00 + 520.00 + 540.00 + 560.00 + 580.00}{5}$$

$$= 540.00 \, \text{ms}^{-1}$$

(b)

$$\sqrt{\frac{500.00^2 + 520.00^2 + 540.00^2 + 560.00^2 + 580.00^2}{5}}$$

$$= 540.74 \, \text{ms}^{-1}$$

Q5

Air contains approximately 21% oxygen and 78% nitrogen.

Each contributes this proportion of the total pressure. Hence partial pressure of oxygen is

$$\frac{21}{100} \times 110 \times 10^3 \, \text{Pa} = 23.1 \, \text{kPa}$$

Q6

$$P = (\rho g h) + P_{\text{atmosphere}}$$

$$= \left(1100 \, \text{kg m}^{-3} \times 9.81 \, \text{N kg}^{-1} \times 100 \, \text{m}\right)$$

$$+ 110 \, \text{kPa}$$

$$= 1.189 \, \text{MPa}$$

$$= 1.19 \, \text{MPa} \text{ (to three significant figures)}$$

Q7

Let percentage be x.

$$\frac{x}{100} \times 1.19 \, \text{MPa} = 23.1 \, \text{kPa (from Q5)}$$

so

$$x = \frac{23.1 \times 10^3}{1.19 \times 10^6} \times 100$$

$$= 1.94\% \text{ (to three significant figures)}$$

Q8

Temperature in kelvins $= 273 \, \text{K} + 20 \, \text{K}$

$$= 293 \, \text{K}$$

$$RT = \frac{mn\langle c^2 \rangle}{3}$$

$$\langle c^2 \rangle = \frac{3RT}{mn}$$

where mn is the mass of 1 mole.

For nitrogen

$$mn = 28.0 \times 10^{-3} \, \text{kg}$$

$$\langle c^2 \rangle = \frac{3 \times 8.31 \, \text{J K}^{-1} \times 293 \, \text{K}}{28.0 \times 10^{-3} \, \text{kg}}$$

$$= 261 \times 10^3 \, \text{m}^2 \, \text{s}^{-2}$$

$$\sqrt{\langle c^2 \rangle} = 511 \, \text{ms}^{-1}$$

For helium

$$mn = 4.0 \times 10^{-3} \, \text{kg}$$

$$\langle c^2 \rangle = \frac{3 \times 8.31 \, \text{J k}^{-1} \times 293 \, \text{K}}{4.0 \times 10^{-3} \, \text{kg}}$$

$$= 1.83 \times 10^6 \, \text{m}^2 \, \text{s}^{-2}$$

$$\sqrt{\langle c^2 \rangle} = 1.35 \, \text{kms}^{-1}$$

Yes, there is a connection. Sound travels faster in gases with faster-moving molecules.

Breathing under water is only one technological feat accomplished by scuba divers. Moving in a controlled and safe way is another – being in control of your movement makes all the difference between an enjoyable, safe dive and a frustrating, risky one. Being under water is strange for the human body – our senses can easily become confused. But being able to move up and down and feeling very light is lots of fun. There are also many dangers, one of the least of which is being eaten by a shark!

READY TO STUDY TEST

Before you begin this section you should be able to:

- define density as $\rho = \text{mass/volume}$, and give its units
- describe phase difference of a wave
- know and be able to use the relationship velocity, $v = f\lambda$
- know that pressure is inversely proportional to volume $P \propto \dfrac{1}{V}$

QUESTIONS

R1 A diver needs a weight belt containing 3.0 kg of lead. It is your job to cut the blocks from a long strip of lead, which is 1.5 cm thick and 5.0 cm wide. What length will you cut? (The density of lead is $11.3 \times 10^3 \text{ kg m}^{-3}$.)

R2 Look at the waves shown in Figure 10.1. One wave is said to occupy 360° for each example. How far apart (horizontally) are the waves shown in diagrams (b), (c) and (d) from that in (a)? Express each answer three ways: in degrees, as fractions of a period, T, and as radians.

R3 Taking v as 330 m s^{-1} what is the wavelength of (a) a 30 Hz bass note, (b) 20 kHz – the upper limit of human hearing?

Figure 10.1
(a) Position–time graph for the regular oscillation of a buoy as waves cause it to move up and down. (b), (c), (d) Position–time graphs (on the same time axis) for other buoys as

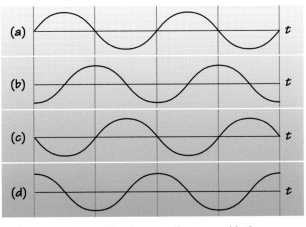

they are moved by the same wave. The buoys all move with the same amplitude and period, but not together – they are not in phase

10.1 The laws of floating and sinking

Being able to predict whether an object will float or sink is something you may have studied at primary school, but it is surprising how difficult and confusing it can be when you are trying to control your movements as a diver. Basically, an object will sink if it is more dense than the liquid that surrounds it. (Divers call this negative buoyancy.) An object floats if it is less dense than the liquid – i.e. it is positively buoyant. If an object has the same density as the liquid it will neither sink nor float. It is then neutrally buoyant. (See Figure 10.2.)

Figure 10.2
Positive, neutral and negative buoyancy

Throughout a dive a good diver adjusts their buoyancy to remain neutrally buoyant. This saves them from wasting energy (and air) maintaining their position. To enable them to adjust their buoyancy, divers wear weight belts, containing lead, and buoyancy control devices (BCs or BCDs) (see Figure 10.3). A BCD can be inflated using air from the diver's tank of compressed air so that they can adjust their buoyancy while under water. Divers also learn to control the amount of air they hold in their lungs to fine-tune their buoyancy to neutral.

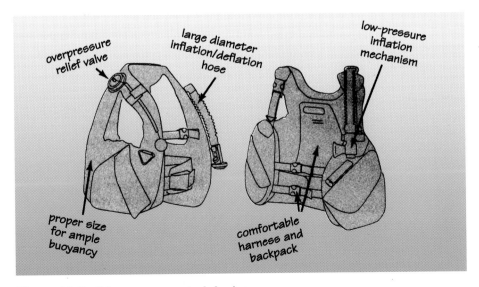

overpressure relief valve

large diameter inflation/deflation hose

low-pressure inflation mechanism

proper size for ample buoyancy

comfortable harness and backpack

Figure 10.3 A buoyancy control device

Floating like an ice cube

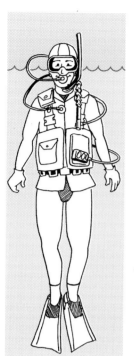

One problem that besets a novice diver and their instructor is the choice of weights that can be worn. Too much weight and the diver will have to put lots of air in their BCD, making movement in the water difficult. Too little weight and the diver will be unable to dive, and be left floundering and embarrassed on the surface as the rest of the class descends. Because the precise density of a diver depends on how fat they are and on the size of their wetsuit, each individual must work out how much weight they need. As a guide, when a diver's BCD is empty they should float on the surface with water around eye level (see Figure 10.4). Then, by exhaling, they will reduce their density to just below that of water, so that they can easily control their descent.

 You have probably noticed that ice, being less dense than water, floats. However, most of the ice cube is below water level. A cork, or a piece of expanded polystyrene, on the other hand, floats with most of the object out of the water, with very little below water level. Why is this?

Figure 10.4
A diver floating with an empty BCD

The cork is *much* less dense than the water, whereas the density of ice is only a little less than water.

How can we predict how far down in the water something will float? This sort of question is not only important to divers, it is also of crucial importance to ships and boats.

Archimedes' principle states that when a body is wholly or partially immersed in a fluid, the fluid exerts an upward force on the body equal to the weight of the fluid that is displaced by the body.

It is fairly simple to explain the existence of an **upthrust** or **buoyancy force** such as F_B in Figure 10.5(b). If no unusual forces act on a liquid, for example when water is in a bucket, the liquid will remain stationary, i.e. in equilibrium.

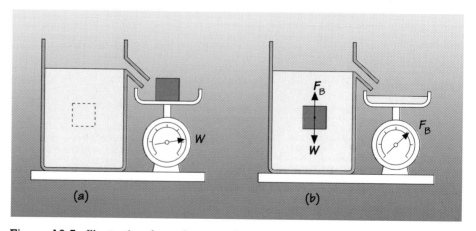

Figure 10.5 Illustrating the existence of an upthrust or buoyancy force

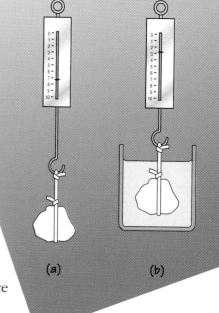

Figure 10.6 Forces acting on a rock when suspended from a spring balance (a) out of water, (b) in water. In (b), apparent weight of rock = weight of rock – buoyancy force

Imagine a cube of water, occupying volume V, in the middle of a can of water (see Figure 10.5a). If no unusual forces act on the liquid, it will remain stationary, i.e. in equilibrium. The weight of the fluid (W) in volume V *must* be supported by an upwards force from the pressure of water beneath V. This upwards force F_B exactly balances the weight, W, of V, equal in magnitude, but opposite in direction. If the liquid in V is replaced by an object of the same volume, the liquid is pushed away (displaced) and the object will experience an upward force of F_B, just as the cube of water would have experienced a force. This force makes things float and gives them buoyancy. An object that is more dense than water appears to become lighter when it is immersed in water (see Figure 10.6). (Try lifting up a friend next time you are in the swimming baths.)

⧫E **Exploration 10.1 Using a hydrometer**

15 MINUTES

Apparatus:

◆ hydrometer ◆ beakers of various liquids – e.g. water, salt solution, methylated spirits

A hydrometer is a device that is designed to measure the density of a liquid. The more dense the liquid, the less volume of liquid the hydrometer will displace before it floats. (When it floats the buoyancy force from the liquid exactly balances the weight of the hydrometer.)

Measure the density of the liquids using the hydrometer, and estimate the uncertainty in your readings.

Is this an accurate method for measuring density? Is it appropriate in all situations?

⧫E **Exploration 10.2 Checking Archimedes' principle**

90 MINUTES

Apparatus:

◆ spring balances ◆ masses (use a variety of objects, some of which will float, whilst others will sink) ◆ top-pan balances ◆ beakers ◆ measuring cylinders
◆ displacement cans ◆ water

Design and carry out an experiment to check Archimedes' principle.

Q1 A diver is correctly weighted with 3.0 kg of lead when they are wearing their normal, spongy neoprene, wetsuit, but they change to a suit with a greater thickness of neoprene for winter. This new suit contains an extra 2.0 kg of spongy neoprene rubber, which has a density of 0.90×10^3 kg m^{-3}. Should they adjust the weight they are carrying? If so, by how much? (Density of seawater = 1100 kg m^{-3}.) ◆

10.2 Controlling buoyancy

It seems strange to many novice divers that they start a dive with an empty BCD. Most people think that divers need a full BCD to start with and then release air from it as they go deeper and deeper. This is wrong and we need to study the physics to understand why.

A diver begins their dive with an empty BCD. By exhaling slightly they decrease their density so that it falls slightly below that of water, and the diver sinks.

As the diver descends, what happens to the water pressure surrounding them?

It increases.

So, as they descend, what happens to the volume of the air and gas-filled spaces in their body and in their wetsuit?

The volume decreases.

As they descend, what happens to their actual weight? (The mass of air they exhale is negligible.)

It is unchanged.

So, as they descend, what happens to their apparent weight?

Because their volume has decreased, the buoyancy force is decreased. Because their weight is unchanged, their apparent weight increases.

The laws of physics – Boyle's law and Archimedes' principle – predict that when a diver descends from floating by exhaling slightly, they will sink faster and faster as they become more and more dense, and apparently heavier and heavier. And that is exactly what happens. Divers need to learn to *add* air to their BCDs as they descend to maintain neutral buoyancy.

E Exploration 10.3 A Cartesian diver

20 MINUTES

Apparatus:

◆ 1–2 litre plastic fizzy drink bottle   ◆ small test-tube (it needs to fit inside the bottle)
◆ Blu-Tack or Plasticene

Fill the bottle with water. Attach a small piece of Blu-Tack around the outside of the open end of the test-tube (to weight it down), and fill the test-tube one-third full of water. Put the test-tube open end down into the bottle and screw the top on the bottle. (See Figure 10.7.) The test-tube should float at the top of the bottle.

Increase the pressure on the test-tube by squeezing the bottle and watch carefully. What happens to the volume of air in the test-tube when the pressure is increased? What happens to the test-tube's buoyancy when the pressure is increased?

Use Boyle's law and Archimedes' principle to explain what is happening. Predict what will happen when the pressure is reduced. Discuss your explanations and predictions with others in your group and with your teacher.

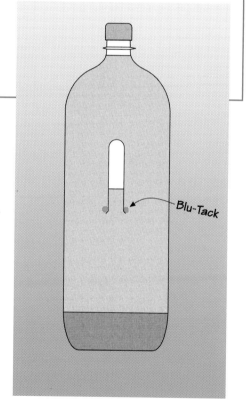

 A diver at 20 m depth is wearing a suitably inflated BCD to be neutrally buoyant. If they want to make a slow, controlled ascent from 20 m to 10 m depth, how should they adjust their BCD?

As they ascend the gas and air in their body and wetsuit will expand, increasing the buoyancy force on their body. They must release air from their BCD, or else they will ascend increasingly rapidly and bob to the surface out of control (possibly risking decompression sickness by ascending too quickly).

Figure 10.7 Apparatus for the Cartesian diver experiment

10.3 Seeing under water

People are well adapted to living on land, surrounded by air, but in an underwater environment our senses are limited or distorted by the water. Divers normally depend mainly on sight, but even this is altered by the water.

Our ability to focus our eyes depends on light bending as it travels from air into the watery fluid, the aqueous humour, inside our eyes (see

Figure 10.8a). The cornea, the tough, transparent outer surface of our eyes, has evolved so that its shape is precisely right for focusing light as it enters the eye from air. The **refraction** (bending) of light depends on light changing speed as it crosses the boundary – from air to aqueous humour in this case. Light travels more slowly in water than in air.

 If the eye is surrounded by water, why is it impossible to focus properly?

Light now enters the eye from water. There is little change in speed from water to aqueous humour, so the light is refracted very little as it crosses this boundary – not enough to focus normally (see Figure 10.8b).

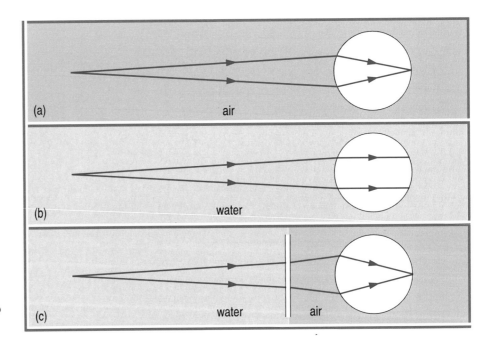

Figure 10.8
(a) The eye focusing normally.
(b) Failing to focus when viewing through water.
(c) Using a mask to focus correctly

(a) air

(b) water

(c) water   air

In order to see clearly under water, divers wear masks (Figure 10.9). These trap a layer of air between the water and the eye, enabling the eye to focus normally (see Figure 10.8c). Any layer of air will do – people have even experimented with special contact lenses that trap a very thin layer of air between the water and the eye.

Figure 10.9
A mask

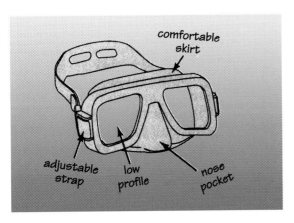

comfortable skirt

adjustable strap   low profile   nose pocket

Wearing a mask to see clearly under water does not alter the fact that the light is travelling from objects that are surrounded by water. When the light passes from water to air it speeds up and refracts. If the water/air boundary is kept flat using a piece of glass or plastic it does not distort the image that we see, but it makes an object appear to be closer than it actually is.

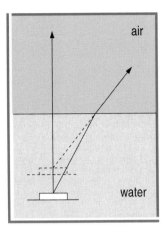

You may have noticed this when looking into a swimming pool. The **apparent depth** of the pool is less than the real depth (see Figure 10.10).

Figure 10.10 Real and apparent depth

 Exploration 10.4 Measuring the refractive index of water by comparing real and apparent depth

Apparatus:

◆ travelling microscope ◆ beaker of water filled to about 6 cm depth ◆ chalk dust
◆ piece of paper marked with a cross

Arrange the microscope so that it can be focused on both the bench and on the top surface of the water without moving the body of the microscope, as shown in Figure 10.11.

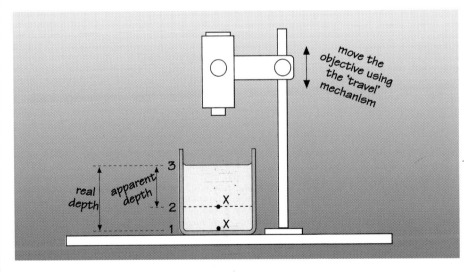

Figure 10.11
Measuring real and apparent depth

Put the piece of paper on the bench and move the objective of the microscope so that it is in focus. Note the position of the microscope (1).

Now place the beaker of water on the bench and move the microscope objective to re-focus on the cross. Note this second position (2).

Sprinkle chalk dust on the surface of the water and focus the microscope on the dust.

Note this position (3).

Use the positions you have noted to calculate the real depth (1 minus 3) and the apparent depth (2 minus 3) of the water.

From the definition of **refractive index** it is possible to prove that the ratio
real depth/apparent depth = refractive index.

Use your results to calculate the refractive index of water. Estimate the uncertainty in your results.

The normally accepted value for the refractive index of water is 1.3. Do your results agree?

 Make a list of the differences between how divers see things on land and how they see them under the water. What problems can these differences cause?

Things seem closer than they actually are when viewed under water. This means that divers usually have difficulty judging distances. They may go too far away from the safety of a line or a dive buddy, or they may think that they are too close to an object. Their mask may fog or become flooded so that they can't see clearly. Silt and debris in the water may limit visibility.

10.4 Hearing under water

Because water is denser than air, sound travels very well under water. It travels faster, and less energy is dissipated as it travels, enabling divers to hear sounds from further away than if they were on the surface. Knowing this, you might be surprised to learn that sound is of limited use to divers.

 Why might it be difficult to use sound normally under water?

Sound is used principally as a means of communication. Divers are unable to speak, because they are not breathing air normally. They can squeak, and make a few noises, but because the sound waves travel faster in water, the sounds are strange and difficult to understand.

A common way for divers to attract the attention of other divers is to hit their tank with a bead or a knife. However, although their dive partner may hear the noise clearly, it will be difficult for them to work out where the noise is coming from. Because sounds travel differently under water we cannot use our normal, instinctive methods of locating the sources of sounds. This can be particularly worrying if, when you are ascending, you hear the sound of a motor from a boat. No one wants to get caught up with a propeller because they are unable to judge the distance or the direction of the boat.

 Exploration 10.5   Listening to sounds under water

10 MINUTES

Undertake this exploration only if you are a confident swimmer.

Next time you go swimming, take some time to listen to what you can hear under water. Try communicating with a friend under water – humming, talking, whistling, squeaking. Can you make any noises?

If you can get permission, experiment with other objects used to make noise on land – ringing a bell or hitting a metal object with a spoon, for example.

Listen carefully to the quality of the sound; how does it compare with the noise you hear through air? Try to locate the source of a sound with your eyes closed; do you experience any problems?

Locating the source of a sound

Having two ears enables the brain to compare the signals from each ear and, by comparing the **intensity** and the **phases** of sound waves at each ear, locate the source of the sound.

 Look at Figure 10.12. For a sound source at S, how will the intensity at the left ear (A) compare with that at the right ear (B)? What will happen if the sound source moves from S to T?

A will record a higher intensity signal from S, so the brain will know that S is closer to A than to B. As the intensity of sound increases the amplitude of vibration at the eardrum increases. This signal is passed on to the inner ear and the brain – so we hear a louder sound. Subconsciously we compare the signals from our two ears. If the signal from the left ear is of higher intensity than the signal from the right, we deduce that the source of the sound is on the left. If the source is only slightly to our left – such as S – the difference between the two signals is small. If the source is closer to the left ear (at T) there will be a much larger difference between the two signals. So, by comparing the intensities of signals, we can begin to locate the course of a sound.

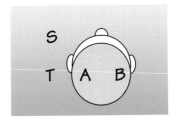

Figure 10.12 Locating the source of a sound by comparing intensity

Because sound travels so much more efficiently in water than in air the brain gets confused if it hears a sound from T in the underwater environment. Sound does not lose as much intensity as it travels in water, so the difference between the signals from the left and right ears is not as great as it is in air and the brain has trouble locating the source of the sound.

The brain also compares the phase of waves at both ears to locate the source of a sound.

 Exploration 10.6   The importance of phase difference

Apparatus:

◆ stereo music system (the music system must have separate speakers, and the speaker wires must be reversible) ◆ a stereo recording (ideally one that makes the position of instruments/performers clear – orchestral recordings are usually best)
◆ stereo demonstration tapes

Listen to a minute or two of the recording with the music system playing normally. You should be able to pick out the position in space, between the two speakers, that the various sounds are apparently coming from.

Now disconnect one speaker and reverse the two wires. The speaker will now be moved exactly out of phase with the way it should be moving. The sounds produced will be out of phase with the ones that should be produced – how does it sound? Can you locate the positions of the various sounds any more?

The phase difference between sound waves arriving at your two ears depends on the wavelength of the waves and the position of the source. Your brain has learned to recognize that sound waves of a certain frequency will produce a certain phase difference if the source is in a certain position. But this depends on the fact that a source producing waves at, say 512 Hz, will produce waves of a wavelength of about

$\dfrac{330\,\mathrm{ms}^{-1}}{512\,\mathrm{Hz}}$, around 0.6 m. The assumption made by your brain is that the

sound waves have travelled through air – a very reasonable assumption if you have spent your whole life surrounded by air!

Under water everything is different. The speed of sound in water is approximately $1500\ \mathrm{m\ s}^{-1}$, as opposed to $330\ \mathrm{m\ s}^{-1}$ in air. That makes the wavelength of waves produced by a source almost five times longer, and makes any phase difference detected by the brain about five times smaller. (See Figure 10.13.)

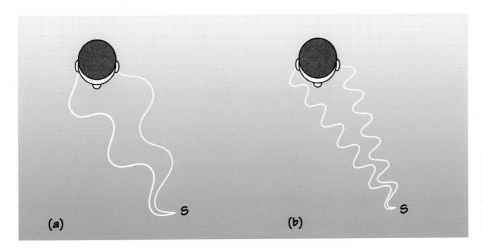

Figure 10.13
Locating the source of a sound by phase difference (a) under water, (b) in air

10.5 Staying warm under water

Breathing, seeing and moving under water are essential ingredients for having fun when diving, but to survive in an underwater environment it is vital to keep warm. Entering open water (lakes or the sea) in Britain wearing only a swimming costume requires a certain degree of bravery, but in the summer the temperature is not dangerously cold. However, scuba diving in Britain requires special, insulating clothing – not as a luxury item, but as an essential piece of equipment.

 Why do divers need insulation when swimmers can make do with a swimming costume?

Divers use much less energy. Swimmers keep themselves warm as they work their muscles, but if divers worked as hard their air supply would not last very long. Also swimmers stay on the surface where, in the summer, the water will be warmed by the Sun more than the water below, whereas divers are surrounded by colder water.

Heat and internal energy

All warm bodies have internal energy, and human bodies are no exception. We are such complicated biological creatures that the temperature of the vital organs of our bodies must be kept at a steady 37°C. If the temperature alters by more than a couple of degrees the biological processes vital to life begin to go wrong, and death is imminent if our temperature is too far out of this range. We are well used to keeping our bodies at a steady temperature in air.

 Suggest three or more methods of increasing your internal energy if you are feeling slightly cold.

Increasing the temperature of the room, adding more clothes, working muscles by doing some sort of exercise.

Suggest three or more methods of decreasing your internal energy if you are feeling slightly hot.

Sprinkling yourself with water, decreasing the temperature of the room, removing clothing, ceasing exercise, using a fan.

In order to maintain a stable body temperature the rate at which internal energy is produced inside the body because of exercise and other metabolic functions (such as breathing) must be balanced by a loss of internal energy to the outside world.

When internal energy is transferred from one body to another it is called a thermal energy transfer.

Q2 A swimmer converts chemical energy into internal energy at a rate of 800 W. If their temperature is to remain steady, at what rate is energy transferred from their body to the water? ◆

Q3 A relaxed diver converts chemical energy into internal energy at a rate of 200 W. If their temperature is to remain steady, at what rate is energy transferred from their body to the water?

Do you think that this diver would be comfortable in the same water as a swimmer if they were wearing only their swimming costume? ◆

How do you lose energy under water?

Divers need to keep warm under water. If their bodies cool down it is unpleasant and even life-threatening. If they have to exercise to stay warm they will quickly use up their air supply, so for successful diving we need to minimize energy loss to the surroundings.

Energy is transferred from a hotter to a cooler body by three processes: **conduction**, **convection** and **radiation**. Conduction occurs whenever there is matter between the two bodies. Energy is passed from atom to atom so that it spreads out from the hotter atoms to the cooler ones. If electrons are free to move in the matter this process can be quite fast because the electrons carry the energy – so metals are good thermal conductors. Water and air are not good conductors, but water, being more dense than air, is the better conductor. Conduction is the method by which thermal energy passes through the skin.

Convection occurs in fluids such as water and air. Hot fluid is less dense than cool fluid and will float on cool fluid. So, if a small volume of fluid is heated it floats upwards, and cooler fluid is drawn in to take its place. This means that cool fluid is continually moved over the warm surface (such as the diver's skin), and the thermal energy rapidly spreads throughout the fluid. In a lake or in the sea the increase in temperature due to the diver's body will be negligible.

Radiation refers to the electromagnetic radiation emitted by all bodies with internal energy. Bodies that are warmer than their surroundings will emit more radiation than they receive from their surroundings, so it is often a significant mechanism of energy flow. Very hot objects such as electric fires and the Sun emit visible electromagnetic radiation as well as longer wavelengths, but warm objects such as people emit only the invisible, longer wavelengths that are called infrared. The amount of energy lost from a body by radiation depends on its temperature, and energy loss by radiation becomes very important when temperature differences are large. Radiation is the only way in which energy can travel through a vacuum, so although it is relatively unimportant to divers it is very important when considering the temperature of the planet and when studying stars.

 Which mechanism of energy transfer is the most significant for a skindiver in cold water (wearing only a swimming costume)?

Convection. Water is a fairly poor conductor, and the diver's skin is not so hot that radiation is very significant.

The commonest way that divers minimize energy loss from their bodies is to wear a wetsuit. A wetsuit does not keep a diver dry, but the water that reaches the skin is trapped in a layer, so that it is unable to convect, and therefore insulates the skin. The suit itself is made from neoprene rubber, which contains gas bubbles and hence has a very low thermal conductivity. By eliminating convection into the water next to their skin divers can be comfortable in water as cold as 10° C. (When you enter the water wearing a wetsuit you still get the cold shock of the water as it enters the wetsuit, but this soon warms up a little and keeps you comfortable.)

For water temperatures below 10° C drysuits are recommended. These suits have tight seals around the ankles and wrists to prevent water entering the suit. Conventional insulation is used inside the suit, and the suit itself may be made of neoprene, like wetsuits. Drysuits prevent the cold shock experienced by divers in wetsuits when they enter the water, but, because the air is squashed upon descent under water, they require their own air supply to keep the insulation fluffed up and effective.

 Drysuit diving requires extra training. It is very important that a diver knows how to control the air supply to their suit. What would happen if the diver, having inflated their suit correctly, ascended rapidly?

The air in the suit would expand and make the diver ascend too rapidly, risking decompression sickness. They also may find that their feet float up above their head – this can be extremely dangerous if a diver ends up unconscious, running out of air with their feet in the air at the surface.

Q4   As you discovered in Exploration 10.4, using the definition of refractive index it is possible to prove that the ratio

$$\frac{\text{real depth}}{\text{apparent depth}} = \text{refractive index}.$$ If a shark appears to be 10 m away, how far away is it really? The refractive index of water is about 1.3. ◆

 Suggested further investigation

Using plastic syringes of various sizes, with the ends sealed with Araldite, and a set of bathroom scales to measure force, verify as best you can:

1   Boyle's law

2   $P = \dfrac{F}{A}$

Achievements

After studying this section you should be able to:

- state and apply Archimedes' principle
- discuss problems of seeing and hearing under water
- calculate apparent depths from real ones and vice versa
- describe the processes of transfer of energy from hotter to cooler bodies.

Glossary

Apparent depth The depth that an object appears to be when submerged in a fluid of refractive index n:

$$\frac{\text{apparent depth}}{\text{real depth}} = \frac{1}{n}.$$

For water, apparent depth < real depth.

Archimedes' principle This states that when a body is wholly or partially immersed in a fluid, the fluid exerts an upward force on the body equal to the weight of the fluid that is displaced by the body.

Conduction The process by which thermal energy flows from atom to atom through a material from hotter to cooler.

Convection The process by which thermal energy flows within fluids. Because fluids flow, hotter atoms can move to areas of cooler atoms, carrying thermal energy. Convection currents often occur naturally because a hotter fluid, being usually less dense, will float on a cooler fluid.

Intensity Unit: watt per metre squared ($W\,m^{-2}$). When applied to sound, it is the rate at which energy passes through a unit area perpendicular to the direction of propagation of the sound. The definition may also be applied to any energy transfer process, e.g. thermal radiation, microwave radiation.

Phase The horizontal position-matching of two sound waves. Two waves that keep 'in step', so that they reach maximum amplitude at the same time, and so on, are said to be 'in phase'. Any perceived phase difference between sound waves as they reach our ears gives us a clue as to the position of the source of the sound.

Radiation The process in which energy transfer is by electromagnetic waves. The best example is energy transfer from the Sun, neither conduction nor convection being possible through the near vacuum of space.

Refraction The bending of light as it travels between mediums of different densities.

Refractive index A measure of how much refraction occurs at an interface between two media. It is equal to the ratio of speeds of light in the two media.

Upthrust (buoyancy force) The upward force experienced by a wholly or partially submerged body due to Archimedes' principle.

Answers to Ready to Study test

R1

Density is given by

$$\rho = \frac{\text{mass}}{\text{volume}}$$

so

$$11.3 \times 10^3 \, kg\,m^{-3} = \frac{3.0\,kg}{1.5 \times 10^{-2}\,m \times 5.0 \times 10^{-2}\,m \times l}$$

where l is the length of lead to be cut. So

$$l = \frac{3.0\,kg}{11.3 \times 10^3 \, kg\,m^{-3} \times 7.5 \times 10^{-4}\,m^2}$$

$$= 0.35\,m \text{ (to two significant figures)}$$

	Degrees	Periods	Radians
(b)	−90	$-\dfrac{T}{4}$	$-\dfrac{\pi}{2}$
(c)	±180	$\pm\dfrac{T}{2}$	$\pm\pi$
(d)	+90	$+\dfrac{T}{4}$	$+\dfrac{\pi}{2}$

R3

$$v = f\lambda$$

therefore

$$\lambda = \frac{v}{f}$$

(a)

$$\lambda = \frac{330\,\mathrm{m\,s^{-1}}}{30\,\mathrm{Hz}}$$

$$= 11\,\mathrm{m}$$

(b)

$$\lambda = \frac{330\,\mathrm{m\,s^{-1}}}{20\times10^{3}\,\mathrm{Hz}}$$

$$= 1.65\times10^{-2}\,\mathrm{m}$$

$$= 17\,\mathrm{mm}\ (\text{to two significant figures})$$

Answers to questions in the text

Q1

The mass of the extra neoprene is 2.0 kg. The volume of this mass of neoprene is given by

$$\text{volume} = \frac{\text{mass}}{\text{density}}$$

$$= \frac{2.0\,\mathrm{kg}}{0.9\times10^{3}\,\mathrm{kg\,m^{-3}}}$$

$$= 2.222\times10^{-3}\,\mathrm{m^3}$$

This volume of neoprene will displace the same volume of seawater, so the mass of the seawater displaced will be given by

$$\text{mass} = \text{volume}\times\text{density}$$

$$= 2.222\times10^{-3}\,\mathrm{m^3}\times1100\,\mathrm{kg\,m^{-3}}$$

$$= 2.444\,\mathrm{kg}$$

The mass of water displaced is 0.44 kg greater than the mass of the extra neoprene, so 0.44 kg of lead needs to be added to the diver's weight belt.

Q2

800 W

Q3

200 W. No, the relaxed diver will lose thermal energy at the same rate as in Question 2 (as conditions are the same), so they will feel cold and will start to shiver. They may even be in danger of hypothermia (i.e. their body core cools so that their body functions start to go wrong).

Q4

$$\frac{\text{real depth}}{\text{apparent depth}} = \text{refractive index}$$

so

$$\text{real depth} = \text{refractive index}\times\text{apparent depth}$$

$$= 1.3\times10\,\mathrm{m}$$

$$= 13\,\mathrm{m}$$

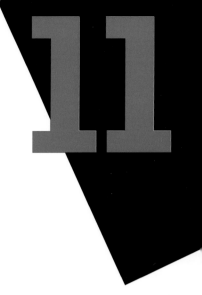

If you think back to the beginning of this unit, you will realize what a lot of physics you have covered through looking in depth at various sporting activities.

To help you to appreciate how far you have come, look back through the list of achievements for each section. If you feel unsure about any of them, go over the relevant section(s) of this unit again. When you feel fairly confident about most of these achievements ask your teacher for the exit test for this unit. When you have done the test, consult your teacher, who has the answers and will probably wish to go through them with you. We hope you have enjoyed learning about the physics of sport with this supported learning unit, and that you want to use more units in the series.

CONCLUSION

Further reading and resources

Part I

British Mountaineering Council, 177–9 Burton Road, Manchester M20 2BB. Tel: 0161 445 4757.

Soles, C. (1995) 'Single-rope buyer's guide: everything you always wanted to know about ropes but didn't know how to ask', *Rock and Ice*, vol. 117, July/August.

Part II

Amateur Swimming Association, Harold Fern House, Derby Square, Loughborough LE11 0AL. Tel: 01509 230431; Fax: 01509 610720.

Frohlich, C, (1979) 'Do springboard divers violate angular momentum conservation?', *American Journal of Physics*, vol. 47, no. 7.

Multimedia Motion CD-Rom. Available from Cambridge Science Media, 354 Mill Road, Cambridge CB1 3NN.

O'Brien, R. (1992) *Diving for Gold.* Leisure Press, Leeds.

Progressive Steps in Diving – A six-video series developed in conjunction with diving coaches. Available from: The Secretary, Media Services, Leeds Metropolitan University, Calverly Street, Leeds LS1 3HE.

Rackham, G. (1975) *Diving Complete*, Faber & Faber, London.

Part III

British Sub Aqua Club World Wide Web address: http://www.cru.uea.ac.uk:80/ukdiving/bsac/index.htm

BSAC (1985) *Sport Diving – The British Sub-Aqua Club Diving Manual.* Stanley Paul, London.

Frohlich, C. (ed.)(1986) *Selected Reprints: Physics of Sports.* American Association of Physics Teachers, College Park, Maryland.

Local dive shops – look in the *Yellow Pages* to locate these. They will be able to show you diving equipment and will have information about local dive clubs and courses.

PADI (Professional Association of Diving Instructors). PADI are an American-based organization, but are the biggest diver-training organization in the world. They publish a huge range of books, magazines, videos and CD-ROMs (as well as organizing diver training programmes and holidays). To illustrate this section we strongly recommend:

    PADI Open Water Diving video
    PADI Open Water Diver Manual (Specify the metric version in English!)
    Scuba Tune-up Multimedia CD-ROM.

These are available through PADI dive centres or from: PADI International Ltd, Unit 6, Unicorn Park, Whitby Road, Bristol BS4 4EX. Tel: 0117 971 1717; Fax: 0117 971 0400; World Wide Web address: http://www.cru.uea.ac.uk/ukdiving/orgs/padi

Acknowledgements

Grateful acknowledgement is made to the following sources for permission to reproduce material in this unit:

Photographs and figures

Cover: Joy Korr climbing in Elorado Canyon, Colorado, USA – photograph by Chris Bonington, Chris Bonington Picture Library; pp. 12, 16, 19, 24, 26: Figures 2.2, 2.5, 2.8, 2.9, 2.18, 2.22 – photographs of Peter Robins, Sarah Lomas and Lakhwinder Gill by Ian Smith; p. 47: Chris Bonington – photograph by Jim Lowther, Chris Bonington Picture Library; p. 67: Climbing Mont Blanc – Chris Bonington Picture Library; pp. 73, 83: Figures 4.10, 4.16 – Edelrid (Edelmann & Ridder, GmbH & Co, Postfach 1165, D-88305 Isny im Allgäu, Germany); p. 92: Mark Lenzi – photograph by David Leah, Allsport; Tracey Miles – photograph by Bob Martin, Allsport; p. 96: Girl jumping from stool – *Multimedia Motion* CD-ROM, Cambridge Science Media; p. 101: Figure 5.4(a) Erica Sorgi – photograph by Al Bello, Allsport; Figure 5.4(b) Cheril Santini – photograph by Jamie Squire, Allsport; Figure 5.4(c) Veroni Ribot – Sporting Pictures (UK) Ltd; p. 124: Greg Louganis – stf Associated Press; p. 160: William James's autonomous diving apparatus – BSAC (1985) *Sport Diving – The British Sub-Aqua Club Diving Manual*, Stanley Paul, London; p. 169: Figure 8.8 – *Illustrated London News*, vol. 72, p. 389 (1878).

The authors and Management Group would also like to thank David Tawney and Mike Burton for their helpful comments and advice whilst writing this unit, and Mike Edge and Adam Southeran of Ponds Forge International Diving Centre and Phil Robbins of The Edge, Sheffield, for their advice and cooperation in the production of this unit.

Index